SOUTHERN SPIRITS

FOUR HUNDRED YEARS OF DRINKING
IN THE AMERICAN SOUTH, WITH RECIPES

ROBERT F. MOSS

TEN SPEED PRESS
Berkeley

Contents

The Old Absinthe House bar in New Orleans, LA,
in the early 1900s. The bar is still in operation today.

Introduction

Sometime in October 2013, 230 bottles of Pappy Van Winkle bourbon went missing from the Buffalo Trace Distillery in Frankfort, Kentucky. Despite a $10,000 reward, no tips were received as to who might have pulled off the heist.

It was the perfect climax to Pappy's meteoric rise. Hailing from a long line of whiskey makers and whiskey sellers, Julian Van Winkle III got into the business with his father in the 1970s. Back then, the only way they could move whiskey was by putting it into novelty-themed decanters shaped like college football mascots. Then, in the 1990s, following the course charted by the makers of single-malt scotches, bourbon distillers started introducing premium lines to the market, which won over new converts to their products. Around the year 2000, a lot of those drinkers started discovering the smooth, long-aged whiskeys sold by Julian Van Winkle.

"We got some really nice ratings," Van Winkle told me, when asked to explain how his products got so popular, "and a lot of word of mouth and a lot of nice press." The real boost came when a few celebrity chefs, including Sean Brock of Charleston's Husk and David Chang from New York's Momofuku, started professing their love for Van Winkle's bourbon. A flurry of magazine articles profiling Pappy followed, and the boom progressed directly to a bubble.

At first, savvy fans could watch the company's Facebook site to learn when the allotment for their state was about to ship, then race to their local retailer to stake out a bottle. That trick doesn't work anymore. Liquor store owners just roll their eyes when greenhorns come in and ask, "Do you carry Pappy Van Winkle?" Bottles float around on the underground market for $500 for the fifteen-year-old bourbon and more than $1,000 for the twenty-three-year-old. Once in demand for its smooth, rich flavor, it's now in demand simply for being in demand.

The rise of Pappy Van Winkle coincided with a more general vogue for Southern food. Restaurants like Seersucker and Peels brought updated Southern classics to New York City. Celebrity chefs on the West Coast started importing Benton's country ham from Tennessee and Anson Mills grits from South Carolina. Indie filmmakers created documentaries to explain pimento cheese to Yankees, and suddenly, from coast to coast, everyone was eating barbecue. Invariably, the drink they chose to sip alongside their Southern fare was bourbon.

And why not? When you ask people today to name a Southern drink, bourbon is almost certainly the first word that springs to their tongues. If they manage to come up with a cocktail, it's bound to be a mint julep (made with bourbon, of course). The funny thing is, from a historical perspective, bourbon is by no means the dominant Southern spirit. It didn't even exist during the colonial era, and it was not widely drunk in most parts of the South during the antebellum days. Yes, plenty of Southerners sipped mint juleps. But contrary to the misty myths of the Old South, they usually weren't sitting on the veranda of a white-columned plantation house, and the liquor in their tumbler was not bourbon. Bourbon's transformation into the dominant Southern spirit happened not during Reconstruction nor the Gilded Age but after Prohibition's brutal scythe laid low the entire American liquor industry, setting Southern drinking back almost a century in the process. It was only in the aftermath of Prohibition's repeal, as the industry reorganized itself into marketing-driven conglomerates, that bourbon emerged as the premier spirit on the Southern bar.

So if it wasn't bourbon juleps on the veranda, what was it that Southerners were drinking all those years? Quite a lot of things, as it turns out, and that's good news for modern drinkers with a taste for history. Peach brandy, rum, Madeira, Cognac, rye whiskey, and locally brewed lager: the history of drinking in the South offers a rich and delicious legacy that can be drawn upon today to open entire new fields of tasting and experimentation.

Booze provides an intriguing lens into history, offering new perspectives on the larger social trends that occurred over the course of centuries. Alcohol helped lubricate the wheels of commerce, for when business-minded folks got together to negotiate and trade, they shared plenty of drinks. In fact, the places where people drank and the places where they conducted business were frequently one and the same. Alcohol taxes were a key source of governmental revenue as well, and excise taxes led to the young United States' first constitutional crisis and, decades later, to the rise of moonshining in the South. At the same time, the legitimate alcohol business helped lead the transition to an industrial, commercial economy, both in terms of large-scale production techniques and the evolution of brand-based marketing. The temperance movement, in its century-long run-up to the failed Prohibition experiment, encapsulated the tensions of a growing and changing society coming to a head, and that movement played out in a formative way in the South that is not frequently addressed in social histories. Prohibition, of course, brought everything to a crashing halt, and once alcohol was legal again, the world of drinking in the South was reshuffled into a totally new set of patterns and preferences.

This book tries to capture the full sweep of that rich, multifaceted story. Each of its chapters opens with a drink recipe or two that are appropriate for that particular point in the narrative. Whether you choose to mix up your own version and sip it while reading is totally up to you, but it certainly wouldn't hurt. We'll start with rum and brandy and traditional colonial preparations, like punches and slings, and enjoy a little fine old Madeira too. We'll sample a range of whiskeys—white corn liquor, aged rye, and old bourbon—and trace the evolution of whiskey making over time. We'll explore the classic cocktails of the Southern bar, like the Sazerac, the Ramos gin fizz, and, of course, the iconic mint julep. They all link up to provide a tasty representation of what people in the South were drinking and how that changed over time.

The South is not, and never was, a monolithic entity. Many different regions and cultures have long existed inside its blurry boundaries. The uplands of Tennessee are very different from the red clay regions of Georgia, which themselves are almost a world away from the marshes of Lowcountry South Carolina and the bayous of Louisiana. To a great extent, the South as a region and the notion of a unifying Southernness was the product of the sectional tensions that led to the Civil War, the ruinous aftermath of the conflict, and the long racial division that followed. The story of drinking in the South by necessity cuts across such arbitrary boundaries and divisions. The narrative takes us up to Baltimore and into Pennsylvania's Monongahela Valley, and it skips over to the Caribbean on occasion too.

The South was not constant in time either. The American South of 1810 was very different from the 1870 version, and even further removed from the version of 1730. A study of drinking habits in the region gives lie to the notion of an isolated, insular South. Much of that concept is tied up in the stereotypes of moonshiners up in the hills, isolated from the world and ready to shoot any revenuers who dared to intrude on their stills. The real story of Southern drink underscores how interconnected the region's cities, towns, and even countryside were with the rest of America as well as the rest of the world. Alcohol, in fact, as an article of trade, was one of the primary things that established that interconnectedness.

Those connections are being restored today as the rest of the country and even the rest of the world starts to discover the rich bounty offered by Southern food and drink. So what better time to take a closer look at what Southerners were drinking over the centuries? There are many fine treasures waiting to be discovered.

1

"Contrary to the Nature of the English": The Failure of Beer and Wine

Most chapters in this book open with a drink recipe, but it might not be appropriate for this particular chapter. Our story begins with the lack of booze, with Englishmen and -women who found themselves in a strange new world, cut off from their traditional tipples and forced to make do however they could, which usually meant cheap substitutes like sour muscadine wine or lousy ersatz beer.

I suppose you could pop open a Bud Light and simulate the effect. After a few sips, though, put the can aside and mix up an Apple Cider Sidecar. It's nothing an early colonist ever sipped, but it incorporates two of the key beverages—apple cider and apple brandy—that were consumed in the first century of the colonial South. If you can find a bottle of Foggy Ridge cider, all the better. It's made in the Blue Ridge Mountains of Virginia using heirloom apple varieties once grown specifically for cider making. You can use a bottle of Laird's for the apple brandy (get the good bottled in bond stuff, not the neutral spirit-based applejack), but if you come across a bottle of Carriage House apple brandy, grab it. It's distilled in Lenoir, North Carolina, from local mountain apples and is an absolute delight.

Apple Cider Sidecar

SERVES 1

2 ounces Carriage House apple brandy

1 ounce Foggy Ridge Serious Cider

½ ounce simple syrup (see page 6)

¼ ounce freshly squeezed lemon juice

1 egg white

Rim a rocks glass with sugar by rubbing a lemon slice along the rim, inverting the glass, and patting its rim in a saucer filled with a layer granulated sugar. Combine the apple brandy, cider, simple syrup, lemon juice, and egg white in a shaker with ice and shake vigorously until frothy, about 30 seconds. Pour into sugar-rimmed rocks glass and garnish with a slice of orange peel.

Simple Syrup

MAKES 1 CUP

1 cup Demerara sugar
1 cup water

Combine sugar and water in a small sauce pan and bring to a boil over high heat. Stir occasionally until the sugar is dissolved, then remove from heat and allow to cool. Kept in the refrigerator, simple syrup will stay good for several weeks.

Note: For the recipes in this book, I recommend using Demerara sugar, which is more like what would have been used in the South before the twentieth century (see note on sugar on page 32).

"Our Drinke Was Water"

In the earliest years of the Southern colonies, settlers wanted to drink like Englishmen and Englishwomen, and that meant drinking ale. Brewed from wheat and barley, it was the daily beverage in the mother country, consumed with meals and in between them too. The ships that brought English colonists to Southern shores carried a generous provision of ale, but once these supplies were exhausted, the settlers found themselves thirsty in a land with few options for a proper drink. In 1607, one of the original Jamestown colonists, Thomas Studley, recorded that after the ships that brought them departed, "there remained neither taverne, beerehouse, nor place of reliefe." After six months in the ship's hold, the barley they brought with them "contained as many wormes as graines" and so "our drinke was water, our lodgings Castles in the ayre."

The Native Americans encountered by the English helped save the new colony from starvation. They provided the interlopers with native foods like corn, squash, and beans, which quickly became staples of the colonists' diet, but the original residents weren't much help on the drink front. Down in Mexico, women brewed pulque from maguey plants and tepache from pineapple, and in the Andes they brewed a corn liquor called chicha. Closer to home, the Iroquois fermented a mildly alcoholic beverage from sugar maple sap, but the Powhatan in Virginia did not make any alcoholic beverages at all, nor did most of the other tribes along the Eastern seaboard. The Brits had to figure out the booze thing on their own.

In 1609, the governor advertised for two brewers to come to the colony, which had grown to three hundred people. Apparently no one jumped at the offer. In 1613, a Spaniard who had been reconnoitering the enemy English outpost wrote home to his government (with great relish, we can guess) that most of the residents of the fledgling colony were sick and desperate to return home because they had "nothing but bread of maize, with fish; nor do they drink anything but water—all of which is contrary to the nature of the English."

Beer wasn't in the cards for the colonial South. Barley, oats, and hops grew poorly in Southern soils, and few Virginian or Carolinian farmers, focused as they were on finding crops from which they could get rich, felt it worth the effort to cultivate them. Even when colonists could get their hands on the necessary ingredients, their brewing results were unreliable at best, since the warm weather rendered the fermented grains too acidic and made the beer prone to spoiling. A thriving brewing industry was established in the cooler climates of Massachusetts and Pennsylvania, and a trickle of this beer made its way southward via intercoastal shipping, but for the first century of colonial settlement in Virginia and the Carolinas, it was a fickle, insufficient supply at best.

Wine was another English favorite, but despite the colonists' dogged efforts, they were unable to produce it in the new land either. In 1584, the first of Sir Walter Raleigh's ill-fated colonial expeditions landed in North Carolina and found a carpet of grapes growing right up to the edge of the surf, where "the very beating and surge of the Sea overflowed them." Two decades later, the settlers at Jamestown found the rivers and bottomlands thick with riverbank grapes and muscadines. In the *Generall Historie of Virginia*, Captain John Smith described these "hedge grapes" and noted that from them "we made neere twentie gallons of wine." The purpose of Smith's book was to promote the colonies to new settlers, so he may have been stretching things a bit when he claimed that this early product "was like our French Brittish wine," meaning French wine imported into Britain. "But," he added, "certainly they would prove good were they well manured."

For decades, colonial leaders maintained a stubborn fantasy that if they just tried hard enough, they could transform the Southern colonies into a wine-growing Eden. In one 1609 tract, a Virginia promoter promised that within a few years the new colony would be producing as good a wine as "any from the Canaries," referring to the Spanish-owned Canary Islands off the northwest coast of Africa. In a letter to the stockholders in the Virginia Company, the colony's governor proposed that "if these natural vines were planted, dressed, and ordered by skilfull vinearoones" (that is, vignerons, or cultivators of vineyards), they might "make a perfect grape and fruitfull vintage in short time."

Wishful thinking. It was not fine wines but a different sort of indulgence—tobacco—that became the cash crop of Virginia. Tobacco transformed Virginia into a boom-minded colony whose residents shared a singular focus on getting as rich as they could as quickly as they could. They poured every ounce of their energy into growing tobacco, and most intended to stay in the new colony for only as long as it took to make a quick fortune and return home. Their houses were little more than temporary shelters roughly constructed of boards nailed to posts set in the ground. Instead of building English-style fenced pastures, they found it easier to fence in their vegetable patches and let the livestock roam free. When Samuel Argall arrived in Virginia in 1617 to assume the office of principal governor, he found a colony in disarray. Only five or six houses remained standing, the church was in ruin, and the stockade fence was broken in pieces. And yet, Argall recorded, he found "the market-place and streets, and all other spare places planted with Tobacco."

These avaricious planters spent much of the earnings from their new cash crop on satisfying their thirsts. Virginians became notorious in England for their love of drink, and ship after ship arrived in the James River loaded with wine and stronger spirits. These private traders' ships functioned, in the words of one settler, as "moving taverns." A dozen or more might be docked at one time along the James, with Virginians crowding on board, doing their best to drink away their tobacco earnings. The governor and council decried "the rates which unconscionable marchantes and maryners doe impose uppon our necessities," and they singled out the "rotten Wynes which destroy our bodies and empty our purses." But those unconscionable merchants kept right on selling.

This monomania for tobacco alarmed King James, who urged the Virginia Company to find other commodities for the new colony. In 1619, the company again tried to jump-start winemaking by requiring every householder to plant and maintain ten grapevines. They sent eight French vignerons and a trove of European grape cuttings to plant in the seemingly fertile soil of the New World. The results were dismal. The prospect of working seven years or more to cultivate a suitable vineyard for wine production held little appeal in get-rich-quick Virginia. In 1622, Captain Nathaniel Butler reported that the colonists had "laughed to scorn" the instructions of the company and their imported vignerons and kept right on planting tobacco. Efforts to encourage beer production had similarly disappointing results. On several occasions, the Virginia Assembly offered a bounty to any colonist who could raise at least two hundred pounds worth of hops. Ironically, the reward for growing something other than tobacco was to be paid in tobacco, or at least a note for ten thousand pounds of it, which could be traded like currency. This did little to spur production.

The experience of the Virginians was repeated decades later in the Carolinas. In drawing up the charter for their new colony in 1663, the lords proprietors focused on the same three commodities—wine, silk, and oil—that the Virginia Company so desired, and with the same dismal outcome. The proprietors instructed their newly appointed governor to set aside twenty thousand acres of good land for vineyards, the first of many doomed experiments to produce a native wine in the Carolina colony. Detractors in England blamed the laziness of the colonists and the incompetence of the vignerons for the failed experiments, but coastal Southern geography simply wasn't suited for wine production. European grapes languished in the sandy soil, their vines steamed by the damp summer heat and blasted by local diseases like powdery mildew and local pests like the grape leaf-hopper and the grape-berry moth. Local grapes were resistant to these blights, but the colonists could produce only a poor, sour wine from them. And thus we have the irony of colonies full of Europeans in desperate want of wine, surrounded by wild vines teeming with grapes that they couldn't do anything with.

In Search of a Local Tipple

Around 1630, the tobacco bubble burst, and the price of the leaf dropped from three shillings a pound to between threepence and sixpence. A large planter could still make a fortune growing tobacco over the course of many years, but it was no longer a boom crop that offered the prospect of cashing in after a single season. The colonists who remained in Virginia undertook a three-decade effort to transform their miserable colony into something that more closely resembled their native England. They planted more corn. In 1634, they completed a six-mile palisade between two creeks to protect their livestock from wolves and Indians. Their cattle and swine flourished, and they began exporting animals to Barbados. The population increased steadily, too, climbing from 2,600 in 1629 to 25,000 by 1660. Tobacco remained the foundation of the colony's economy, but it now supported an ecosystem of related trades, like coopers who made hogsheads (barrels) for shipping the leaves and carpenters who built tobacco sheds and houses.

Virginians also turned their energies toward producing their own forms of strong drink so they could stop squandering their incomes in floating taverns. Importing beer and wine from England was not only costly but unreliable, too, since casks leaked and their contents frequently arrived spoiled. In the seventeenth century, there was little coastwise shipping and only a handful of vessels from Pennsylvania or New England landed in Virginia each year, so bringing in cider or beer from the Northern colonies was not a sufficient option. The attempts to find a reliable beverage that was palatable and intoxicating but not prohibitively expensive underlies the entire history of drinking in the South up until the Civil War.

Southern colonists turned to fruits to make alcohol, and they soon settled upon two primary ones: apples and peaches. Apples thrived in cooler climates, so cider was more common in Virginia than in coastal Carolina. Orchard keepers and gardeners began growing crab apples and "bittersnaps" for cider, which had higher tannins and more acid and sugars than eating or cooking apples. Peaches became the fruit of choice in the warmer parts of the Carolinas, and they were fermented into a concoction known as peach mobby. Initially, brewing and cidering were small-scale domestic pursuits and, being kitchen activities, were practiced primarily by women. That remained the case through the end of the seventeenth century. Cookbooks imported from England provided lengthy instructions for fermenting cider and mead. A typical kitchen in Williamsburg, Virginia, contained a full array of cidering equipment: tubs, casks, and kettles for fermenting and skimmers and haircloths for straining.

Virginians drank cider in great quantities, and ambitious planters stockpiled as much as a 150 gallons of it at a time in their cellars. In 1676, colonist Thomas Glover recorded "there are few Planters but have fair and large Orchards, some whereof have twelve hundred trees and upward." Those trees bore a wide variety of English apples "of which they make a great store of Cider." It was common for large planters to produce one hundred gallons or more per year by the end of the seventeenth century. Though mechanical presses were becoming available, most large plantations—including that of Robert "King" Carter, one of the largest landholders in the colonies—still depended upon workers to "beat cider" by hand in wooden troughs, and they managed to produce quite a volume.

The slaves at Carter's Corotoman plantation made more than twenty butts of cider—almost three thousand gallons—in the first two weeks of the August cidering season in 1722. Much of this was likely sold to nearby residents, since small farming households, which had little cash to purchase imported spirits, often turned to the large plantations when their own cider supplies ran low.

Though apples and peaches were the primary fruits for fermenting, Southerners used whatever they could get their hands on. The family of Martha Washington possessed a prized manuscript called the *Booke of Cookery* that contained handwritten recipes passed down from one generation to the next. Included are instructions on decocting and brewing as well as recipes for a range of wines made from lemons, gooseberries, blackberries, and elderberries. The processes for making all of these are pretty similar: the housewife mashed or bruised the fruit, mixed it with water and loaf sugar, and let it stand for days or weeks to ferment before filtering and bottling it.

As the eighteenth century opened, Southern colonists were still trying to figure out how to brew something akin to the beer of their native land, but obtaining the ingredients remained the tricky part. The planter and historian Robert Beverley recorded that, in Virginia, "the richer sort generally brew their small beer with malt, which they have from England." Barley could be grown in the colony, Beverley claimed, but because there were no malthouses to parch it, the inhabitants chose not to sow it. "The poorer sort brew their beer with molasses and bran," he added, and also "with Indian corn malted by drying in a stove; with persimmons dried in cakes, and baked; with potatoes; with the green stalks of Indian corn cut small, and bruised; with pumpions [pumpkins], and with batates Canadensis [Jerusalem artichoke]." Colonists also brewed a sort of beer from molasses, sassafras, and, instead of hops, "the Tops of Firr-Trees." They put these in a kettle with water, boiled it, then allowed it to ferment. Corn was the grain that grew most readily in the Southern colonies, so frequently, Southerners had to resign themselves to make their "beer" from it. The kernels were coarsely crushed and mixed with water and allowed to ferment, resulting in a sour but alcoholic beverage. Women sometimes added honey to this mixture to create a sort of modified mead.

Such improvised beverages were, at best, poor substitutes for proper beer and wine. The local cider was far from perfect either. Apples were in season only from late fall to early winter, and the orchards might not produce in years that had a late frost or summer drought. Unfenced cows and pigs wreaked havoc, stripping the trees of their bark and killing them. Cider improved with age, but only if you had a cool place to store it and, preferably, an airtight container in which to keep it. Few small planters had storage cellars, glassware was rare and expensive, and only the best and most expensive barrels would keep cider fresh. Most cider turned to vinegar quickly, so many Virginians had to drink it raw and unimproved by age. July was generally the driest month, since the previous year's cider supply had long been exhausted or gone bad and the new crop of apples were not yet ripe.

There was, however, one surefire way to make apple cider or peach mobby durable enough to last through a Virginia or Carolina summer: distill it into brandy. It's hard to pin down precisely when Southern colonists began distilling, since writers from the era often used the terms *brew* and *distill* interchangeably. The term *brandy* was commonly applied to any alcoholic beverage made from fermented fruit—not necessarily one that had been passed through a still. By the opening of the eighteenth century, though, it appears that distilling was common on the larger Virginia plantations. In 1705, Robert Beverley noted that if a planter tended an orchard properly, within six or seven years it could produce a sufficient supply of apples "from which he may make store of good cider, or distill great quantities of brandy." Peach trees were even easier, requiring no grafting, and bore fruit just three years after planting. Beverley felt that peaches made "the best spirit next to grapes."

Early Southerners had two main ways of making spirits: drop distilling and rise distilling. In drop distilling, the fermented fruit juice was poured into the still's upper container, which was heated over a fire so that the alcohol would boil, rise to the top, and then drip down a pipe to a lower collecting container away from the heat. Rise distillation worked in the opposite direction, with a fire beneath the bottom container of the still and the boiling alcohol rising up a pipe so it could be collected in an upper container. Both methods were dangerously prone to explosion, took hours to complete, and generally produced spirits with plenty of impurities. Early stills were unable to produce anything close to pure alcohol, but distilled apple brandy could reach 60 proof (30 percent alcohol), which was strong enough to keep through the heat of summer.

A. The Still   L. A Pewter Crane

B. The Worm-tub   M. A Pewter Valencia

C. The Pump   N. Hippocrates's bag or Flannel

D. Water-tub   Slieue

E. A Press   O. Poker Fire-shovel Coe-rake

F.F.F. Tubs to hold the goods   P. A Box of Bungs

G.G.G.G. Canns of different size   Q. The Worm within the Worm-tub

H. A Wood Funnel with a iron-nosel   mark'd with prick'd lines

I. A large Vessel to put the Fains   R. A Piece of Wood to keep down

    or after-runnings   the Head of the Still to

K. Tin-pump   prevent flying of

P. Fourdrinier Delin et Sculp

Early distilling equipment, 1738.

Typically, only large planters—those with estates worth £250 or more—could afford stills, which were among their most valuable assets. At this stage, distilling, like cidering, was largely a woman's enterprise. Estate inventories commonly listed stills among the other contents of the kitchen. Fathers usually willed their stills to their sons, but they often stipulated that the wives or daughters be allowed to keep the equipment and use it during their lifetimes, the property passing into the sons' hands only upon the women's deaths. There was at least some distilling going on in the early colonial cities too. In 1704, the Carolina Assembly passed a fire-suppression act that included restrictions on stills. The opening provision notes that "several people keep stills and still-houses in Charleston, to the great endangering of their own and their neighbors houses." The act forbade any still exceeding ten gallons without a license from the commissioners.

Like most strenuous labor on Southern plantations, the production of alcohol was often performed by slaves. The first Africans arrived in Virginia in 1619, but their legal status remained ambiguous until the system of chattel slavery was formalized in the second half of the seventeenth century. By the 1680s, enslaved Africans had begun to eclipse indentured European servants as the primary laborers in Virginia. Slaves were present from the very beginning in the Carolina colony, and by 1710, just four decades after the arrival of the first European settlers, more than half of Carolina's population was enslaved. It is now well understood that West Africans played a foundational role in shaping the foodways that emerged in the Southern colonies—a distinctive food culture that blended African, European, and Native American ingredients and techniques. But there has been much less investigation into how African alcohol traditions may have shaped Southern drinking culture.

We do know this: the Africans who were enslaved and brought to Southern shores arrived with a culture of making and consuming alcohol. In the non-Muslim parts of precolonial Africa, people made palm wine and brewed beer from corn, sorghum, millet, and even bananas. Alcohol played a role in weddings, funerals, initiation rites, and harvest festivals, and intoxicating beverages were tightly linked to spirituality. In Akan society, palm wine was considered a sacred fluid that opened communication between the living and ancestral worlds. Families would pour libations to seek favor from ancestral spirits and help individuals recover from illness. During weddings, the bride and groom would exchange drinks before witnesses and pour libations for the gods and their ancestors. Alcohol was used by Igbo men as gifts for their intended brides' families, and at West African funerals, liquor was drunk heavily and also sprinkled on the graves of the deceased to help bridge their transition to the spirit world. It is little surprise, then, that the Africans who were enslaved and brought to the British colonies took readily to drinking alcohol there and were soon closely involved in the production of cider and brandy too.

In the early years of Virginia, a ration of alcohol was included as part of the labor agreement for servants, and that ration might account for more than one-third of his or her entire cost of employment. As indentured servitude gave way to slavery, alcohol was provided to—and often made by—enslaved workers too. A small farming household with one or two slaves consumed around ninety gallons of cider and twenty-one gallons of distilled liquor each year. A plantation with twenty slaves would consume 450 gallons of cider and more than 100 gallons of brandy per year. Black or white, free or enslaved: Southerners needed their drink.

Alcohol Consumption in the Early Southern Colonies

Let's pause for a moment and reflect on why having something alcoholic to drink was such a big deal in the Southern colonies. For starters, there was very little to drink that was not alcoholic. A good milk cow of that era produced only one quart a day, and most Southerners let their cows roam free in the woods, so milk remained expensive and in short supply. Long before pasteurization and refrigeration, there was no way to stop apple, pear, and plum juice from fermenting and becoming alcoholic. Tea and coffee were expensive luxury items until the eve of the Revolutionary War. There was water, of course, but on the coastal plains the supply was unreliable and frequently unhealthful. The rivers teemed with insects and waste, and in tidal areas they would became filled with slime and filth at low tides. Shallow wells were easily contaminated by the bacteria that caused typhoid fever, especially during warm weather.

Alcohol was far safer to drink, and it had other virtues too. It relieved pain and was, in fact, one of the few effective medicines available. There's also this simple fact: the colonists loved to tie one on. They came from traditions of heavy drinking and continued those habits in the New World. In describing the recreation and pastimes of Virginians, Robert Beverley commented that "there is the most good nature and hospitality practiced in the world, both toward friends and strangers," though he noted, "this generosity is attended now and then with a little too much intemperance."

Early Southerners drank pretty much all day and at any occasion. At meals, men and women would dine and drink together. At other times, colonists tended to drink in same-sex groups, with the men frequently doing their drinking outside the home, either outdoors or in taverns.

Virginians loved feasting and dancing, and just about any occasion was an excuse for a celebration. The rules of hospitality required that a guest be served the best food and the best liquor that the house could provide. When a Frenchman named Durand of Dauphiné visited Virginia in the 1670s, he remarked on the lack of wine and the sheer amount of hard liquor consumed by Virginians. Each time someone new joined a drinking party, custom required that he be toasted, which got to be quite an undertaking as groups grew to twenty or more.

The tavern, or ordinary, became the center of drinking culture in the colonial South. While the terms *tavern* and *ordinary* had distinct meanings in England, they were used pretty much interchangeably in America. Often an ordinary operated out of someone's house, and for at least the first century of Southern colonial life, they remained very houselike in their appearance and accommodations. A typical establishment had a large room with tables, benches, and a broad fireplace with receptacles for pipes and tankards. They were places where people could gather to drink, converse, sing, argue, and pass the time. Most served meals, and they were all supposed to provide overnight accommodations for travelers and their horses. Gambling was an integral part of tavern life. A French visitor to a Virginia tavern found at night "Carousing and Drinking in one Chamber and box and Dice in another, which continues till morning." Billiards and cards were common gambling games too.

When men, women, and alcohol mingled in taverns, there was bound to be a little hanky-panky. In 1627, Captain William Eppes arrived at a Virginia tavern, and over the course of the evening, he and six other guests put away three gallons of wine. At the end of the night, Captain Eppes staggered to his feet, pulled off his clothes, and retired to one of the beds in the common sleeping room. Another guest, Mrs. Alice Boise, asked Captain John Huddleston if he were going to share the bed with Captain Eppes. Huddleston declined, so she took the space instead. Initially, Mrs. Boise lay atop of the covers with her clothes on, while Captain Eppes lay beneath them. Before long, though, the other guests in the room heard "a great busselling and jiggling of the bed." The noise occurred again in the middle of the night and once more two hours before dawn. Eppes was hauled into court and charged with misconduct and lewd behavior, but he beat the rap. The justices found that while Eppes was clearly "in drink," it was "not proved or manifest" that he and Mrs. Boise had "offended the law."

Taverns and ordinaries were by no means the only places where Virginians would indulge in alcohol. In fact, there were few places, it seems, where they wouldn't indulge. In the modern South, Baptist and Methodist churches still have dry wedding receptions in the fellowship hall, but colonial Virginians routinely drank in church. Royal holidays were a great occasion for boozing it up too. In 1688, officials in Rappahannock County, Virginia, spent ten thousand pounds of tobacco to provide alcoholic beverages to celebrate the birth of King James II's son. Drinking was an inseparable part of militia musters, which drew men from all over the county, and many women and children came along to see the spectacle and join in the merriment. Though the muster itself might last only a few hours, the entire event would occupy the better part of two booze-soaked days.

Court days were all-male affairs, and they were occasions not just for settling judicial matters but for conducting business and debating politics as well. Most county courthouses had a tavern located conveniently next door. In jurisdictions that lacked a courthouse, court sessions were often held inside the taverns themselves. In Virginia, some judges rewarded jurors with a round of drinks for each verdict delivered. An indentured servant in Northampton County who was caught after running away from his master confessed that he had waited until a court day to steal a bridle and saddle and attempt his escape since he knew everyone would be too drunk to notice him.

Blind justice, it seems, was often blind drunk, for judges routinely drank on the bench. Perhaps the best indication of just how much they consumed is the law passed by the Virginia Assembly in 1676 that restricted drinking by judges. It by no means prohibited judges from drinking on court days. Instead, it specified punishment for any justice of the peace who became "soe notoriously scandalous upon court dayes at the court house, to be soe farre overtaken in drinke that by reason thereof he shalbe adjudged by the justices, holding court to be uncapable of that high office." The punishment for being too crocked to see in your own court was a fine of one thousand pounds of tobacco for the first offense, two thousand pounds for the second, and removal from office only if it occurred three or more times.

Women put back their fair share of beer, cider, and brandy too. They drank at meals and at sewing circles. Drinking during childbirth was a common practice in Virginia, and the woman giving birth was expected to have prepared alcohol and cakes for female neighbors who would gather for the lying-in period before, during, and after the birth. Alcohol ushered

Virginians out of the world too. Far from being somber events, funerals were quite the occasion for a party, especially in the more rural areas, where people would travel from miles around to pay their respects to the dead. Whenever Virginians had visitors, hospitality required that they provide their guests with refreshment, and the fact that someone was dead didn't let them off the hook. In the upper ranks of society, men were expected to set aside funds to provide drinks for the guests at their own funerals. If they didn't, the cost would be deducted from their estates. These weren't trivial sums either. At one York County funeral, mourners put away twenty-two gallons of cider, twenty-four gallons of beer, and five gallons of brandy. The executors for John Grove, a planter of rather modest means, subtracted one thousand pounds of tobacco to pay for his funeral.

Nothing goes together like booze and firearms, and the South has a long history of that too. In 1624, the Virginia Assembly, in an effort to save scarce gunpowder, passed an ordinance making it illegal for anyone to "spend powder unnecessarily in drinking or entertainments." The law seems to have been widely ignored. It was common, once a man was laid in the ground, for attendees to fire a fusillade of shots over the grave. Frequently, the memorial shots continued long after the ceremony concluded. At the funeral of Major Philip Stevens of York County, more than ten pounds of powder were expended. This could get problematic when the attendees had been drinking all day. Due to the sheer number of accidents, the Lower Norfolk County court in 1668 prohibited the discharge of firearms at a funeral unless an officer of the militia was present to supervise.

By the end of the seventeenth century, funeral revelry had gotten so notorious that some of Virginia's more conservative residents tried to rein it in through the terms of their wills. Ralph Langley of York County dictated that his executors buy no more than six gallons of brandy for his burial, while George Jordan of Surry County explicitly prohibited guns from being fired over his grave. Edmund Watts of York County declared that because of "the debauched drinking used at burials, tending to the dishonor of God and religion, my will is that no strong drink be provided or spent at my burial."

From the earliest days, colonial leaders worried about drunkenness among their citizens. In 1632, the Virginia Assembly specified that anyone convicted of being drunk would be fined five shillings, to be paid to the churchwardens of the parish in which the offense was committed. The fine was upped to ten shillings in 1691, and if the guilty couldn't pay, they would be placed in the stocks for three full hours. In 1668, the assembly limited each county to just two licensed taverns and specified that those should be near the courthouse and public places such as ports, ferries, or great roads in order to accommodate travelers. This restriction, the act stated, was needed because "the excessive number of ordinaryes and tipling houses" were frequented by "a sort of loose and carelesse persons who neglecting their callings mispend their times in drunkennesse." The same act fined anyone keeping a "tippling house" without license two thousand pounds of tobacco, half of which would go to the informant who ratted the business out.

Early tavern regulations walked a fine line between suppressing drunkenness and ensuring that responsible citizens had access to an affordable supply of wholesome drink. The first Virginia law regulating ordinaries, passed in 1639, dictated that an establishment charge no more than twelve shillings for "a meale or a gallon of beer" due to "the great plenty of provisions." In 1644, the assembly began licensing ordinaries, and it capped the price of a gallon of strong beer at eight pounds of tobacco. Tavern keepers could charge no more than fifteen pounds of tobacco for French wines, twenty pounds for those from the Portuguese-owned island of Madeira, and thirty pounds for a gallon of Spanish wines. Eighty pounds was allowed for "the best sorte of all English strong wares" and forty for brandy or aqua vitae.

As the seventeenth century closed, Southerners had found their booze. It wasn't always the best drink, but it was better than water. Alcohol had become fully integrated into the core institutions of the emerging societies of Virginia and Carolina. The dream of transforming the South into a flourished vineyard still lingered, but for the time being, Southerners were making do with home-brewed cider, ersatz beer, and locally distilled apple and peach brandy, augmented by as much of the good stuff as they could afford to import from Europe. It was good enough for a start, but colonists still thirsted for a more potent and more affordable drink.

2

"That Damn'd Devil's Piss":
The Rise of Rum

To start things out, let's mix up a rum punch. It has not only rum in it but sugar, too, along with a little citrus, which captures the convergence of trade in the coastal South in the eighteenth century. If you want to be truly authentic about it, do not give in to temptation and put any ice in your punch. There was no ice to be had in the South during this era, and its introduction at a later time was an important milestone in Southern drinking. (You will be forgiven if, after a sip or two of room-temperature punch, you backslide and plunk in a couple of cubes.)

Rum Punch

SERVES 12 TO 15

1 bottle Smith & Cross
Navy Rum (see note on
rums, page 32)

Juice of 12 limes

I cup simple syrup (page 6)

2 cups freshly brewed
green tea

Combine the rum, lime juice, simple syrup, and tea in a large glass or ceramic jug. Shake a few times to mix, then allow to rest in a cool place (you can refrigerate if you like) for several days. Serve at room temperature if you dare, or pour over ice in a glass.

The Rise of the Rum Trade

The Southern colonies needed not just a reliable supply of drink, but an inexpensive one too. They found just that in the island colonies that lay a short voyage away in the Caribbean. The product was called rum, and it quickly became the main tipple of the colonial South. It was a truly colonial American beverage, created by Europeans in the New World and consumed there too. Rum greased the wheels of commerce and helped define new trading patterns. It helped open the American interior to trade from the coastal cities, and it influenced the colonists' interactions with the Native

American population—and that population's near destruction. There was nothing elegant nor refined about rum, but there was nothing elegant nor refined about the times either.

There's a handy rule of thumb for explaining the differences among the various types of spirits: brandy is the distilled essence of wine, whiskey the distilled essence of beer, and rum the distilled essence of sugar. If you're inclined to be more a little colorful, though, you could borrow rum historian Wayne Curtis's memorable description that rum is "the distilled essence of industrial waste." The sugaring process began with cane, which was put into a large press and squeezed to extract the sweet juice, and that, in turn, was boiled in massive copper cauldrons until reduced to a nearly crystallized syrup. As the juice boiled, dirt and impurities rose to the top, and these scummings were removed. The reduced cane syrup was then cooled and cured in clay pots with holes in the bottom, through which waste matter would ooze. That waste was molasses, a dark, sticky, sweet liquid that could not be further refined or crystallized.

There wasn't much a sugar producer could do with molasses, since there was no demand for it on the islands and it was expensive to ship anywhere else. Around the middle of the seventeenth century, though, planters realized that the sugars remaining in molasses could be fermented by wild yeasts, and if they put it in a still, they could extract the alcohol. So they took the waste from the sugaring process—the skimmings from the boiling, the lees from the bottom of the pots, the water used to clean everything out—and mixed it in a large cistern. They let this so-called wash rest in the tropical heat until natural yeasts caused it to bubble and ferment, then added molasses. After about a week, fermentation ceased, and the wash was transferred to the main vat of a pot still and heated over a fire. The steam rose and moved through the worm, a length of copper tubing cooled by water, where the alcohol condensed out of the vapor. The resulting spirits were either put into a cask for storage or passed through the still again to be double distilled.

The end product was called rumbullion, which later was shortened to just rum. Kill-devil was another popular term for the spirit at the time, and it seems a fairly accurate description of early rum's harshness. Wayne Curtis surveyed the historical record and concluded that "no seventeenth-century account has surfaced that had anything nice to say about the taste." A French priest named Jean-Baptiste-Labat pronounced it "rough and disagreeable," while another visitor to the West Indies concluded it "a hot, hellish, and terrible liquor." Ned Ward, a British wit and travel writer who had visited the Caribbean just after the turn of the eighteenth century, described rum memorably as "that damn'd Devil's Piss."

What rum lacked in flavor, it made up for with an intoxicating kick, which is all it really needed to find a market. Rum first began seeping out of the West Indies around 1650, arriving as a cask or two loaded by a captain for his crew on the voyage and then, as more American colonists got a taste of the stuff, as a regular article of trade. Soon the money generated from the by-products of sugar making were enough to offset the entire cost of sugar cultivation, meaning that the money from sugar sales was almost entirely profit. Through the early 1700s, almost all the rum exported from Barbados and Antigua was destined for the North American colonies since no export market existed yet in England or Europe. Barbados was the largest exporter, shipping some 680,000 gallons per year, while Antigua exported 236,000 gallons and Saint Kitts and Montserrat shipped around 14,000 each.

That rum from the Caribbean found a ready market in Virginia and the two Carolinas, which split into separate colonies in 1710. That year, English explorer John Lawson visited the area north of Cape Fear and found planters producing wheat, corn, beef, pork, tallow, and hides. Sloops from Barbados and New England regularly docked to trade rum, sugar, salt, and molasses for those Carolina products In 1711, John Urmston, a missionary to North Carolina from the Society for the Propagation of the Gospel in Foreign Parts, described North Carolina residents as fiercely independent individuals who "live by their own hands of their own produce," using whatever they could spare to trade for foreign goods. "Many live on a slender diet to buy rum sugar and molasses," he noted.

Drinking rum seems to have taken precedence over just about everything else, including religion. Urmston found that three of the colony's five precincts had no churches at all. The other two never got around to finishing theirs. One had no floor, just loose benches placed upon the sand. At the other, the door was left standing open since the key had long been lost, and it became a shady refuge for hogs and cows in the summer. An aggrieved Urmston convinced the assembly to mandate that the people select a vestry of twelve men in each precinct to build a proper church and hire a clergyman. Urmston attended the initial vestry meetings and found them "very much disordered with drink." They "quarreled and could scarce be kept from fighting" and broke up without accomplishing a thing. In another precinct, the vestry met in an ordinary where "rum was the chief of their business."

It wasn't long before a few wily Yankees figured out that they could make a buck off of Southerners' thirst for rum, and they started importing cheap molasses from the West Indies and distilling it in New England. Boston's first rum distillery was established in 1700, and by 1770, there were 141 distilleries in the American colonies, mostly in Boston, Providence, and New Haven. That new domestic supply helped lower the cost of rum and further increase its popularity. When William Byrd II of Virginia was surveying the disputed boundary between Virginia and North Carolina in 1728, he observed that in Norfolk, merchants exported beef, pork, flour, and lumber to the West Indies in exchange for Caribbean-made rum. But out in the countryside, Byrd noted, "Most of the Rum they get . . . comes from New England, and is so bad and unwholesome, that it is not improperly call'd 'Kill-Devil.' " That fiery beverage, he added, "breaks the Constitution, Vitiates the Morals, and ruins the Industry of most of the poor people of this Country."

Rum was the drink of an ambitious people, rough around the edges but hearty and lively, and it became an increasingly important part of the commercial life of rising cities like Charleston and Williamsburg. The 1730s were Charleston's first boom decade, and that boom was fueled in part by rum. The rice economy was just becoming fully established, creating for the first time a thriving import/export trade. A tremendous amount of rum arrived on ships from Barbados and Antigua, which sold their cargoes of liquor and filled their holds with rice for the outbound journey to England. In 1735 alone, 134,000 gallons of rum arrived in the port, passing through the establishments of more than sixty different merchants. Charleston, at this stage, was still a rough-and-tumble place where the luxuries of the elite life were not yet enjoyed. In 1738, Robert Pringle, one of Charleston's leading wholesale merchants, wrote to a London trading partner that it would take at least six months to sell a shipload of Madeira wine in Charleston, there being a huge backlog of supply already on the market. "This is a place of not great consumption for Wines," he explained.

Pringle advised his London partner to have his men in the West Indies, if they could not ship sugar to England, to instead load their holds with rum and sail it to Charleston, "there always being a great demand for Rum here." This three-legged pattern followed the trade winds, and it became the standard route for ships engaged in the Charleston trade. A typical ship would depart a British port, make its way down the European coast past Portugal, and stop off at the island of Madeira or one of the Azores, where it would take on a load of locally produced wine. From there it would cast off for the long journey across the Atlantic, riding the trade winds to Barbados or Antigua. Upon arriving in the West Indies, the captain would sell the wine and invest the proceeds in rum, sugar, and molasses. Next, he would island-hop his way over to the Gulf Stream, which carried his ship up the Florida coast to Charleston, where rum and sugar were in high demand. In Charleston, the ship would be loaded with rice or, if rice was out of season, with deerskins and naval stores like pitch, tar, and turpentine. Finally, the captain would set sail up the Carolina coast to Cape Hatteras and from there head out into the open Atlantic for the return voyage to Europe.

The pattern was very much the same up the coast in Williamsburg, where tobacco, not rice, was the primary cash crop. Ships tended to leave British ports, perhaps with a stop at Madeira along the way, and sail to Barbados, and from there to either the James or the York Rivers in Virginia. The cargoes on the inbound ships included everything from salt and molasses to finished goods like iron pots and straw ware. Some ships, especially those that had touched off at Madeira, carried a few pipes (casks) of wine. But the one item that was present on virtually every ship that landed was rum. It arrived by the barrel, tierce, and hogshead. It was payment for the commodities produced by the colony, which appear in the manifests for the outbound voyages and were almost always bound to a British port, including planks and staves, skins and furs, wheat, and, more than anything, tobacco.

Punch Houses and Taverns

Much of the rum that arrived in Charleston and Williamsburg never left the city limits. From December to March, the peak shipping season, the Charleston harbor was filled with masts and the streets swarmed with sailors. They gathered in punch houses, like the Two Brewers on Church Street and the Pig and Whistle on Tradd, where they ladled strong punch out of large common bowls. The city's merchants and artisans as well as planters visiting town from the countryside preferred the public taverns, where they could eat salted fish, wild game, and rice flour puddings while drinking their rum in the form of slings, flips, and toddies.

The Pink House Tavern in Charleston, which opened in 1712 about five blocks from
the river, was one of the first taverns in the city to be built away from the waterfront.

The most prominent Charleston drinking spot during this period was
Shepheard's Tavern. Its owner, Charles Shepheard, arrived from London,
deeply in debt, around 1720. He set out to revive his fortunes by building a
tavern at the corner of Broad and Church Streets, and it became popularly
known as the "Corner Tavern." Its public long room was called the Court
Room, for it was rented by the province for holding court. In October
1734, a notice appeared in the *South Carolina Gazette* that tickets were
on sale for *The Orphan, or the Unhappy Marriage*, to be performed at
Shepheard's on October 17—the first known public performance of a play
in the colonies. The first American opera performance took place in the
Shepheard's long room, too, when Colley Cibber's *Flora, or Hob in the Well*
was performed in 1735.

Up in Virginia, Williamsburg was both the capital and the social center
of the colony. Men regularly traveled in from the countryside to attend

court and transact business, and when they did, they needed a place to eat, drink, and sleep. At any one time, between eight and fourteen licensed taverns served Williamsburg's two thousand residents. Most were located close to the capitol building along the town's main thoroughfare, and they served different types of clientele. The gentry patronized the Raleigh and Wetherburn's, while Shields Tavern was popular with both locals and travelers of the lesser gentry and upper middle ranks. Marot's Ordinary had a large public room with a wide fireplace and a small bar in one corner along with a garden room for private gatherings and a lodging room on the first floor. Marot's patrons included William Byrd and other members of the gentry, and they enjoyed a generous supply of imported wines.

After Jean Marot's death, his widow, Anne, married Timothy Sullivant, and they operated the tavern until 1738. In the 1740s, John Shields, who had married one of Anne Sullivant's daughters, took over the tavern and kept it until his death in 1750. As this progression suggests, the real continuity in the operation of taverns tended to lie not with the men, but with the women associated with them. In the case of Marot's Ordinary, it is likely that Anne Sullivant was the one actually running the tavern, and she passed the business on to her daughter. In both Virginia and the Carolinas, the tavern license and the sign over the door usually bore a man's name, but a woman—typically the license-holder's wife or another family member—actually ran the day-to-day business.

The laws of the period give us a good sense of what wines and liquors patrons were consuming in taverns. In 1695, a Carolina statute instituted price controls, capping Madeira wine at three royalls per quart, other wine from the Western Islands at two royalls, and domestic beer, ale, cider, and rum punch at sixpence. Later ordinances fixed prices for stout, ale, and other malt drinks. The purpose of these regulations was to ensure consistent, affordable prices for patrons, but they made tavern keeping a precarious business. The basic service of food and drink didn't turn a profit, so owners had to offer a range of additional services. They rented private rooms to wealthy travelers and provided rooms for locals to drink, smoke, converse, and gamble. Tavern keepers frequently were paid through barter, not cash, and their daybooks and ledgers recorded the cash value assigned to bartered goods. Many also extended credit to their patrons, which made their enterprises even riskier. When Charles Shepheard of Charleston died in 1748, his estate included 750 pounds in bad debts.

Gadsby's Tavern, Alexandria, Virginia.

Another constant theme in tavern regulations was the desire to control the sale of alcohol to slaves and indentured servants. The black populations of both Charleston and Williamsburg were sufficiently large to allow slaves a degree of anonymity in the crowded taverns. As early as 1693, the governor of South Carolina complained of the "very disorderly houses" in Charleston that sold strong liquors to great numbers of black slaves, whom he claimed were drawn in from the countryside "knowing they can have a drinck . . . for mony or what else they bring." In 1744, a Charleston grand jury named twelve establishments that had been caught selling liquor to slaves. None of these actions seemed to have much effect on the market. Despite seven decades of laws and regulations, in 1772, a correspondent to the *South Carolina Gazette* was still complaining that "at all times, nay, even at noon-day, many dram-shops are crowded with negroes."

Sailors were a constant worry to the authorities too. As tavern historian Sharon Salinger judiciously puts it, sailors "subscribed to an ethic of nonaccumulation." That is, they blew through money like drunken sailors. When they landed in port and were paid their wages, they did everything in their power to ensure they sailed out on their next voyage with empty pockets and a splitting headache. Broke sailors caused no end of trouble in port cities. In Virginia, sailors currently under pay were prohibited from being served in taverns without a license from their shipmaster, and those that had been discharged were required to show a signed document from their captain indicating as much. In 1743, Charleston prohibited tavern keepers from extending more than ten shillings in credit, and a few years later the legislature attempted to limit sailors to spending only one hour per day in a tavern. Most tavern owners blithely ignored such regulations. In 1759, Captain Robe of the snow Africa took out a notice in the *South Carolina Gazette* announcing that he had learned of several tippling houses that were entertaining his sailors and that he would refuse to pay any debts incurred by his crew and prosecute the tavern owners under the law.

Outside the port cities, taverns played a much smaller role in the drinking culture. Planters were explicitly exempted from the laws that regulated city taverns and liquor sellers, and many served as the liquor dealers for their neighborhoods. A handful of rural residents did get licensed to operate proper taverns, but these were rather poor operations in the sparsely settled plantation districts and not the centers of social activities they were in cities. "Strangers are always welcome [in homes] and genteelly treated," one Frenchman traveling through Virginia recorded, making it possible to travel through the length of the colony and pay only for ferry crossings. John Gerard DeBrahm, who journeyed through South Carolina in 1769, noted that "the Hospitality of this province makes traveling through this Country very agreeable, pleasant, and easy." Visitors were routinely invited into private homes for tea, suppers, and even lodging, so they didn't have much need for taverns.

Sampling Colonial Rum

Before we go any further, let's address the nature of rum and rum drinks in the colonial era. If you are thinking of Bacardi when you're imagining old Southern rum, you're not even in the same ballpark. The original rum was the product of the pot still, an inefficient device that left lots of impurities in the finished product. Caribbean rum makers later began using better stills and aging their products in oak casks, but during rum's heyday it was raw, white, and as harsh as moonshine. Such rum was characterized by something called hogo, a West Indian corruption of the French *haut goût* ("high taste"), which was often used to describe rotting meat. When applied to rum, it meant, as one ninenteenth-century commentator put it, "the strong and somewhat offensive molasses-like flavor of new rum." From the very beginning, rum was routinely mixed with other ingredients, particularly sour and sweet ones, for the simple reason that it was the only way an average drinker could stomach the stuff.

As David Wondrich explains in his book *Punch* (2010), there are four primary ways to make raw spirits more drinkable, and they all have to do with handling congeners, the impurities and other parts of the distilled spirit that aren't pure ethyl alcohol or water. You can mask congeners with aromatic flavorings, like the juniper berries in gin; filter them out with charcoal, as is done for vodka; mellow them by letting the spirits age in wooden casks, as whiskey makers do; or mix the spirits with enough sweet and sour substances like sugar and citrus that you can't taste the harsh stuff. The last was the strategy employed by most rum drinkers in the colonial South: heating it with sugar to make a flip, soaking orange and sugar in it for weeks to make a shrub, or blending it with lemon, sugar, and spices for massive bowls of punch.

William Byrd noted that North Carolinians, when entertaining guests, always set before them a "Capacious Bowl of Bombo." This was a mixture of equal parts rum and water mixed with long sugar, the Carolinians' term for molasses. As the good humor began flowing and the contents of the bowl got low, they would top it off with pure rum. That capacious bowl was a key element of colonial-era drinking, for slow-steeped, made-in-bulk drinks were the order of the day. The bombo bowl reflects the sociable nature of colonial drinking, where people from all walks of life—local residents, travelers from somewhere else, and sailors and slaves who legally weren't supposed to be there—gathered in common rooms to partake of a dram or twelve.

More sophisticated than bombo was punch, which brought additional flavors to the bowl. It originated in the colonies of British India, where it was usually made with arrack—a hard spirit distilled from coconut sap, palm tree sap, or rice wine—that was diluted with water, sweetened with sugar, and cut with citrus and spices. Overseas adventurers brought punch home to England, where it flourished in London's coffeehouses and clubs. From there, it spread to the Western Hemisphere, arriving in Barbados in the 1650s. In 1668, the colony's governor endorsed a local citizen for office because he was "a man of good reason, and at a bowl of punch I dare turn him loose to any Monsieur in the Indies." (Now there's a politician with his priorities straight.) Punch appears in tavern regulations in Charleston as early as 1686 and in Williamsburg by 1709. The English preferred brandy in their punch, but colonists adapted the British recipe to the liquor they had most readily at hand, which was rum.

Punch recipes from the colonial South vary widely, but they share four basic elements: citrus peel–infused rum, a sugar syrup of some sort, a blend of fruit juices, and then more rum. Harriott Pinckney Horry, who married into a prominent South Carolina family and lived at Hampton Plantation near present-day McClellanville, recorded an entry for the Duke of Norfolk Punch in her receipt book (as recipe books were known), which she began compiling in 1770.

Harriott Pinckney Horry's Duke of Norfolk Punch ❧

Boil twelve Gallons of Water, as soon as it Boils put in twelve pounds of loaf Sugar and the Whites of thirty Eggs. Let them boil a quarter of an hour, and when cold strain it very clean through a coarse cloth into a rum Cask; then put in five quarts and a half of Orange juice, and three quarts and a half Lemon juice straind. Peel thirty Oranges and thirty Lemons very thin, steep the Peel in a Gallon of rum four days, strain the rum off into the Cask adding four gallons more of rum. It will be fit to bottle in two Months. Care must be taken not to shake the Cask when drawing off.

Horry notes that the punch base should be weakened with water "to the palate" at serving.

Another popular rum preparation was shrub. One must be careful when looking for recipes for it today, because shrub evolved over time and modern versions bear only a faint resemblance to the colonial-era variety. In his book *How's Your Drink?* (2009), for instance, Eric Felten identifies shrub as a vinegar-based fruit syrup that would be mixed with rum or brandy when drunk. Many recipes for shrub cocktails call for blending such a syrup with rum and club soda or seltzer, but those are modern incarnations. Like punch, shrub was a technique for cutting the harshness of spirits by infusing them with sharp flavors and letting time go to work. The typical additions are fruit—especially citrus—and sugar. Far from a flavoring syrup, shrub was one the earliest forms of ready-to-mix drinks.

The 1736 *Dictionarium Britannicum* defined shrub as "a compound of brandy, the juice of Sevil oranges, and lemons kept in a vessel for the ready making of punch at any time, by the addition of water and sugar."

Here is Harriott Pinckney Horry's recipe for shrub, adapted from her receipt book from the 1770s:

Shrub

SERVES 24

1 gallon old rum

4 pints Seville orange juice (see note)

1 pint lemon juice

3½ pounds sugar

Put the rum, juice, and sugar in a jug and let it sit for two months, shaking it every day. Let contents settle one last day before pouring off and serving.

Note: If you make this recipe with modern-day navel or juice oranges, you will likely end up disappointed with the results. Back in Horry's days, the oranges would have been Seville oranges, which are quite flavorful but very bitter and acidic. If you can find Seville oranges, by all means use them. Otherwise, use 2⅔ pints lime juice and 1⅓ pints orange juice along with the pint of lemon juice.

The same treatment used to convert rum into shrub was applied to brandy as well. In her receipt book, Horry included formulas for plum brandy and raspberry brandy, both of which were made by steeping fruits in brandy in a jug for many weeks. She also provided instructions for ratafia: peach pits soaked in brandy then mixed with sweet wine, orange-flower water, and sugar and allowed to infuse in the sun for six weeks. A golden cordial was made from one gallon of brandy infused with citron or lemon peel, sugar, almonds, peach kernels, cinnamon, and cloves and allowed to sit in the sun for several weeks before being strained and bottled for use. In her *Booke of Cookery*, Martha Washington had her own recipe for a brandy-based shrub. It calls for one quart of brandy, one quart of white wine, and one quart of springwater. To that, one adds three sliced lemons and one pound of sugar, stirs well, and lets sit in a covered pot for three days before straining and bottling.

Making Colonial Shrub 🐘

If you want to re-create the original flavor of Southern punches and shrubs, it's worth making the effort to track down the right ingredients, for rum and sugar are quite different today than they were back in colonial times. Most modern rums are smooth, column-distilled products that are far milder than their colonial-era ancestors. But there are a few versions out there that are made in old-style pot stills and have that the good old hogo bite of colonial rums. There's Lemon Hart and Wood's Old Navy rum, two dark rums that hail from the Demerara River region of Guyana, and Wray & Nephew white overproof rum from Jamaica, a high-test clear rum with a solid pot-still foundation. My favorite is Smith & Cross, a 114-proof London dock-style Jamaican rum created by importer Eric Seed to re-create the style of rum that was prevalent in Jamaica before the advent of the column still. A 50/50 blend of two pot-stilled Jamaican rums, it's made not from cane juice or molasses alone but from the full range of byproducts from sugar production—the molasses and the skimmings and the syrup bottoms.

The sugar matters too. In the colonial era, sugar was not the white granular stuff we use today. During the colonial era, loaf sugar came in dense, bullet-shaped cones. It was light brown in color due to retained molasses and therefore had a darker, more complex sweetness. To create a close approximation today, use a raw sugar such as Demerara, turbinado, or if you can find it, jaggery, an unrefined whole cane sugar common throughout the Caribbean, Asia, and Africa. (You can often find these sugars in your local Indian or Asian grocery.)

Punch and shrub took time to make properly, needing weeks of steeping in a cask before they were ready to enjoy. A more expeditious way to turn raw rum or brandy into a palatable beverage was to drink it as a toddy or a sling. It's not exactly clear what the difference between a toddy and a sling is. David Wondrich has surveyed early recipes and concluded, helpfully, that "toddy was perceived as a hot drink that you could also make cold, and sling as a cold one that you could also make hot." Hot or cold, you didn't need much else besides your liquor—just a little water, sugar, and maybe some spices. And by "cold," it really just means that the drink included water that was not hot, which would be pretty much room temperature in the South and might better be termed "warm toddy."

I haven't been able to turn up an actual recipe for toddy from the eighteenth century, but considering how simple a drink it was, it's not surprising that no one bothered to write down instructions. In the mid-nineteenth century, Jerry Thomas recorded one in his seminal bartender's guide *How to Mix Drinks, or the Bon-Vivant's Companion* (1862), and it's quite simple.

Jerry Thomas's Toddy

SERVES 1 OR 2

1 teaspoonful of sugar
½ wine-glass of water
1 do. brandy (that is, ditto, meaning one wine-glass)
1 small lump ice

Stir with a spoon.

For hot toddy omit the ice, and use boiling water.

Note: In Thomas's day, a wine-glass was a measurement of about four fluid ounces, so this is a pretty stiff drink, unless you are sharing it with a friend. That lump of ice, I should note, would have been unavailable in the colonial South.

But precise recipes aren't necessary, for toddy was something mixed to each individual's taste. A host would provide the sugar and water, plus a toddy stick to be used to mix the beverage. You could make toddies and slings from just about anything. Gin slings tended to be popular in the mid-Atlantic and New England states, but rum and brandy were the leading ingredients in the South. This simple formula—a generous dose of rum or brandy cut by a little sugar and a little water—became the foundation for an entire generation of mixed drinks of the South. One early variant was sangaree, which takes its name from the Spanish word for blood and essentially applies the toddy treatment to red wine.

Sangaree and Negus ❧

Miss Leslie's Complete Cookery (1851) provided the following instructions for making sangaree: "Mix in a pitcher or in tumblers one-third of wine and two-thirds of water either warm or cold. Stir in sufficient loaf sugar to sweeten it." By adding lemon juice, Mrs. Leslie notes, "you may make what is called negus."

Rum, Wine, and the Founding of Georgia

The fourth Southern colony, Georgia, was founded in 1733, and it was under very different circumstances than Virginia and the Carolinas. By then, the English had more than a century of experience living in the New World, including many years of establishing and regulating a reliable supply of drink. Georgia's founder, James Oglethorpe, wanted to take his colony in a very different direction. He aspired to create a society based upon the concept of agrarian equality, where colonists would hold small parcels of land and there would be no stark class distinctions. Unlike Carolina's lords proprietors, who tried to administer their colony from afar in London, Oglethorpe came to Georgia with the first group of settlers. During the summer of 1733, he witnessed scores of colonists die in the new, unfamiliar climate. Though the concept of a "seasoning" was well known from the experience of Virginians and Carolinians, Oglethorpe concluded that the deaths were at least partially to blame on alcohol. He thought that the colonists' strength had been sapped by too much strong drink—specifically, by too much rum. The chiefs of the nearby Indian nations also lodged complaints against rum, with which white traders were plying their people and creating "great disorder."

To address these concerns, Oglethorpe secured legislation from Parliament that dictated that "no Rum or Brandys nor any other kind of Spirits or Strong Waters" could be imported into the new colony nor sold to any persons, whether English or Native American. Oglethorpe was not opposed to alcohol in and of itself. He simply wanted to limit his colony to wholesome beer and ale. He was himself a lover of wine and had a vineyard of his own back home in England at his estate in Surrey, and undeterred by the repeated failures of Virginians and Carolinians, he dreamed the old Southern dream of transforming his new colony into a center of wine production.

The original settlers of Georgia arrived with a variety of vine cuttings, and they selected a ten-acre plot on the east end of Savannah to become the Trustees' Garden. This area was to serve as an experimental farm for growing potential cash crops like flax and hemp, as well as mulberry trees for silk production, and, of course, grapes for making wine. Unfortunately, the colonists picked about the worst spot possible for such a tract. The soil was exceptionally sandy, and the summer heat parched the trees and vines planted there. The trustees didn't have much luck with their help either. The Georgia Trustees hired a botanist from Scotland to oversee their garden, but he died en route. His successor was captured by the Spanish, and the third candidate, who actually made it to the colony, quit after a few years. The grapevines, unsurprisingly, languished in the Georgian climate, just as they had in Virginia and the Carolinas. Silk production fared a little better, but not enough to create a marketable product. In 1748, the Trustees' Garden was abandoned.

Just across the Savannah River to the north, the Carolinians snickered at Oglethorpe's prohibition. They considered rum mixed with water to be "the cheapest, the most refreshing, and nourishing drink for workmen in such foggy and burning climate." Most Georgians must have agreed, for they regularly made their way across the Savannah for a few snorts. After fourteen workingmen drowned when their boat capsized as they were rowing to visit an alehouse on the South Carolina side, Oglethorpe tried to have the offending alehouse shut down, but to no avail. Boats from Carolina regularly carried loads of rum into Savannah too. Magistrates had the kegs seized and destroyed whenever they found them, but the booze kept right on flowing.

In 1738, a "notorious retailer of rum" named Scott was hauled into court on the charge of selling "Punch and plain Drams" within his home. The judge instructed the jury to find Scott guilty, but they returned with an acquittal. This, colonial secretary William Stephens recorded in his journal, was "so barefaced and scandalous a Proceeding" that the jury was sent out again to reconsider. When they returned with another not guilty verdict, the judge threw up his hands and released Scott. "The people here will not yet easily think Rum-selling a crime," Stephens commented, "till some can be brought to understand it with Severity."

The authorities never did bring Georgians to that understanding. Stephens noted that in Savannah "private Rum-Shops were become as common among the People, in Proportion, as Gin-Shops formerly at London." After 1742, the government gave up any pretense of enforcing the ban, which was officially repealed five years later. Rum was the drink of the Southern colonists, and there was little their governments could do to change it.

Rum and Native Americans

Most Native American tribes in the South neither made nor consumed alcohol prior to the arrival of Europeans. But once strong drink was available, they took to it readily, and often with disastrous results. John Lawson, traveling among the Sewee in 1700, found rum already widely in use. He noted that the Sewee (who called it oonaquod) would "part with the dearest Thing they have, to purchase it." In 1728, William Byrd recorded that Nottoway town, which then had a population of about 200, was the last significant pocket of Native Americans within the bounds of settled Virginia and that "nothing has been so fatal to them as their ungovernable Passion for Rum." Fur and skin traders took rum deep into the backcountry, using a round of rum to open negotiations and even more to close the deal. They exchanged kegs of rum for skins, furs, and even slaves. Journals and travelogues record shocked accounts of Native American drinking binges that led to chaos and disorder. "In these frolics," naturalist William Bartram recorded, "both sexes take such liberties with each other, and act, without constraint or shame, such scenes as they would abhor when sober." John Lawson likened rum to smallpox, a plague visiting destruction upon the native residents.

When reading such accounts, one must keep a cautious eye out for the inherent biases of English writers. The assertions that no Native American could handle strong drink—that rum instantly turned each and every one into a lurching, out-of-control lunatic—are often part of a more general portrayal of Native Americans as wild, uncontrollable savages. This much is certain, though: Native American leaders weren't happy about rum traders and the alcohol they peddled, and they repeatedly petitioned English governments to restrict the rum trade or ban it altogether. Some colonies did pass such laws, though they were routinely circumvented. As early as 1691, Carolina prohibited the carrying of "rum, brandy, or spirits whatsoever" to sell to the nation of Indians along the Savannah River, and it renewed such acts regularly through at least 1707. A primary reason that the Trustees of Georgia tried to prohibit rum from the new colony was because the area's tribal chiefs petitioned them to do so.

Such bans proved ineffective, and throughout the eighteenth century, more and more rum made its way into Native American hands. A woman named Mrs. Russell operated a tavern along the so-called Cherokee Path in South Carolina, and on three separate occasions in the 1740s, she presented bills to the colonial government for tabs run up by Cherokee and Catawba chiefs drinking punch and drams when they were visiting the governor. Alexander Hewatt, writing in 1779, attributed the dramatic decline of the Native American population to several causes, including the loss of rich hunting and fishing grounds, deaths through war, and smallpox. "But of all causes," he wrote, "the introduction of spirituous liquors among them, for which they discovered an amazing fondness, has proved the most destructive."

By this point, rum was fully entrenched in all aspects of Southern life, from the wealthiest planters to the enslaved Africans upon whose backs the planters' fortunes were earned, from the very sailors who brought the spirits to Southern ports to the Native Americans who were being pushed ever farther into the backcountry. The dark side of rum drinking—violence, destitution, illness, and debt—were readily apparent, and colonial leaders made continued efforts to suppress them, but with little success. It was a young, rough, and independent-minded society, and strong spirits were an inherent part of it. Rum and brandy, punch and toddies: these formed a firm foundation for a Southern drinking culture that would continue to grow and expand as the colonies matured.

3

Southern Drinking on the Eve of the Revolution

Rum and brandy are two spirits that aren't frequently found together in the same cocktail, which is a bit surprising considering how thoroughly they dominated the Southern drinking scene in the last decades of the colonial era and how nicely their flavors merge when combined. We opened the previous chapter with an authentic large-batch punch. Let's bend the rules a little this time and mix up an iced, single-batch punch. It's adapted from the recipe that appears in *The Ideal Bartender*, a slim volume published in 1917 by Tom Bullock, the longtime bartender at the Saint Louis Country Club and the first African-American bartender to publish his own recipe book. If you use good apple or peach brandy instead of the imported grape stuff, it will be all the more thematically appropriate.

Brandy Punch

SERVES 1

Crushed ice

2 ounces apple or peach brandy (or substitute regular brandy)

1 ounce strong Jamaican rum (see notes on rums on page 32)

1 ounce freshly squeezed lemon juice

2 teaspoons simple syrup (page 6)

1 slice orange

1 piece pineapple

Fill a cocktail shaker three-quarters full with crushed ice. Add the brandy, rum, and lemon juice and shake until well mixed, 10 to 20 seconds. Pour contents of shaker into a large bar glass and garnish the rim with the orange and pineapple slices.

Alembics and Brandy:
The Expansion of Southern Distilling

The French and Indian War marked an important dividing point in the history of the Southern colonies. Erupting in 1754 as an extension of the Seven Years' War in Europe, it interrupted trade and put the brakes on the surging plantation economy. By the war's end in 1763, Britain had secured control of the entire eastern half of North America, including seizing Florida from Spain. Access to land in East Florida and the opening of new territory in Georgia fueled the growth of plantations, and the export of rice increased from 61 million pounds in 1764 to 83 million in 1770.

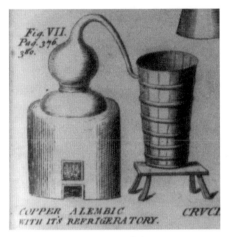

Copper alembic with water-cooled worm.

Not coincidentally, the nature of drinking in the South changed considerably in the years just after the French and Indian War. Rum, for starters, got a lot cheaper. The British government lowered the duty on spirits imported from Spanish and French colonies, which encouraged West Indian planters to expand their production and led to an oversupply that depressed prices. In 1763, rum from Barbados, Antigua, and Saint Kitts was selling in Savannah for less than three shillings per gallon, and the most prized Jamaican rum was selling for just four. At the same time, more and more brandy was being produced domestically. The improved alembic still, or side still, arrived in Virginia in the 1760s. With older stills, the alcohol vapors had to rise up a long straight tube to a condensing chamber high above. With the alembic, a copper coil connected the heating container with the collection container, and the coil was immersed in a basin of cold water. The coolness made the alcohol condense more quickly, and the steam didn't need to travel nearly as far. This allowed stills to be smaller, less expensive, and less prone to break.

As the volume of domestically produced liquor grew, more and more of it took the form of peach brandy. Peach trees set fruit several years earlier than apples, allowing a farmer to produce his own liquor that much quicker. They grew well in the warmer climate of the non-mountainous regions of the South too. Traveling through Virginia in 1773, Josiah Quincy found orchard after orchard planted with ten to twenty acres of peaches, the purpose of which was "the making of brandy, a very favorite liquor." An advertisement in the *Georgia Gazette* in 1769 offered for sale a five-hundred–acre farm near Augusta, a key feature of which was an eight-acre peach orchard from which "a great quantity of peach brandy" could be made. The estate sale of Samuel Hipkins's Virginia plantation included "a valuable new still that works 60 gallons or more" along with 130 gallons of peach brandy.

Almost all of this brandy was being consumed locally, since there wasn't an export market for peach brandy. And local consumption was prodigious. Philip Vickers Fithian recorded that, in addition to four hogsheads of rum, the family of Colonel Robert Carter in 1774 put away 150 gallons of home-distilled brandy per year. Fithian noted that in August he found a local squire having his people "shaking the trees to prepare the peaches for brandy." There is even some indication that Southerners actually preferred local cider and brandy over imported rum. Virginia merchant William Allason explained to his overseas partners that their rum, which was mostly consumed as a substitute when brandy was scarce, sold poorly when planters had bumper crops of apples and peaches and could make their own brandy.

Not everyone was a fan of the peach spirits, though. Thomas Anburey, a British officer who served under General John Burgoyne during the American Revolution, recorded the arrival of British troops to Charlottesville in 1779 and noted that many of the officers, to ward off the cold, "drank rather freely of an abominable liquor, called peach brandy, which, if drank to excess, the fumes raise an absolutely delirium." It did the trick, though, and Anburey noted that "in their cups several were guilty of deeds that would admit no apology."

During his time in Virginia, Anburey had several opportunities to observe brandy being made. Having done so, he wrote, "I no longer am

surprized at this spirit having such pernicious effects when drank to
excess." Anburey described Virginians gathering the fruit, putting it into
small vats, and allowing it to sit until "it is in such a state of putrefaction,
as to be extremely offensive to approach it." The peaches were then
pressed and their juices distilled. Anburey recalled asking several local
inhabitants whether, instead of letting the peaches rot, it might be better
to simply bruise them while ripe and immediately press them. It's not
clear whether Anburey meant that, once strained, the juice should be
allowed to ferment before going in the still or whether he just didn't
understand how the whole fermentation process worked. Nevertheless,
the Virginians answered diplomatically that they believed Anburey's way
might be better, but the other way was how it usually was done. He was
armed, after all.

Fruit Brandy Today ❧

If you're trying to re-create the experience of old-time peach brandy,
don't just grab any old bottle off your local liquor store shelf. That
would, in all likelihood, be a peach-flavored brandy liqueur, made
from a grape-based brandy (and a pretty cheap one, at that) that's
dosed with peach flavoring and sugar. For a long time, it was almost
impossible to find brandy distilled from actual peaches or apples.
Fortunately, with the rise of craft distilling in recent years, several
small artisan producers have started making real fruit brandies
again. Here are a few:

* Carolina Distillery, Lenoir, North Carolina: Carriage House apple
  brandy (white and aged versions)
* Tom's Foolery, Chagrin Falls, Ohio: Tom's Foolery applejack
* Peach Street Distillers, Palisade, Colorado: Jack and Jenny peach
  brandy and pear brandy
* Dutch's Spirits, Pine Plains, New York: Dutch's Spirits peach brandy
* ÆppelTreow Winery & Distillery, Burlington, Wisconsin: apple
  brandy, pear brandy
* Old World Spirits, Belmont, California: oak-aged O'Henry peach
  eau-de-vie

It's apparently quite difficult to make peach brandy well, which is why, even with the flourishing of craft distilleries, so few are trying their hands at it. In 2010, a group of distillers gathered at the reconstructed distillery at Mount Vernon to try to re-create a historical version of the peach brandy that was periodically produced in George Washington's distillery. Lance Winters of California's St. George Spirits told the *Washington Post*, "The toughest thing is finding peaches in this country that are worth distilling." Today's peaches were bred for long shelf life and "supermarket appeal." Back in the eighteenth century, Winters speculated, "the fruit was probably much better." With no additional sugar added during distilling, all the sugars to be converted into alcohol and give flavor to the brandy must come from the peaches themselves.

One might expect apple and peach brandy to range in color from a pale yellow to deep golden brown, and, indeed, many of the brands that are available on the market today do. That color, though, comes not from the fruit but from the barrel in which it's aged. Apple and peach brandy emerge from the still perfectly clear. Barrel aging does wonders for fruit brandies, imparting the same rich caramel and oak flavors that it does to whiskey. But the spirits imbibed in the colonial era would have been young and clear, as the practice of barrel aging (especially with toasted or charred barrels, which impart extra color and sweetness) did not come around until the nineteenth century. All of the distilleries that make apple and peach brandies today are barrel aging their products, but a few also sell an unaged version. Carolina Distillery in Lenoir, North Carolina, for instance, sells what they call white apple brandy, and Colorado's Peach Street Distillers sell an unaged eau-de-vie version. If you want a smooth sipping spirit, by all means go for the aged brandies. If you're trying to get closer the type of apple or peach brandy that would have been enjoyed in the South before the Revolution, look for the clear spirits.

Improved Cider, Commercial Distilling, and Beer

The late colonial period also saw important innovations in cidering. Cider presses and troughs became much cheaper. Grafting produced the Hewes crab apple, a small, sturdy fruit that grew more quickly than other varieties, allowing a planter to start producing cider from a new orchard several years sooner after planting. Its flesh was fibrous and tough, so it essentially filtered out its own pulp when pressed, leaving a clear white juice. That juice was sweeter, too, and the higher sugar content caused faster fermentation. Other varieties like the Taliaferro, Roan, and Gloucester White had similar properties. When combined with the newly available alembic stills, these apple varieties made it much easier for small farmers to distill an improved cider into an apple brandy that didn't spoil, resulting in a great expansion of both cidering and brandy distilling, especially in Virginia, where apple trees were more abundant than in the colonies farther south.

The advances in ingredients and distilling technology inspired a few practical men to undertake commercial distilling on a large scale on the eve of the American Revolution. At least two commercial distilleries operated in Norfolk in the 1770s, and two more in Alexandria. In 1771, Jamieson, Campbell, Calvert, and Company of Norfolk advertised that "at our Rum Distillery here may be had a constant supply of that Article." Down in Savannah in 1767, Henry Snow advertised himself as a "distiller from London," making and selling a variety of liquors that included "Fine Georgia Geneva" (that is, gin) along with aniseed water, caraway water, brandy "equal to the French," mulberry brandy, Vizney or Turkish brandy, ratafia, and cinnamon and citron waters.

Snow doesn't seem to have made a go of his distilling business, and other early commercial distillers struggled too. Several decades after the experiment to produce wine had proven a failure, a distillery was constructed on a lot that once was part of the Trustees' Garden in Savannah. Little is known about this distillery except that it was advertised for sale in 1770 and the offer included "all its utensils and a quantity of molasses," so we can assume it was producing rum. By 1773, Daniel Roberdeau, a Philadelphia merchant who had a plantation in Alexandria, Virginia, saw his West India rum trade declining and decided to create his own supply in Virginia. He secured £3,000 to build a stone distillery house, a grain storehouse, a cooper's shop, and a woodyard. The operation included two stills with the capacity to work 2,500 gallons along with a third still with a 600-gallon capacity to produce low wines. By April of the next year, Roberdeau and his distiller were advertising "Alexandria Rum, which they engage to be equal in quality, strength, agreeableness of smell, and good flavour, to any made on this continent." It was for sale for cash or "country produce." The Revolution disrupted Roberdeau's business. Just a few months after he announced his rum for sale, Roberdeau was named a brigadier in the state militia, and he also served in the Continental Congress from 1777 to 1779. In 1781, he declared bankruptcy, and the distillery equipment was sold at a sheriff's sale, bringing a quick end to Alexandria rum.

After the end of the French and Indian War in 1763, Southerners returned to their century-old ambition of brewing their own beer, though the short supply of ingredients forced brewers to be creative. Malted barley was reused in multiple boils, the first producing double beer, with the most sugar and therefore the most alcohol. A second boil produced table beer, and the final one small beer, which would have had much less alcohol, though still enough to prevent it from spoiling. Brewers also turned to alternative ingredients like spruce as a hops substitute, providing bitterness and flavor to what became known as "spruce beer."

It wasn't until the eve of the Revolution that a Southerner was able to make brewing a going concern. Edmund Egan arrived in Charleston from England in the early 1760s after serving as an apprentice to a London brewer. Around 1765, he went into business with John Calvert and opened a brewery. By 1766, the pair were advertising double-brewed spruce beer, table beer, and small beer for sale, but they struggled to obtain ingredients. Egan ended up buying barley seeds, giving them away free to local planters, and guaranteeing to buy whatever they grew. By 1773, Egan announced that "having long laboured under many Disadvantages," his brewery was now complete and "amply supplied with a stock of best malt and hops." He also adopted a catchy new slogan to use in his advertisements: "Let the beer Justify itself!"

By all accounts, it did. The *South Carolina Gazette and Journal* wrote that Egan's beer was "superior to most of that imported from the Northern Colonies." Henry Laurens wrote to a Northern merchant that there was little use in selling imported beer in Charleston because "most of the Tavern keepers here, seem to prefer Carolina Brewing to that of Philadelphia." By the mid-1770s, Egan had bought out his investors and made himself the sole owner of the brewery, and he was bringing in almost £20,000 in annual revenue. His Magazine Street operation had a one-hundred-foot-long malthouse, a kiln, an imported grinder with cast-iron rollers that could process a hundred bushels of malt a day, two large copper kettles, and many barrels and bottles. It was worked by eight slaves—two coopers and six trained brewers—all of whom were apparently owned by Egan.

THE Subscriber, being support-
ed by Gentlemen of Fortune in this Province
who have determined to promote the BREWERY in
Charleftown, under his Management and Care, Gives
Notice, that he will pay, in ready Money, *Fifteen Shillings*
per Bufhel, for Summer or Winter BARLEY, and *Five*
Shillings per Pound for HOPS, both to be good in their
Kind, delivered at the BREW-HOUSE, at any Time from
the 1ft of *September*, 1771, to the 1ft of *February*, 1772.
Any Perfon inclined to plant BARLEY, may be fup-
plied by him with SEED, upon Condition of returning
him a like Quantity, and felling to him the overplus of
the Produce, upon the Terms above mentioned.
                                    EDMUND EGAN.

To ensure a supply of ingredients, pioneering Charleston brewer Edmund Egan gave barley seeds
to farmers and guaranteed he'd buy the crops.

As brewing and distilling grew more commercial in nature, alcohol
production moved from the woman's realm of cooking and housekeeping
into the male-dominated world of trade. Brewing and distilling instructions
gradually disappeared from women's cookbooks and started showing up
in the pages of agricultural manuals. By the 1760s, men no longer made
provisions in their wills for their wives to retain the use of their stills after
their death; instead, they passed them directly to their sons.

Drinking on Plantations and in the Backcountry

In the latter half of the eighteenth century, the institution of chattel slavery
became ever more embedded in the political, economic, and social life
of the South. As it did, elite whites grew increasingly wary of alcohol use
among slaves. Grand jury records from the Georgetown and Orangeburg
districts in South Carolina in the 1770s note numerous "tippling and
gaming houses" along the public roads, some of which were thought to be
"dealing with and enticing Negroes." In 1766, James Houstoun repeatedly
placed advertisements in the *Georgia Gazette* demanding that whichever

persons were buying provisions and grain from his slaves cease doing so and stop selling them "rum, brandy, or other spirituous or strong liquors" in return. In both Virginia and the Carolinas, lower-class whites were frequently the ones supplying alcohol to slaves. Overseers and neighboring farmers regularly exchanged rum or brandy for money or bartered goods like chickens. In some cases, whites and blacks drank together, particularly at horse races or when gambling at cards or dice.

It had long been the practice of planters to supply drink to their enslaved labor force. In the Chesapeake region, slaves typically received a daily ration of a pint of cider. During the harvest, most men and women received between a half-pint and a pint of rum per day. In 1766, Henry Laurens expressed amazement that on one of his Lowcountry South Carolina rice plantations, thirty gallons of rum were consumed in less than three months, but he sent along an additional ten gallons of Jamaican rum nevertheless.

Toward the end of the eighteenth century, though, many planters started reducing or even eliminating alcohol rations. In 1793, George Washington observed that "others are getting out of the practice of using spirits at Harvest," but decided that since his slaves "have always been accustomed to it, a hogshead of Rum must be purchased." But the enslaved portion of the Southern population knew how to get their hands on alcohol when they wanted it. Though not officially sanctioned by the government, slaves maintained their own economies, accumulating currency in the form of money or goods for barter. Skilled slaves whose labor was rented out were often allowed to keep a portion of the money they earned, and they frequently spent it on alcohol. Landon Carter of Virginia decided to provide his slaves with only one shirt, not two as was customary, in the hopes of forcing them to buy linen to make a second shirt "instead of buying liquor with their fowls." At Henry Laurens's Wambaw plantation, a man named Amos had a "great inclination to turn rum Merchant," and he frequently sneaked parcels onto Laurens's schooner for trading at other plantations along the Santee River.

Hundreds of miles inland from the coastal rice plantations, a new type of Southerner was beginning to carve out homesteads in what was known as the backcountry of the Carolinas. While some of these frontier residents had migrated westward from Charleston or coastal plantations, many more were Scotch-Irish Presbyterians and Baptists who had made their way down into the Piedmont from Pennsylvania and Virginia in search of land. As they came, they converted Indian paths into wagon roads and established fords and ferries at stream and rivers, creating a new transportation network in a largely unsettled land.

Charles Woodmason was an itinerant Anglican minister who traveled that backwoods network extensively in the 1760s, and he found the region to be soaked with rum. This was the era of the Great Awakening and the New Light Baptists, who believed that there was no scriptural basis for infant baptism and insisted upon a conscious conversion experience. These days, Southern Baptists are known to be pretty abstemious, at least in public. (It's well known that if you are going to invite a Baptist to go fishing, you'd better invite two. If you invite just one, he'll drink all your beer.) That was not at all the case in the colonial days. Drunkenness and brawling prevailed at militia musters and public venues, Woodmason found. Taverns remained jammed with patrons, and "a much greater Quantity of Rum is now expended in private families than heretofore." The Baptists even drank heavily at their own assemblies, and Woodmason judged that half of the attendees at evening meetings were there not for the Holy Spirit but for the more worldly variety.

Reverend Woodmason decried intoxication, but he had no problem with rum itself. In fact, his inability to get his hands on rum was a constant grievance in his journals. As soon as the Baptists and the Scotch-Irish Presbyterians learned Woodmason was an Anglican minister, all hospitality ceased. He was routinely denied lodging, food, and drink at taverns (even though at one of them, he noted, the owner had "2 Barrels of Rum in the House"), and he soon learned to carry with him "my own Necessaries," which included biscuit, cheese, sugar, coffee, tea, and a pint of rum.

The tavern had played a minor role in the social life of coastal plantation districts, but in the backcountry it was among the earliest and most important economic institutions. While in theory a place for travelers to find accommodation, in practice these taverns catered mostly to a local clientele. In 1751, an anonymous clergyman groused to the *Virginia Gazette* that "Ordinaries are now, in a great Measure, perverted from their original Intention and proper use," which was the "Reception, Accommodation, and Refreshment of the weary and benighted Traveller." Instead, they were now serving "the very Dreggs of the People" from the local community, who gathered there to drink, play cards, and engage in "Vice and Enormities of every other kind."

For backcountry men, the tavern was the primary social center of the region, offering food, drink, and amusement as well as a place to conduct business, talk politics, and gamble at cards and dice. Some, like Cantey's in Pine Tree Hill (the original name for Camden, South Carolina), were large establishments with public rooms and lodging. Others, like William Mitchell's near the Wateree River, were little more than houses where, as one Carolinian put it, "there was Lickuar to sell." In 1755, the village of Salisbury, North Carolina, contained eight houses. Four of them functioned as inns or taverns.

Women did not typically do their drinking in taverns, but they were frequent customers nevertheless, for the tavern also served as the neighborhood liquor store. In his study of the account records of taverns in Rowan County, North Carolina, historian Daniel Thorp found that more than half of the entries in men's accounts were for individual drinks like drams and toddies that were likely consumed there on the premises. Women's accounts were almost exclusively for liquor in larger quantities, suggesting they were taking it home for themselves and their families to consume. Rum was by far the most popular purchase, though a fair amount of wine and beer was sold too.

Charles Woodmason blamed taverns (and not his own preaching) for low attendance at his church services. He found that Saturday was the day most backcountry residences chose to "fully indulge themselves in Drink," which would allow them to sleep it off on Sunday—skipping church in the process—and still be fit to attend to their business on Monday morning. Woodmason decried the fact that most backcountry magistrates either kept stores or taverns, complaining, "Thus Vice and Wickedness is countenanc'd by those whose Duty is to suppress it—but their Interest to promote it." Joseph Kershaw managed the store at Pine Tree Hill, where he sold everything from food and drink to clothing, tools, and seed. According to Kershaw's daybook, alcohol made up one-eighth of his business (the largest item, making up one-third of his sales, was cloth). Rum was the top-selling beverage, followed by wine, and he handled a small amount of gin and brandy too. Most of this liquor made its way into the backcountry via boat and wagon from either Charleston or Norfolk.

Planters and farmers periodically traveled into town to conduct trade and attend court, and when they did, they generally ended up drinking heavily. Englishman Nicholas Cresswell arrived in Virginia in 1774, and he lived in the colony for three years. His journals record his visits to Williamsburg while the House of Burgesses was in session. Cresswell lodged at Mrs. Vaube's tavern with "all the best people" of the colony.

"All are professed gamesters," he wrote. "Especially Colonel Burd." He meant William Byrd III, who had served as a colonel during the French and Indian War then returned home to Virginia to drink and gamble away his family fortune. All day long, statesmen and observers scurried from the Capitol building to the tavern for a quick dram, and once the sessions were adjourned for the evening, Mrs. Vaube's was filled with "carousing and drinking in one chamber and box and dice in another." The festivities lasted straight through until morning.

Booze was an indispensable part of the electoral process. In the 1758 election for the House of Burgesses in Virginia, George Washington spent almost forty pounds on spirits to treat voters, including fifty gallons and one hogshead of rum punch. Theodorick Bland Jr., a planter and politician from Virginia's Prince George County, wrote in 1765 that "our friend, Mr. Banister, has been very much ingaged since the dissolution of the assembly, in swilling the planters with bumbo, and I dare say from the present prospect, will be elected a burgess."

It's a little hard to pin down exact statistics for the alcohol consumption of people three hundred years ago, but just about every scholar who has attempted it has come to the same conclusion: people during the colonial era drank a lot. Historian W. J. Rorabaugh estimates that between 1700 and 1770, annual hard liquor consumption in the American colonies rose from 2 gallons per capita to 3.7 gallons. By 1770, an average adult white male drank seven shots of rum per day, while an average white woman drank a quart of hard cider daily. Children consumed alcohol daily too— often in the form of the lower-alcohol small beer—as did most slaves.

Over the course of the eighteenth century, Southerners had established their favorite forms of drink. Brandy—both domestic and imported—was still a prized tipple, but rum was the workhorse, drunk in the dockside taverns in coastal towns, on tobacco and rice plantations, and way out in the backwoods too. In Virginia, though, tobacco had made a small number of planters wealthy, and farther south in the Carolinas, rice had made an even smaller number of planters even wealthier. These men could now afford to import fine wines and brandies from Europe and the Atlantic islands, and they were thirsty for something more elegant and rare. If it was something they could use to flaunt their wealth and lord over everyone else while getting their drink on, well, all the better.

4

Three Times Around the Horn: Madeira Emerges

If you've never tasted Madeira before, you're not alone. It's a wine that was almost lost to history. Mannie Berk, the president of the Rare Wine Company, is trying to change that. He teamed up with Ricardo Freitas, the managing director and winemaker for Madeira's Vinhos Barbeito to produce the Rare Wine Company's Historic Series, which not only recognizes the wine's long history but also aims to introduce wine lovers to its rich, complex flavor. Each wine in the series is blended from vintage Madeiras to match the particular style that would have been enjoyed in a colonial American city, including Savannah, Charleston, and New Orleans (which, at the time, was a colonial French city).

For this chapter, then, get yourself a bottle of the Rare Wine Company's Charleston Sercial or their Savannah Verdelho. Both are old-style Madeiras, the most esteemed wine of Southern planter society. Like port, Madeira is a fortified wine, so it often gets lumped in with the ports on store shelves. The few consumers who are aware of Madeira today tend to treat it as a sweeter dessert-type wine like port, and for good reason, since that's how most twentieth-century incarnations of the wine were. But that wasn't always the case. "It used to be that Madeira was not just a dessert or after-dinner wine," Berk told me. "It was drunk throughout an entire meal." Following the historical preferences of the Southern palate, the Charleston Sercial is much drier than the style preferred in Northern cities like Boston and New York.

If you don't mind being a touch anachronistic, you could also incorporate that Madeira into any number of fine cocktails. That particular category of drink, in which spirits are cut with herbal bitters, didn't emerge until around 1800. But if Southern gentlemen had known about it, they would have thoroughly enjoyed the Creole Contentment, which Charles Baker Jr. included in his classic bar guide *The Gentleman's Companion* (1939). It combines rich Madeira with that other spirit beloved by the Southern elite: barrel-aged Cognac brandy.

Creole Contentment

SERVES 1

1½ ounces Cognac

1 ounce Madeira

½ ounce maraschino liqueur

1 dash orange bitters

Maraschino cherries (for optional swank)

Combine Cognac, Madeira, maraschino, and bitters in a tall bar glass filled with ice. Stir well and strain into a martini or coupe glass.

You could garnish the cocktail with cherries (Baker reports that the original recipe given to him by a friend called for one each of red, green, and white maraschino cherries), but as Baker adds, that would be "sheerest swank. It is a good drink and needs little trimming."

The Rise of Madeira

Despite repeated efforts, Southern colonists had consistently failed to produce a drinkable domestic wine, so those with a taste for the grape had to import it. Much of what they purchased came from the Azores and the Canary Islands, two archipelagos in the Atlantic that belonged to Portugal and Spain, respectively. A trickle more came in from the Spanish and Portuguese mainland. But the single largest source of the wine drunk in the South during the colonial era was a tiny, three hundred-square-mile island off the coast of Morocco. Its name is Madeira.

The island first started exporting wine to Europe in the sixteenth century, and British merchants began trading Madeiran wine in the 1640s, selling it first in England proper and then shipping it to the far-flung

A view of the island of Madeira in 1840.

British colonies. Madeira enjoyed an advantageous position in the Gulf Stream, which carried westward-bound ships leaving European ports right past the island, so it was a natural spot from them to resupply before making the long trek across the Atlantic. Before long, casks of Madeiran wine were arriving in the ports of the newly settled British colonies in the Caribbean and the American mainland.

In the 1660s, mercantilist political maneuvers gave a boost to British merchants' Madeira trade. The Navigation Acts prohibited any European goods from being imported into or exported out of any British colony unless they were transported on British ships and shipped first to England for inspection and the payment of duties. After King Charles II of England married the daughter of the king of Portugal, though, Parliament exempted the Portuguese islands of Madeira and the Azores from the rule, giving British merchants on Madeira a virtual monopoly on the wine trade with the West Indies and the American colonies. For most of the eighteenth century, more than three-quarters of the wine imported into British North America came from that one tiny island in the east Atlantic.

Madeira needed a geopolitical advantage to get a leg up in the trade, since it never would have made it on the quality of its wine alone. In the early eighteenth century, Madeira was by all accounts a cheap, bare-bones sort of table wine. As the export market developed, though, Madeira vintners and exporters began improving their products to meet the demands of a rising class of consumers.

The planters in the Southern colonies were precisely those sorts of consumers. Having secured their fortunes with rice and tobacco, one of the first things they spent their new wealth on was imported wine. By the late 1730s, the shipping news in Virginia papers was filled with a steady parade of ships arriving from London via Madeira, and their cargoes invariably contained plenty of wine. Madeira was even better suited to the Charleston trade because the Carolinians had something that the Madeirans very much needed: rice. A brisk exchange developed, and ships loaded with barrels of Carolina Gold rice frequently set sail directly for Madeira, returning home with holds filled with pipes of wine. As Southern elites drank more wine, they began to develop specific preferences and tastes that made them more selective buyers. In response, Madeiran producers began to improve their products to compete in a nascent connoisseur's market. Exporters became masters not just of logistics but of blending wines too. Older Madeiras tended to lose their color as the pigments precipitated out of the liquid and settled to the bottom of the bottle or cask. By blending wines of darker and lighter shades, exporters could achieve the color most desired by their customers. When a particular year's production was poor, an exporter might mix in an older wine of better quality to improve it.

Before long, exporters were competing on their blending skills, and the price of good Madeira began to rise. Even more important was the introduction of fortification, in which brandy or some sort of distilled alcohol was added. The practice seems to have been driven primarily by the exporters' American customers, who found it helped the wine stand up better to the months it would spend at sea and in wholesalers' warehouses. In the 1750s, one American customer of the Madeira merchant Francis Newton complained that the wine he ordered had arrived too acidic, since Newton did not put "a bucket or two of brandy" in each pipe as other houses did. The Madeiran winemakers and exporters quickly adopted "the American practice," as many called it, and by 1762 it was being used by the majority of Madeira's exporters. Fortification helped control the flavor and color of the wine, smoothing the acidic bite, killing bacteria, and stopping further fermentation. A new, unfortified Madeira was reddish in color and sweet to the taste; the more brandy that was added, the paler the wine's color and the drier the flavor. A heavily fortified wine was also much higher in alcohol content, and Madeiras could range anywhere from 10 to 29 percent alcohol by volume.

Madeira was shipped to the Southern colonies in wooden casks made of white oak. The most common size, known as the pipe, was a round barrel that was considerably longer than it was wide. Usually holding 110 gallons, it likely took its name from its resemblance to the barrel of a musical pipe. Those pipes received a serious shaking during transport as the ship crested one wave after another. During a voyage to America via the Caribbean, the temperature in the holds could reach 120 degrees Fahrenheit, so the wine would essentially lie cooking in its cask for weeks if not months.

It didn't take too long for Madeira drinkers to notice the unusual and highly desirable effect that this heat and agitation had on their wine. Most wines can be ruined by heat, which quickens oxidation and encourages the growth of harmful bacteria, but the extra alcohol in fortified Madeira warded off the damaging effects of heat. The agitation during a six-month journey softened the added brandy's kick and improved the wine's flavor. Madeira was the ideal wine for the South, because it not only held up well in hot climates but, as one exporter put it, "the more 'tis exposed to Sun-beams and heat, the better it is."

If a little heating and rocking was good for the wine, exporters reasoned, a lot must be even better. They started sending their wines on the longest, warmest routes possible. As early as 1750, distributors were intentionally shipping wines to the American colonies via long routes through the West Indies. A pipe of Madeira that traveled first to America and then on to Europe would sell in London for ten to twelve pounds more than one shipped from Madeira to England directly. Starting in the 1770s, exporters began shipping the wine on journeys all the way to India or even China before delivering it to Charleston. "Three times around the Horn," referring to the Horn of Africa, became a common expression for properly aged and shaken wine.

Over the course of half a century, these advancements transformed Madeira into an esteemed luxury good. At the opening of the eighteenth century, imported wines were no pricier than imported spirits and barely more expensive than ale or beer. Around 1750, that began to change. Wine historian David Hancock conducted a survey of probate inventories in South Carolina and concluded that between 1732 and 1741, the average value of all estates was $721 and the average values of estates that included a stock of wine was $1,041. But the average value of estates that included Madeira wine specifically was considerably lower than average at $616, suggesting that before 1740 Madeira was a cheap wine most likely to be found in less prosperous households. A similar survey of estates between 1765 and 1774 shows a rapid change in just three decades. In that latter survey, the average value of all estates was $1,131, but the average values of estates that included Madeira was $5,220.

Between the 1750s and the 1770s, a swarm of British merchants— many of them former sea captains—set up shop on Madeira to serve the growing American market. These Brits had the social and commercial connections to establish wide trading networks in the British colonies, and instead of just buying and exporting local wine, they soon started buying grapes and making the wine themselves. For the Southern trade, most merchants began either with a connection in Charleston or with planters along the Chesapeake and the rivers of the Carolinas. At first, they conducted business largely through correspondence, with aspiring merchants writing to old friends or acquaintances in distant ports, requesting them to place an order and to refer new customers to them.

After the 1750s, as competition grew, the island firms took to sending representatives to visit American cities every few years to drum up new business. By the 1770s, most Madeira merchants had set up full-time representatives in the colonies to manage their distribution.

Early on, the wine trade in the South was largely a wholesale business that dealt in barrels and casks, for ceramic and glass containers were expensive and rare. Taverns bought wine by the pipe (110 gallons) or barrel (31 gallons), and they rented smaller jugs or bottles to their customers, who brought them into the tavern to be refilled on a regular basis. By the 1760s, though, the domestic manufacture of glass had made bottles more widely available. They weren't suited for long-distance shipping, but they were fine for customers to use to carry wine home from stores. The retail wine business boomed. Four times as many shopkeepers in Charleston carried wine in 1765 than had just a few decades before. Customers could buy or rent bottles, corks, decanters, and glasses from their local wine merchant. A few wealthy planters in the backcountry might order wine directly from exporters in Madeira, but most who wanted more than they could buy at their local tavern would purchase it from importers and wholesalers in the Eastern seaports. In the last half of the eighteenth century, proprietors of general stores began stocking wine too.

By the eve of the Revolution, Madeira had become so expensive that many Southerners started switching to cheaper wines from the Canary Islands, but that only increased Madeira's cachet among those who could afford it. In 1771, the wealthy Lowcountry South Carolina planter John Drayton requested from his Madeira merchants "a couple of pipes of madeira for my use, of the finest flavor. Silkey-soft & smooth upon the palate—no ways ruff, sweetish & a little more Malmsey in it than usual." By 1759, just a few months after he married Martha Custiss, George Washington was ordering barrels of wines from the best Madeira houses, like the Newtons and Scott, Pringle, Cheap & Company. In 1768, Washington ordered vine cuttings from Madeira hoping to establish a vineyard at Mount Vernon, though this venture does not appear to have succeeded.

Of the Founding Fathers, Thomas Jefferson was the greatest lover of wine. Though he later became a passionate champion of French wines, thanks to his service as the American minister to France, before the American Revolution the wine Jefferson drank most often was Madeira. In the late 1760s, while still a bachelor and newly elected to the Virginia

House of Burgesses, Jefferson began recording in his account book an inventory of his wine cellar at Shadwell, the plantation he had inherited in Albemarle County, Virginia. In October 1769, he noted that he had on hand sixty-nine bottles of "Lisbon" and fifteen bottles of Madeira. He increased his purchases after moving into the newly completed Monticello in 1770, and in his lifetime, he bought and cellared more Madeira than any other wine. In 1776, he acquired a pipe of six-year-old Madeira, which contained more than five hundred bottles worth of wine.

Like other wealthy planters, Jefferson bypassed wine shops and wholesalers and placed his orders directly with winemakers. This was by no means a simple process. It required ordering by letter, specifying the ship, the captain, and the ports of entry and exit for the wine along with finer details, such as how it was to be packaged and how the shippers should pay for the wine and duties. That was just the beginning. Bottles were unreliable and burst during shipping, so Jefferson ordered his wine in pipes and had it bottled at Monticello. Often the bottles cost more than the wines they contained. Many of his shipments were lost to storms, and more than once pirates raided the ships carrying his wines from Europe. The troubles continued even after the wines arrived safely on Virginia soil. Jefferson was particularly plagued by "rascally boatmen" on the Potomac and the James Rivers, who tapped his barrels, drank much of the wine, and refilled them with water.

The Drinking Habits of the Southern Elite

In 1779, Alexander Hewatt wrote of Charleston, "With respect to wine, Madeira is not only best suited to the climate, in which it improves by heat and age, but also most commonly used by the people in general, though French, Spanish, and Portuguese wines are likewise presented at the tables of the most opulent citizens." Hewatt delineated the city's drinking habits markedly along class lines. "Where rum is cheap," he noted, "excess in the use of it will not be uncommon, especially among the lower class of people; but the gentlemen in general are sober, industrious, and temperate."

This last assertion should probably be taken with a grain of salt, for by all accounts most Charleston gentlemen had but a passing acquaintance with sobriety. In colonial Charleston, William J. Grayson recalled in his autobiography, it was the custom at dinner parties to lock the doors to the dining room and allow no one to leave. The end of the feast would find the weaker drinkers passed out under the table and the stronger ones staggering home. Grayson himself recalled seeing a group of Revolutionary War veterans, after a dinner at one of their party's houses, "going the rounds to each others houses, as long as they could walk, drinking and breaking the wine glasses and tumblers."

In March 1780, in the midst of the Revolution, Francis Marion attended just such a Charleston dinner party at the home of a fellow officer. The host locked the doors, and as the drinking escalated, Marion, who was not a heavy imbiber, began to panic. Determined to escape, he threw open a second-story window and jumped from it, breaking his ankle in the fall. Because of the injury, he left the city to recuperate and, by chance, was not captured when the British took the city in May. Marion went on to organize a small unit of irregulars in the Pee Dee region of South Carolina that harried the British with quick, guerilla-style surprise attacks, earning himself the nom de guerre of Swamp Fox. You might call his clumsy exit from the Madeira party a lucky break for the Americans.

Francis Marion escaping the madeira party.

Cognac

It wasn't just fine wines that elite Southerners developed a taste for as they began to amass their wealth. They also started importing a particularly prized version of brandy called Cognac. Its trade developed along lines similar to those of Madeira wine, as British merchants moved to the Cognac region of France and established export firms. Many of those names might be recognized by brandy lovers today. Jean Martell arrived in Cognac from Jersey in 1715. Rémy Martin founded a firm in 1724. A good bit later in 1765, an Irishman named James Hennessy started trading in Cognac brandy too. Like Madeira, Cognac evolved over the course of the eighteenth century from a cheap, low-end booze into an expensive connoisseur's product. Brandy started out as a way to make something salable from grapes that were deemed to be unfit for wine. The base of brandy is weak and acidic, but once it's double distilled into raw spirits and aged in wooden barrels, a remarkable transformation occurs. Evaporation concentrates the spirits, and the wood of the barrel softens them, adding flavors from the oak and allowing a nuanced bouquet to develop.

In the seventeeth century, Dutch merchants bought French wine and took it back to Holland for distillation, and they found that the wine from the Cognac region was particularly well suited for a smooth final product. Soon, winemakers from Cognac started doing the distilling themselves. As the decades passed, the quality of their product improved. Cognac became renowned for its delicacy, being one of the few brandies that could be sipped straight and did not have to be cut with water to be bearable. In the latter half of the eighteenth century, as its popularity and prestige were spreading, it was often spelled "Coniac" or "Cogniac." The British and Irish were the main consumers of brandy, but the rising elites in the American South took a liking to it too. In December 1764, an advertisement in North Carolina's *Newbern Gazette* listed "Coniac brandy" for sale alongside "choice Madeira and Fyall wines." "Cogniac" brandy appears occasionally for sale in the 1770s, and by the 1780s, merchants in Charleston and Alexandria were routinely advertising it by the pipe, by the anchor (a European measure equivalent to 10 gallons), and by the gallon. Its prestige continued to grow over the next half century.

By the time of the Revolution, elite Southerners had defined their preferred high-end tipples. As the aristocratic, almost-feudal society further cleaved the wealthy elite from those who toiled in bondage, fine

Madeira and Cognac became a badge of sophistication that cemented the position of the small number of people at the top of the social and economic hierarchy. In the minds of ambitious planters and merchants, at least, you were what you drank in this emerging elite South.

5

Revolutionary Spirits:
An Interlude

This recipe was contributed by R. H. Weaver, the head barman at Husk Restaurant in Charleston. I like it because it blends two liquors that are not often mixed in the same glass—rum and whiskey. That's appropriate for this chapter, for the American Revolution marked the point where these two essential Southern spirits met.

Tiki the Hut

SERVES 1

2 ounces Rittenhouse rye

½ ounce Smith & Cross Jamaica navy-strength rum

½ ounce Velvet Falernum

½ ounce black walnut orgeat (see page 61)

Whole allspice, for grating

Combine rye, rum, Velvet Falernum, and orgeat with ice in a mixing glass and stir. Strain into a cocktail glass and grate a little allspice over the top.

Rum and Madeira were two of the most valuable imported goods in the colonies, so it is not surprising that they became embroiled in the trade and taxation controversies that led to the American Revolution. For more than a century, the wine imported from Madeira had not been subjected to any import duties. Molasses from non-British colonies had been taxed at the rate of sixpence per gallon since 1733, but American colonists had routinely evaded those duties and smuggled in whatever molasses they needed to make rum. After the French and Indian War, though, the British crown started taking a hard look at the financial affairs of their colonies. Britain had taken on significant debts defending their provinces, and Parliament felt it only fair to recoup that money by increasing taxes on their colonies. The colonists saw matters a little differently. In a time of rising expectations, the question of taxation led to a decade of tension that culminated in the American Revolution.

Black Walnut Orgeat

MAKES ABOUT
1 QUART

½ pound black walnut
pieces

2 to 3 drops orange-flower
water (if desired)

Put walnut pieces in a pot and cover with water (around 2 cups). Bring to a boil and allow to simmer for 20 minutes. Strain liquid through a colander into a bowl and reserve for later. Return nuts to pot, cover with water, bring to a boil again and simmer 15 minutes. Strain through a colander, again reserving the liquid. Taste a nut to test for residual flavor. It should be fairly tasteless, but if it still has strong walnut flavor you can repeat the boiling an additional time.

Combine the reserved liquids and strain first through a fine mesh strainer then again through a cheesecloth to remove any grittiness. Measure the "milk" by volume and sweeten with 25 perfcent Demerara sugar by volume. (For example, 32 ounces of milk should be sweetened with 8 ounces of sugar.) Return sweetened milk to the saucepan over medium-high heat, stirring periodically, until sugar is dissolved.

Allow to cool and flavor with a few drops of orange-flower blossom water, if desired. This step isn't necessary but adds a unique hint of floral notes. Can be stored in the refrigerator for several weeks.

In 1764, Parliament passed the Sugar Act, which imposed a new duty of seven pounds on a tun (that is, two pipes or 220 gallons) of wine imported directly from Spain or Portugal and a lower duty of four pounds if the wine was sent first to Britain and imported to the colonies from there. The measure also cut the existing tariff on molasses in half, but the government made it clear that this time they intended to actually enforce it. The next year, Parliament passed the Stamp Act, which levied additional taxes on legal documents, newspapers, and magazines.

In February 1767, the militia companies from several counties in North Carolina marched to the town of Brunswick and articulated their feelings on the tariffs by refusing to let a cargo of stamped paper be landed. An alarmed governor, William Tryon, tried to placate the militiamen at their next muster in New Hanover by treating them to a whole barbecued ox and several barrels of beer. When called to the feast, the jeering soldiers poured Tryon's beer into the ground and pitched the ox untasted into the Cape Fear River. Seven years later, a bunch of Yankees donned Mohawk garb and chucked three shiploads of tea into Boston harbor, and for some reason that's the protest that everyone remembers. Wouldn't it be much more fun to celebrate liberty with a Carolina beer bash instead of a tea party?

A BARBECUE AND THE RESULT.

North Carolinians pay their respect to Governor Tryon.

Despite the ox and tea pitching, Parliament stuck to its guns, and over the next few years continued to put additional duties on imported goods like glass, paint, tea, and paper. In October 1774, the First Continental Congress responded with a nonimportation agreement in which the colonies pledged that, starting in December, they would no longer import goods from Great Britain or Ireland, nor wines from Madeira, since that trade was dominated by British merchants. By April 1775, traditionally the busiest time of year for the wine trade, the Madeiran exporters were feeling the pinch. That same month, fighting broke out in the Massachusetts towns of Lexington and Concord.

Troops on both sides of the conflict were fueled by rum. Alcohol was considered an essential part of soldiers' rations, providing much-needed calories at a time when food, if available at all, was frequently spoiled. Rum lent warmth when clothing was in short supply, and it relieved pain too. Drinking alcohol was generally safer than drinking water, and it was also thought to reduce fatigue. Soldiers were given extra rations of alcohol before battle and as a reward afterward.

How to supply soldiers with their needed drams became a big point of contention within the military and the American government. Rum, cider, and beer were typically purchased from licensed sutlers who followed the army camps, and at first military leaders tried to steer them away from rum, believing cider and beer to be healthier for the troops and less likely to cause drunkenness. But soldiers liked their spirits strong. They sold their clothes and personal belongings to purchase rum and, in some cases, stole liquor outright. George Washington tried twice to forbid rum sales to his troops, sentencing sutlers caught selling rum to two hundred lashes. Soldiers caught purchasing rum could be court-martialed, deprived of their rations, and whipped. But the Continental Army continued to struggle to supply its troops with sufficient ale or beer and increasingly had to embrace rum out of necessity.

On numerous occasions in 1776 and 1777, George Washington approved the supplying of rum to troops. In his general orders on July 13, 1777, he directed, "As the weather is bad, and the ground wet, the General orders a gill of rum to be served to each man immediately." In August 1777, he wrote to John Hancock, "The benefits arising from the moderate use of strong Liquor have been experienced in All Armies, and are not to be disputed." That same month, Washington wrote to the Continental Congress that his men lacked almost any kind of vegetables and, more worrisome, "neither have they been provided with proper drink—Beer or Cyder seldom comes within the verge of the Camp, and Rum in much too small quantities." It was to these wants that he ascribed "the many putrid diseases incident to the Army."

Getting their hands on rum, though, soon became difficult too. As Washington told Hancock, "Our Imports of Spirit have become so precarious—nay impracticable on account of the Enemy's Fleet, which infests our Whole Coast." As a result, "Our Soldiery cannot obtain such Supplies, as are absolutely necessary, and if they are fortunate enough to get any, it is from the Sutlers at most extravagant rates." At Yorktown,

Virginia, in May 1777, Nicholas Cresswell found rum to be twenty to thirty shillings per gallon, where it once had gone for two shillings. In January 1778, Washington wrote to General Casimir Pulaski that "the Scarcity of Rum is so great that the Infantry can only have it dealt to them on certain occasions." He ordered the construction of public distilleries and appointed men to buy not molasses but grain and to distill it for the army. In August 1778, Washington issued a general order that men would be allowed one gill either of rum or of whiskey each day, when it was available to be had. A gill (about four fluid ounces) was the standard dose received before marching into battle, too, and it was doubled in cold or wet weather.

A century before, Southerners had embraced rum out of necessity when imported brandy was scarce and expensive. Once rum became expensive and scarce, too, they turned to a new substitute: whiskey distilled from rye and corn. Traveling through Virginia in 1779, the British officer Thomas Anbury found the accommodations at the typical rural ordinary to be quite meager. Such ordinaries, he wrote home to Britain, consisted of "a little house placed in a solitary situation, in the middle of the woods." There was little fare beyond eggs, bacon, and corn hoecakes, and the only liquors were peach brandy and whiskey. Those happened to be the two main spirits that could be produced locally. While it's not completely accurate to say that whiskey was born at the same time as our country, it's not all that far from the truth.

Rye Whiskey and Corn Liquor

If you want to get a feel for what early whiskey was like, pour a shot. Don't use a bottle of bourbon or even rye. You need white whiskey, which, fortunately, has been in vogue in recent years (often labeled legal moonshine). Best of all would be to get your hands on a bottle of Anchor Distilling's Old Potrero, an unaged whiskey made from rye. It's distilled by Fritz Maytag of San Francisco's Anchor Brewing, the makers of Anchor Steam beer. In 1993, Maytag set out to re-create the type of whiskey made back in the colonial era, before the advent of aging whiskey in charred oak barrels, and the results are quite lovely. If you can't find Old Portrero, a bottle of white corn liquor will do, but don't bother with anything that's too fancy or expensive. And please don't pour it over ice: few Southerners would have had such a luxury in the early nineteenth century. Just mix it with a little water and sip.

If that does the trick for you, then you're all set. If you find it a bit harsh and unpleasant to swallow—and I imagine you will—do what most Southerners did back in the early days of whiskey: mix a toddy.

Whiskey Toddy

SERVES 1

1 teaspoon sugar (see note on sugar, page 34)

2 ounces hot water

2 ounces whiskey

Put the sugar and water in a small bar glass and stir until combined. Add the whiskey and stir. Take a sip of the toddy and savor its raw power. It's not a great drink, especially if you're using unaged whiskey, but it's authentic.

The Rise of Whiskey

Chronologically, the emergence of whiskey coincided neatly with America's birth, and it proceeded to grow up with the country. Whiskey reflected the strong streak of independence ingrained in the character of the frontier

South, and it even sparked the young country's first constitutional crisis. As the frontier grew more civilized, whiskey did too. It became a primary article of commerce in regions that were striving to become economically self-sufficient, and it helped Southerners break their long dependence on imported booze.

Today when most people think of whiskey drinking in the South, they think of bourbon, that mellow, slightly sweet spirit distilled from corn. But there's an equally long and proud tradition of drinking rye whiskey in the South. In fact, when you are reading an account from the nineteenth century and it mentions whiskey, the odds are that, unless the setting was Kentucky, the liquor being drunk was actually rye, not bourbon. A host of bourbon historians and fanciers have dug deeply into that spirit's history, and they've meticulously documented each Kentucky distillery, tracing the men who ran them and the brands they produced. Rye whiskey hasn't received nearly the same amount of attention. In many old accounts, the author just refers to "whiskey" and doesn't specify whether rye or corn was its primary ingredient or even where it came from. To be honest, in the really early days, there wasn't a whole lot of difference between the two.

Around 1718, new types of ships started arriving in the port of Philadelphia. These vessels sailed not from London or Bristol but from Liverpool, Belfast, or Carrickfergus, and their passengers hailed from the counties that bordered the Irish Sea. They spoke English with lilting brogues, and many were desperately poor, fleeing their homes in Ireland, Scotland, and the north of England to escape high rents, low wages, and starvation conditions inflicted upon them by English landlords. What started out as a small trickle of newcomers grew with each of five main waves of immigration, the final two in the 1750s and the 1770s. Though there was plenty of rum available on the Pennsylvania frontier, these new immigrants brought with them a long tradition of distilling a different spirit, one they called whiskey (originally usqebaugh). In Scotland, they made it from malted barley—that is, barley that had been steeped in water, allowed to partially geminate, and then dried. They used the same distilling methods in Pennsylvania as they had on the other side of the Atlantic, but in in their new homes they generally started not with their traditional barley but rather with rye.

And that raises an interesting question: which came first, the whiskey or the rye? Most whiskey histories say rye. It was the principal grain raised in western Pennsylvania, the story usually goes, but there wasn't much domestic demand for it and no export market either. So farmers with excess rye on their hands started distilling it into whiskey. An economist would find this explanation a little screwy. A bunch of farmers move out to the remote parts of Pennsylvania and start growing rye for some random reason, then look around and realize that nobody wants to buy the crop they just put so much effort into growing? "Well," they say with a shrug, "I guess we could always make whiskey out of it."

The history books have it exactly backward. As was the case throughout the American colonies, corn was the principal food grain of western Pennsylvania—the first crop settlers put in the ground and the one that they could depend upon to keep them nourished. Rye and wheat were luxury grains, if you will, planted and grown only after a region was settled and the food supply secure. In a 1787 letter to the *Edinburgh Review*, Dr. Benjamin Rush, the noted Philadelphia physician and author, described the different "species" of frontier settler. The first moved to a new patch of uninhabited land, cleared a few acres to grow corn, and built a small cabin of rough-hewn logs for himself and his family. He typically moved on after a few years, and his rude homestead was purchased by a second type of settler, who improved the rough-hewn cabin, built a large barn, and planted an orchard with two or three hundred apple trees. In addition to Indian corn, he sowed wheat and rye. The latter, Rush noted, "is cultivated chiefly for the purpose of being distilled into whiskey."

The desire for whiskey led to the cultivation of rye, not the other way around. The distillers' preferred grain in Scotland was barley, but as an Irish-born schoolteacher living in Pennsylvania wrote, "Rye grows exceeding well here. Barley does not do so well here as at home." Rye produced nearly one-third more spirit than wheat and a much higher quality one than corn, so it was the next obvious choice.

All that whiskey making created a huge demand for rye. In August 1777, wealthy planter Charles Carroll wrote to Benjamin Franklin that while wheat was selling at six shillings, "rye sells as high as 10s. per bushel; the distillers give that price to distill it into whisky; stills are set up in every corner of the country." In November 1778, the state of Pennsylvania forbade distilling whiskey from "wheat, rye, barley, malt, or other grains," but they amended the measure less than a year later to exempt rye and barley that was distilled by the same farmer that grew it. The reason was simple: citizens, "especially such that are at a distance from any sea-ports," needed rye and barley to distill into whiskey "as is absolutely necessary for the consumption of their own families."

Whiskey distilling may have started in Pennsylvania, but it soon became an inseparable part of frontier life in the Southern states too. As Benjamin Rush put it, "The migrants from Pennsylvania always travel to the southward." That meant down the east side of the Appalachian Mountains into western Virginia and then into the Carolinas and northern Georgia, and they took whiskey distilling with them. For decades, that whiskey was produced mostly on a very small scale for use by the distillers' families and neighbors. Rye was the preferred grain, but settlers would make whiskey from whatever they had most readily on hand, and on the frontier, that was usually corn. In 1780, the French Marquis de Chastellux, traveling through the Virginia backcountry, stopped at a public house and had "an excellent supper," though he noted that "wheyski was our only drink, as it was on the three days following. We managed however to make a tolerable towdy [toddy] of it."

The first whiskey was likely distilled in Kentucky just after the first corn harvest in 1775. The first permanent settlements were established in the mid-1770s by Virginians and North Carolinians who came across the mountains through the Cumberland Gap and by Pennsylvanians who came down the Ohio River, all of whom shared a long tradition of distilling and undoubtedly brought their stills with them. By 1781, the retail sale of whiskey in Kentucky taverns was being regulated, and in 1789, Daniel Stewart advertised for sale "a Copper Still of 120 Gallons Capacity, with a Good Copper and Pewter worm." On either side of the Appalachians, early distilleries were frequently linked to a milling operation, which would grind grains for farmers in the neighborhood and receive as payment a portion of the milled grains. The miller could convert these more effectively into a salable product by distilling them into whiskey. Most stills were small, with a capacity of four to ten bushels. Distilling was typically a winter activity, taking place after the rye and corn were harvested and farmers had sufficient time on their hands before the spring thaws came.

Whiskey Leaks to the East

In a 1794 poem entitled "Eulogy on Whiskey," Absalom Aimwell wrote, "Strong art thou O WHISKEY on the high mountains, and strong is thy brother Brandy in the vales below." It's a good summary of the situation.

For the first few decades of its history, whiskey was something consumed almost exclusively in the mountainous frontier regions, and tipplers on the eastern seaboard stuck to rum and brandy. Before long, though, whiskey distilling started reaching the scale necessary to produce an article of commerce, and it was only then that whiskey began to be consumed in any significant quantities outside the mountains.

In the years just before and after the Revolution, few roads existed in the western part of Pennsylvania, so packhorses were the primary means of transportation. The farmers in a western community would unite in the fall and send a horse train eastward loaded with furs, whiskey, and ginseng. The dozen or more wiry, surefooted horses headed east for several weeks until they reached a depot where the roads were good enough to support wagons and their cargo could be transferred. The pack train then made the long return trek west bearing salt and iron.

By the mid-1770s, rye whiskey was appearing occasionally in merchants' ads in Pennsylvania and Maryland newspapers, and in 1777, an ad in the *Virginia Gazette* offered "casks of old Whiskey" for sale at William Pitt's store in Williamsburg. A little farther down the coast, Cudworth, Waller & Co. of Charleston were advertising whiskey for sale by 1783 alongside the more common Jamaican and West Indian rum. These were just scattered appearances, though, a little whiskey leaking out of the hills and getting put up for sale. It wasn't until the 1790s that whiskey started being sold on a regular basis in seaport towns, and it was not bourbon or corn liquor but rye from western Pennsylvania, Virginia, and North Carolina. This trade was made possible by new wagon roads that led from Philadelphia into the whiskey-distilling regions of central Pennsylvania. The whiskey that traveled down these roads sold very cheaply, one contemporary commentator noted, "owing to its badness." Early whiskey was, quite simply, a cheap drunk, its primary appeal being that it was much less expensive than brandy imported from Europe or rum from the West Indies.

Rum's Last Stand

The trade between the new American nation and the British colonies in the West Indies never fully recovered after the Revolution. The Navigation Acts still prohibited sugar planters in the West Indies from trading with nations other than England, so they could no longer ship rum to the newly independent United States. For a short while, American distillers could obtain molasses from French and Spanish islands, but in 1783, because of a dispute over American settlers entering Spanish Florida, Spain closed its Cuban ports to American ships. Rum was selling at nearly three times the price it had in 1774, and prices for imported brandy were rising, too, thanks to increased consumption in Europe and the war-related interruption of supply.

The South didn't give up its rum without a fight, though. A number of enterprising Southerners undertook to distill it themselves, and for a brief two decades there was a flourishing rum distilling industry in the South. Many of these early commercial distilleries are known only by the records of their being sold. In the early 1780s, three men bought a tract of land in Charleston and created the Rumney Distillery. After one of the partners died in 1784, the distillery and the property, including its three copper stills, were put up for sale. This was no small-time operation. It occupied ten acres of land extending from the harbor inland, including a wharf on a navigable creek plus a dwelling house and several outhouses. It boasted three stills, two with capacities of 1,250 gallons each and the third with 625 gallons. The sale notices claimed the stills were "allowed to be the best and most substantial ever imported into America."

Hassell Street was the center of Charleston's distilling industry, with at least three distilleries operating on it in the 1780s. John Michael and his partner Jonathan Sarrazin owned one of them, and in 1787, the *Charleston Morning Post* declared, "The profits arising from this Distillery when carried on to any considerable extent are too obvious and well-known to require any enumeration." (Today one wishes that they had taken the trouble to enumerate them.) At some point, Sarrazin parted ways with Michael and set up his own competing business on the same street. A third Hassell Street distillery was owned by Colonel Richard Lushington, a respected local merchant and commandant of the Charleston militia. He operated it for several years but sold it in October 1785. By 1790, it was being run by Daniel Latham, with "three stills, a horse and dray, and stock in trade." Charleston's rum industry peaked around 1796, when there were seven distilleries in operation in the city.

Charleston wasn't the only Southern city distilling rum. In 1788, the land, houses, stills, utensils, and other improvements belonging to "the late distillery near Wilmington, in North-Carolina" were put up for sale. Advertisements noted the nearby supply of wood and position near the fountainhead of the stream that "together with the market for the consumption of rum" made it one of the best prospects in the United States. In the late 1790s, John Fitzgerald, who served as George Washington's aide-de-camp during the Revolution, operated a rum distillery in Alexandria, Virginia. But Southern rum distilling was short-lived. The same forces that made imported rum more expensive also made it harder and more expensive for distillers to get their hands on the molasses they needed to make their own. All the while, cheap rye and corn whiskey was flowing in from the western regions in greater and greater volume.

The Whiskey Rebellion

George Washington had a problem. His new government was up to its eyeballs in debt. To finance the Revolution, the Continental Congress and the individual states had collectively borrowed more than $80 million. To pay off that debt, Alexander Hamilton, Washington's secretary of the Treasury, proposed levying new taxes against luxury goods like coffee, tea, and—most significantly—distilled spirits, the making of which had become a substantial commercial industry. On March 3, 1791, Washington signed into law the first excise tax on domestically produced spirits.

The measure had a built-in inequity that made it particularly repugnant to frontier distillers, for it taxed them differently than those in towns and villages. Distillers in towns paid a tax of nine cents on each gallon of spirits produced. In the countryside, where stills couldn't be easily monitored, distillers had to pay an annual flat fee based upon the capacity of their stills and the estimated amount of spirits that would be produced if they ran at full capacity for a four-month distilling season. But few rural distillers ran their stills for four months straight. Some, especially the smaller ones, operated their stills just a few weeks out of the year. The tax, furthermore, had to be paid in hard currency in an era when most farmers had little or no cash and conducted most transactions through barter. Whiskey itself was so frequently used for barter on the frontier that it was almost a form of currency itself.

As one might have expected, fiercely independent mountaineers didn't take kindly to such a policy. An excise officer was supposed to establish an office in each county, but residents in many areas did their best to persuade him to take up another line of work. In Kentucky, revenue collectors had their papers stolen, their horse's ears cropped, and their saddles slashed to pieces. Colonel Thomas Marshall, the chief collector for the state, was hanged in effigy and the stuffed dummy representing him was dragged through the streets of Lexington. The protest was most severe in four frontier counties in western Pennsylvania, where as many as five thousand stills were in operation. Revenue collectors were harassed, beaten, and tarred and feathered. Distillers who paid the tax found their stills riddled with bullet holes. In a further outrage, offenders charged under the tax law were ordered to appear in the federal court at Philadelphia, a long and expensive journey of three hundred miles. The law was amended in 1792 and 1794 to lighten the tax burden, but it did little to placate the citizens of western Pennsylvania, who saw little difference between the actions of the new, distant government in Philadelphia and those of the earlier distant government in London.

Things turned violent in the summer of 1794. On the morning of July 19th, fifty "whiskey boys" from the Washington County militia confronted John Neville, the local collector, and demanded that he resign his position and relinquish all his records on distillery taxes. Neville refused, and shots were fired, but Neville and his slaves were holed up in secure positions within his house and managed to hold off the attackers, who eventually dispersed. A detachment of eleven federal soldiers from nearby Fort Pitt volunteered to defend Neville and his household, and the next day they found themselves surrounded by a mob numbering four hundred or more. Again gunfire erupted, and in the exchange, one of the attackers was killed and several of the soldiers were wounded. Neville managed to escape under the cover of a thicket, and the Fort Pitt soldiers surrendered. The mob burned Neville's house and outbuildings to the ground.

In the weeks that followed, antifederal anger raged across the country-side. A group of rebels ambushed a mail carrier and found letters written by Pittsburgh residents condemning the attack on Neville, which turned the frontiersmen's anger upon the town. David Bradford, a wealthy lawyer and the most active antitax leader, called for members of the militia units from the four counties to gather. Seven thousand men heeded the call, assembling at Braddock's Field near Pittsburgh and threatening to storm the federal Fort Fayette and to burn Pittsburgh to the ground. The noble residents of Pittsburgh responded by kicking the three letter writers out of town and, in a crafty move, sending conciliatory barrels of whiskey to

Tarring and feathering a revenue collector during the Whiskey Rebellion.

the assembled mob, which proceeded to get drunk and, the next morning, staggered back home to their farms.

The counties around Pittsburgh remained in active revolt through the month of August, and President Washington decided he could no longer ignore this brazen challenge to the new federal government's authority. He mobilized a force of thirteen thousand militiamen from Pennsylvania, New Jersey, Virginia, and Maryland, placing them under the command of General Henry "Light Horse Harry" Lee. They arrived in western Pennsylvania in October 1794 after an arduous trek over the mountains made even more difficult by mud from heavy rains. The standoff ended with a whimper. In the face of the federal-led militia, the rebel force fractured and largely disbanded. The chief leaders of the rebels and as many as two thousand of their followers fled into the mountains. Of those men remaining, it was difficult to determine whom to prosecute. The federal force marched back to Philadelphia with just twenty prisoners, intending to make them serve as examples. All but two were acquitted. And thus the Whiskey Rebellion sputtered to an end.

The military action against the western Pennsylvania rebels was an important moment in American political history, for it established once and for all the power of federal law over state residents. It also cost the new national government $1.5 million, almost one-third of all monies raised during the entire duration of the excise tax. The levy was quietly repealed by the Jefferson administration, and with the exception of a brief few years between 1813 and 1817, whiskey remained unencumbered by excise taxes until the Civil War.

George Washington and Distilling

Ironically, the very man who suppressed the Whiskey Rebellion became a distiller himself not long afterward. In 1796, George Washington engaged James Anderson, a Scottish immigrant, to serve as his plantation manager. Anderson was an experienced distiller and convinced his new employer to undertake whiskey making at Mount Vernon. It required a significant investment, and to raise the capital for construction, Washington had to call in debts from friends, including Light Horse Harry Lee. By March 1798, a new 2,250-square-foot, stone-walled distillery was complete, and it contained five copper pot stills and fifty mash tubs. Washington's liquor was sold simply as whiskey, but it was what today we call a rye whiskey, since it was made with 60 percent rye, 35 percent corn, and 5 percent malt and barley. Like all whiskey of the era, it was unaged, meaning it was stored in barrels only as long as it took to sell it, so it would have been largely colorless. The distillery produced 4,500 gallons in 1798 and almost 11,000 in 1799, making whiskey Washington's single largest source of all-important cash in an era when most agricultural business was conducted in credit and trade. While much of the whiskey was sold to local farmers—Washington wrote in a letter that "demand for this article (in these parts) is brisk"—almost half was sold to Alexandria merchants, who then resold it in their retail stores. Rye whiskey proved the most profitable product of Mount Vernon, and within a year, Washington's had become one of the largest and most productive distilleries in the young United States.

The run of the Mount Vernon distillery was brief. George Washington died in 1799, and Martha Washington followed in 1802. Mount Vernon passed into the hands of Washington's nephew Lawrence Lewis, who leased out the distillery. Within a decade, the building had fallen into disrepair, and many of the stones from its walls were carted away for other uses.

Plenty of other Southerners outside the mountains also experimented with commercial whiskey distilling in the early years of the republic. Robert Squibb's distillery in Augusta, Georgia, sold whiskey for a dollar a gallon, made from barley and rye grown by local farmers, and a distillery operation just south of the new state capital at Columbia, South Carolina, had two stills and consumed three thousand bushels of grain in a season. Whether in the mountains or the lowlands, most distilleries at this stage were small, single-still concerns producing just a few hundred gallons of spirits a year. They used a simple process of heating the mash, vaporizing the alcohol, and condensing it into whiskey. Early whiskey stills were essentially the same as those used on the coast to distill brandy and rum. The old copper pot still was kettle-shaped with a round bottom, topped by a head with tapering neck that connected to the condenser (or worm), which was a spiral of copper or pewter tubing that was immersed in a tub through which cold water circulated. Fermented "beer" (the soured mash combined with barley malt and yeast) was poured into the pot and heated over flames. The alcohol vapor rose and passed through the chilled worm, which liquefied it again, and it was drawn off through a cock.

George Washington's distillery—one of the best in the country—was an expensive stone-walled structure, but in the mountains areas a stillhouse was often just low-roofed shack with a mud floor and one side open to weather. That open side was essential to keep gasses from building up, for whiskey distilling—with its highly flammable ethyl alcohol and open flames from the boiler fires—was a dangerous business. Stillhouses were generally located far away from houses, barns, and other structures, since explosions and fires were par for the course. In the first decades of the nineteenth century, whiskey was no darker than a pale amber color. It was stored in barrels for transport, but just long enough to get the liquor to its destination, not to mellow it with age. Those barrels were not charred inside, either, so there would be no filtering effect nor coloring from charcoal. Up until the Civil War almost all whiskey was white—raw, colorless, and hot as fire.

The 1810 census revealed just how widespread Southern distilling had become. Pennsylvania, which produced 6.5 million gallons of spirits per year, was the country's leading state in terms of the volume produced, but Virginia (2.4 million gallons) actually had more distilleries in operation, and Kentucky (2.2 million gallons) and the Carolinas (1.7 million gallons) had a respectable representation as well. Unfortunately, these figures lump grain and fruit distilling together into a single category, so we can't tell precisely how much of the spirits being produced in Virginia and the Carolinas was rye or corn whiskey versus peach brandy, nor how much was being produced in the mountainous parts of the states versus the coastal plain. The editor of the census volume did note that domestic spirits were made "principally from rye, apple, and peaches," with molasses, oats, corn, buckwheat, wheat, and potatoes being used less frequently. Outside of New England, rum distilling was a marginal enterprise at best—meaning those rum distilleries in Charleston seem to have been out of the picture by 1810. For domestic production, whiskey and brandy were the future.

When it came to drinking whiskey, most Southerners just swapped it for rum in their usual libations. "The chief end of whiskey," a correspondent for the *Alexandria Gazette* wrote in 1827, "is to make toddy, flip, and punch." The toddy—whiskey cut with water and sugar—was perhaps the most common preparation in the Southern interior. Here's how Captain Simon Suggs, Johnson J. Hooper's fictional Alabama backwoodsman, made his: First he drew a glass of whiskey from a barrel, then dropped a lump of brown sugar in it and stirred it with his finger, "looking intently in the tumbler, the while." He tasted the liquor, added a little more sugar, then finally drew his finger from the tumbler and drew it through his mouth before knocking down half the glass at one gulp, and, after a brief pause, polishing off the rest. (Feel free to use a spoon to stir yours, if you are the more refined sort.)

Better Whiskey, Roads, and Rivers

One big barrier stood between whiskey and commercial success: you had to be really desperate to drink it. "The very name of whiskey is nauseous to some men," Harrison Hall wrote in his 1818 distiller's guide. "And when they taste some of that which is offered for sale in our cities, the reality is found to be ten times worse than the idea, and they are completely disgusted." Another advocate argued that because of "the slovenly, imperfect manner in which our whiskey is manufactured and the badness of its quality, the opulent part of the community do not consume much of it; but import rum, brandy and gin from abroad."

The early years of the nineteenth century witnessed a series of innovations that greatly improved the quality of American whiskey. For starters, distilling technology got better. In 1794, Colonel Alexander Anderson patented a steam still that used a single boiler to heat two stills simultaneously. Seven years later, he added a patent for a condenser to heat the wash. Henry Witmer built on Anderson's ideas, and in 1805 he patented a more compact rig—popularly called the patent still—and the two men's inventions quickly gained wide use. Between 1802 and 1815, more than one hundred patents were issued for distilling devices, amounting to 5 percent of all American patents during that period.

A distiller with a 110-gallon patent still could produce nine runs a day instead of the three possible with a common pot still. Farmer-distillers could buy new copper stills in dry goods stores that had double or triple

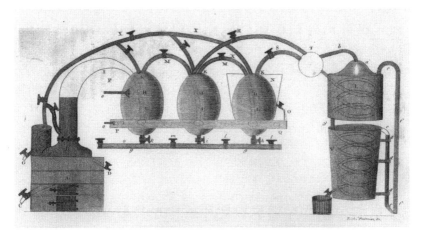

A patent still, 1818.

the capacity of their old hand-fashioned ones. New tools and techniques made for a more consistent process too. Instruments like thermometers and hydrometers made the fermentation and distilling more controlled, and distillers' manuals encouraged their readers to avoid "sour, dirty yeast" and ensure "cleanliness in every matter." The use of a second distillation became prevalent in the 1810s and 1820s, and many distillers adopted two stills, a larger one for the first run and a smaller for the second.

At the same time, advances in transportation and distribution made it possible for distillers to get their products to new markets. In 1803, Thomas Jefferson plunked down $15 million to purchase the Louisiana Territory from the French, giving Americans—especially the farmers and distillers working along the Ohio River and its tributaries—access to the vital port of New Orleans. In the hills of southwestern Pennsylvania, long flatboats shaped like cigar boxes navigated the shallow waters of the Monongahela River as they twisted and flowed through the green forests to Pittsburgh, bearing casks and barrels filled with whiskey from hundreds of distilleries that dotted the riverbanks. In Pittsburgh, they would be loaded upon barges and schooners and sent down the Ohio to Cairo, Illinois, and from there down the Mississippi all the way to New Orleans. In 1816, the *American Telegraph* reported that Monongahela flour and whiskey commanded better prices in New Orleans than the produce of any other part of the western country.

At first, navigation on the Mississippi depended on the annual rise of the waters, which occurred in the fall, when seasonal rains made the upper rivers navigable. Over the next two decades, a series of dams and locks alleviated some of the worst choke points on the river, and more and more commerce flowed every year. The trade was accelerated by the introduction of steamboats. In 1811, the *New Orleans*, designed by Robert Fulton and Robert Livingston and built in Pittsburgh, was deployed to the lower Mississippi, where it provided passenger and freight service between Natchez and New Orleans. Henry Miller Shreve's *Washington* began service in 1816, sailing from New Orleans to Louisville in twenty-five days. In 1814, New Orleans saw twenty steamboat arrivals. That number increased to 1,200 a year by 1835. Steamboats could carry large amounts of cargo not only down a flowing river but up it too. The result was a revolution in the distribution and trade of whiskey from the western states.

Similar improvements were needed for whiskey to be able to travel eastward to markets on the Atlantic seaboard. Construction of the National Road, the first major highway built by the federal government, began in 1811 at Cumberland, Maryland, on the Potomac River. By 1817, the road had crossed the Allegheny Mountains through to Uniontown in western Pennsylvania, and by 1820, it had reached Wheeling, Virginia (now West Virginia), where it met the Ohio River. Conestoga wagons could now cross the Allegheny Mountains and make the three hundred-mile journey from Pittsburgh to Philadelphia in about three weeks. Within four years, a series of private turnpikes were completed that connected the National Road all the way to the port of Baltimore on the Chesapeake Bay.

By the 1820s, so-called western whiskey was available in large quantities to consumers throughout the South. For those who could afford it, Madeira remained the preferred wine and brandy the preferred spirit, but whiskey was the new, low-priced alternative. It was harsh and white but plenty strong and improving in quality with each passing year. Whiskey's foothold in the South was established, and its popularity would only increase in the decades that followed.

7

The Cocktail in Antebellum New Orleans

Just after Christmas in 2011, my wife and I sat down for an afternoon meal at Commander's Palace in New Orleans. A Sazerac seemed the natural thing to sip, and when mine arrived, the waiter placed in front of me a rocks glass holding about two inches of ruddy liquor, a twist of lemon peel bobbing inside. "Enjoy," he announced stentoriously, "America's original cocktail!"

It's a great spiel for the tourists: that New Orleans is the birthplace of the cocktail and that the Sazerac—rye whiskey mixed with sugar, bitters, and absinthe—is the original formula. Popular legend says it was invented by a local pharmacist named Antoine Amédée Peychaud, who used his personal line of bitters to flavor toddies. He measured them out with a double-ended egg cup known as a coquetier, a word his English-speaking friends transformed into "cocktail."

Not exactly. The Sazerac is a wonderful drink, but by no stretch of the imagination is it America's original cocktail. We'll get around to discussing all of that, but first, let's mix up something that more accurately represents what was being imbibed in New Orleans in the 1830s.

Brandy Cocktail

SERVES 1

2 sugar cubes

3 or 4 dashes Peychaud's bitters

2 ounces good French brandy

Splash of water (optional)

Put the sugar cubes in a rocks glass and dribble the bitters on top of them. With a flat muddler, crush the sugar cubes and stir until almost dissolved, adding a few drops of water if needed. Pour in the brandy and, if you are looking for an old-style cocktail, add a generous splash of water and stir well.

If you are of more modern sensibilities and insist on a cold cocktail, omit the water and chill by filling the glass with ice, stirring, then straining the cocktail into a second glass to drink. (The melted ice will take the place of the water.)

The Bitter Truth About Cocktails

The notion that New Orleans was the birthplace of the cocktail has been thoroughly discredited by other writers, so let's put it to bed quickly. The word *cocktail* used as the name of a drink appeared in print as early as 1803, and it has nothing to do with *egg cups*. In 1806, *The Balance and Columbian Repository* defined it as "a stimulating liquor, composed of spirits of any kind, sugar, water, and bitters," and the author noted that it was commonly called a bittered sling. The cocktail was a simple variation on the sort of toddies and slings that people had long been employing to cut the bite of harsh liquors. The addition of a little bitters was the defining characteristic.

Note that in our cocktail we used brandy, not whiskey. It is true that barrel after barrel of whiskey was being floated down the river to New Orleans to be sold, but it doesn't appear that many New Orleans residents were actually drinking it. Whiskey was an article of trade—cheap, harsh stuff that you sold to people out in the backcountry who were too poor to be high-living sports, so that you, in turn, could use the proceeds to become a high-living sport. In New Orleans, the money made from buying and selling whiskey—and from buying and selling cotton and flour—went to buy fine wines and brandies imported from Europe.

By the time it became an American city, New Orleans was already eighty-five years old, and its French-speaking population continued to grow in the early nineteenth century, as the Haitian Revolution of 1804 sent a flood of refugees that included white planters and their slaves along with free people of color. The French and Spanish influence usually gets credited with making New Orleans an exotic and unique city, and, in particular, for giving it a distinctive drinking culture. That Latin influence certainly is an important factor, but equally important was commerce. New Orleans in the 1830s was an internationally connected boomtown, and that outburst of economic energy as much as anything is what stimulated its thirst.

The New Orleans of the 1830s was, as one contemporary observer put it, "the great emporium of trade" for the entire Mississippi valley. New visitors were captivated by the levees lining the river, which dominated travelers' sights on their first approach to the city. They composed a world in miniature, where, as one writer recalled, "one may meet with the products and people of every country in any way connected with commerce." The levees served as both wharf and market, and at least forty steamboats and fifteen hundred or more flatboats at any one time lined the banks along the upper part of the city, laden with the produce of the up-country. The air was filled with a loud jumble of English, French, Spanish, German, and even more exotic tongues. Winter was the season of trade, drawing twenty thousand visitors to the city and swelling its total population by half.

In 1834, one visitor described the vessels he found on the New Orleans levees: "Some are laden with flour, others with corn, others with meat of various kinds, others with live stock, cattle, hogs, horses or mules . . . and some are full with what is infinitely worse, 'Old Monongahela' whiskey." Above all, though, what was flowing in was bale after bale of cotton, which the newly planted farmlands of Mississippi, Arkansas, Alabama, Louisiana, and Texas were just beginning to produce. Imported goods flowed into New Orleans, too, arriving on European ships via the Gulf, and their cargoes were broken into smaller portions and sent upriver on the returning steamboats.

New Orleans' economy had boomed despite frequent outbreaks of malaria and a cholera epidemic in 1833 that claimed nearly one thousand lives. Its population grew from 17,242 in 1810 to 27,176 in 1820, when it eclipsed Charleston to become the largest city in the South. It then doubled in the space of a decade, growing from 46,082 in 1830 to 102,193 in 1840, making it roughly the same size as Baltimore and trailing only massive New York City (which crossed 300,000 residents that year) as America's largest city. As more Americans arrived in New Orleans, a fierce rivalry developed between the French-speaking Creole population in the city proper and the Anglophone Americans living in the neighborhoods uptown from the French Quarter. Originally called the Faubourg Sainte Marie (French for the "St. Mary Suburb"), uptown quickly became known as the American sector or the First Municipality. (Today it goes by the more prosaic Central Business District.)

And that brings us back to the cocktail. New Orleans did not invent it, but the city took to the drink quite readily. It flourished at the places where men came together for trade and sociability, which in antebellum New Orleans meant coffeehouses. The most famous was the Exchange Coffee House, which opened in 1806 in a two-story brick building on Conti Street—a meeting place, market, auction house, tavern, and gambling parlor all rolled into one. Men could buy a drink, gamble at cards, and trade in everything from ships and real estate to flour and cotton. They could buy and sell human beings there, too, for New Orleans by this point had become the nation's largest slave market.

In 1811, the Exchange moved from Conti Street to an establishment operated by Bernard Tremoulet at the corner of Chartres and St. Louis Streets. Now called the Commercial Coffee House (in French, the Café de Commerce), it offered "the best refreshments that can be procured in town." Ship captains left letter bags there, the proprietors collected newspapers and maritime lists for use by its patrons, and it was where the civil sheriff auctioned off seized property. Two years later, Tremoulet fell into financial difficulties, and the building was taken over by Pierre Maspero, who renamed it the New Exchange Coffee House and installed Philip Alvarez to manage the place. (Remember the name Alvarez; he shows up again later in the story.) A long, two-story wooden building with a sand floor, it had a bar running the entire length of the main floor, and the upstairs housed gambling and billiard tables. The full list of beverages Maspero offered has not survived, but brandy must have been served in large quantities, for at one point he was sued by his landlords for not paying them for a 116-gallon pipe of brandy worth $217. Maspero was embroiled in an eviction lawsuit with his landlords when he died in September 1822, leaving behind a wife and four small children.

The New Exchange changed hands a few times following Maspero's death and ended up being taken over by a man named John Hewlett, who figures prominently in many accounts of the cocktail in New Orleans and is often misidentified as James. He promptly renamed the establishment Hewlett's Exchange, enlarged the building, and transformed it into the finest barroom in the city. The main area was lit by four brilliant chandeliers with twelve lamps each, and in an era before electric lights those chandeliers had a stunning effect. One visitor recalled that, as he and his companions entered from the dimly lighted street, "our eyes were dazzled by the noon-day brightness shed from innumerable chandeliers." The term *coffeehouse* was pretty much a misnomer by this point. The bar had "its peculiar dazzling array of glasses and decanters," one traveler wrote, "containing 'spirits'—not of 'the vasty deep' certainly, but of whose potent spells many were apparently trying the power, by frequent libations.' Each of the café's many small tables were occupied by three or four men "sipping negus"—port wine mixed with hot water, spices, and sugar— and "puffing their segars," while even more crowded around the large circular bar. The walls were decorated with, as one visitor put it, paintings "of the most licentious description, and though many of their subjects were classical, of a voluptuous and luxurious character." He also quickly noted, "This is French taste however."

The Exchange Coffee House was just one of many such establishments in New Orleans. The Café des Ameliorations was frequented by "militantly unreconstructed" Creoles, while the Café des Emigres was the favorite haunt of French planters who had fled the slave uprisings in Santo Domingo. The Gem Restaurant occupied a building at 17 Royal Street that was originally the home of a Spanish grandee. In the early part of the nineteenth century, it was something of a magnet for duelers, who passed challenges over the small tables or the mahogany bar. In all of these cafés, from early in the morning until late at night, men could be found playing dominoes, "with a tonic, often renewed and properly sangareed" and enveloped in the smoke of "their eternal segars." One visitor estimated there were at least one hundred coffeehouses in the city, doing business throughout the day.

Hotels were another reliable place to find a drink, and in the 1830s, the five-story Bishop's Hotel was the city's largest. It had two fronts, one on Camp Street, the other on Common. Its barroom stretched more than one hundred feet in length, and one writer vouched that it was "universally allowed to be the most splendid in America." He described it on Sunday morning as being crowded with more than one hundred gentlemen, some talking in pairs, others quietly smoking, reading papers, and sipping their morning potations. On the bar, he noted "a row of rapidly disappearing glasses, containing the tempting, green-leaved, mint-julep."

Booze wasn't just for breakfast in New Orleans hotels. Henry Durell made his first visit to the city in 1835, and he described the men at his hotel lining up in a narrow passageway for the midday "dinner" at 3:00 p.m. A gong rang promptly on the hour, and the doors to the dining room opened. The guests shouldered their way in and filled the chairs on either sides of a very long table. Servants hurried back and forth, and nothing could be heard but "the clashing of knives and forks, and the other collaborators of mastication." In the space of five minutes, the diners—planters, farmers, and merchants and their clerks—had devoured their food, and then the conversation commenced. The talk immediately turned to trade: what each man bought and sold that day, and what they were looking to buy next. All the while, Durell noted, they were drinking wine and sipping brandy and water. He also observed that it was a ritual for drinking men to call "touch" and clink their glasses together before imbibing. He called it "this Southern custom" and related the story of a congressman from Mississippi who nearly lost his life complying with the custom when "his glass broke in his hand, and he swallowed one of the fragments."

It was in this atmosphere that the city's preferred tipple evolved from toddy to cocktail. Henry Durell succinctly described the difference between the two: a brandy toddy is "a little water, a little sugar, and a great deal of brandy" while a brandy cocktail is the same drink with "the addition of a shade of Stoughton's bitters." Bitters are alcoholic concoctions themselves—high-proof spirits infused with herbs, spices, roots, bark, fruit peels, and flowers. Long before they made their way into cocktails, bitters were being drunk on their own as a sort of medicine, being touted as relieving everything from fevers to upset stomachs. Sometime in the late nineteenth century, tipplers came to realize the salubrious effects of bitters when mixed with liquor.

Stoughton's Bitters, which Durell singled out as the defining ingredient in a brandy cocktail, was one of the most popular varieties before the Civil War. It was first patented in England 1712 and was being sold in the South by the eve of the Revolutionary War (often in counterfeited versions). Many other players entered the Southern bitters market in the early part of the nineteenth century. Boker's Bitters was founded by Johann Gottlieb Boker in 1828, and Dr. Hoofland's Celebrated German Bitters were manufactured by C. M. Jackson in Philadelphia and sold throughout Kentucky, Tennessee, and Louisiana. Angostura, the brand of bitters that is best known today—and, in fact, was until just recently almost the only brand that could still be found in American bars—were created in Venezuela by German-born doctor J. G. B. Siegert to treat stomach ailments suffered by Simón Bolívar's soldiers. Although they were being sold in England during the 1830s, they do not appear to have made their way to the South until after the Civil War.

In the twentieth century, the word *cocktail* came to be applied to mixed alcoholic drinks more generally, but in the heyday of the New Orleans coffeehouse, it referred to a very specific formulation. Be it Stoughton's or Boker's, it was that touch of bitters that literally made a drink a cocktail.

The Great New Orleans Hotels

The hotel bars described by Henry Durell and others were an important innovation of the antebellum era. Colonial-era taverns had been scarcely distinguishable from private houses. What passed as the bar was essentially a small wooden cage in which liquor was dispensed and locked up when it was time for patrons to retire to bed—and often those patrons not only shared a room with strangers but shared a bed too. The first hotels offered private bedchambers as well as public rooms that were far larger and more luxurious than anything found in even the most high-end taverns.

By the 1820s and 1830s, most of the features of the modern hotel had emerged: grand entryways, lobbies, and front desks on the ground floor and guest rooms on the floors above, arranged along long corridors with numbered doors. One of the most essential features was the grand hotel bar, which is where hoteliers made their real money. Open to use by hotel guests and visitors alike, it was always on the ground floor, usually directly off the main lobby and sometimes with a separate entrance to the street. The bar was a general gathering place, where storekeepers, merchants, travelers, politicians— most with a cigar clamped firmly in mouth—would congregate. It was a place for transacting business, exchanging news, debating politics, and swapping gossip, and it operated morning, noon, and night. "To drink with a friend when you meet him is good fellowship," Captain Frederick Marryat wrote. "To drink with a stranger is politeness, and a proof of wishing to be better acquainted." He also noted that drinking in the morning was a general custom in the United States, "although much more prevalent in the South and West, where it is literally, 'Stranger, will you drink or fight?' "

Grand hotels were constructed in all the major antebellum Southern cities, but none was grander than those in New Orleans. As trade in the city grew, Hewlett's Exchange became too small and antiquated to handle the traffic. In March 1835, a group of American businessmen organized the Exchange Company and broke ground for the Merchant's Exchange on Royal Street near Canal, right at the point where the American sector met the French Quarter. At the same time, they were planning to build a grand new hotel a few blocks away to be called the Saint Charles. The Creole business community wasn't pleased by this turn of events, and they organized a rival company, dubbed the Improvement Bank and New Orleans Improvement Company. The Creole group purchased the entire block of St. Louis Street between Royal and Chartres, which included Hewlett's Exchange, with plans to reproduce the feel of the Rue de Rivoli, Paris's famed commercial street.

The hotel race was on. Construction began on the Saint Charles, commonly called the Exchange Hotel, in the summer of 1835. The cornerstone for the Improvement Company's hotel, to be called the Saint Louis, was laid in 1836. The Saint Charles opened for business first in February 1837. Designed by the firm of Dakin & Gallier, it cost nearly $800,000 to build. The portico facing Saint Charles Street had six Corinthian columns and a flight of marble steps leading up to the hotel. Inside, spiral staircases made of marble curved around the sides of an open gallery all the way to a 46-foot-diameter dome topped by turret from which, 185 feet in the air, you could take in sweeping views of the entire city. Cotton and sugar planters flocked there from across the South, and the rotunda became the de facto cotton exchange and chamber of commerce for the city. Guests could take their brandy cocktails in the octagonal basement barroom, which was seventy feet in diameter and encircled by Ionic columns beneath a twenty-foot-high ceiling.

Saint Charles Hotel, 1869.

Some four blocks to the northwest on St. Louis Street, the Creole efforts got off to a little slower start. First, the Improvement Bank built the City Exchange, which extended from Royal Street to the rear of the old Hewlett's Exchange and combined in a single building the functions of an exchange, a hotel, a bank, ballrooms, and private stores. This so-called New Exchange included a rotunda devoted exclusively to business that was surrounded by arcades and galleries for recreation. The operations of the

Southern Spirits

old Hewlett's Exchange were moved into the new building, and in 1837, the old Exchange building was destroyed. The plan was to build in its place a wing containing the Improvement Bank, bathing rooms, and dining rooms, but the financial panic of 1837 slowed construction and forced the company to scale back. When it finally opened in October 1838, though, it still had luxurious saloons and a grand ballroom with elegant chandeliers.

Less than two years later, the Saint Louis Hotel—"the most gorgeous edifice in the Union" —caught fire and burned to the ground, as early hotels were prone to do. The company quickly rebuilt, though, and the new version exceeded the original's splendor, including a massive four-story building topped by a dome reminiscent of the Capitol building in Washington, DC. It was meant to be a place where aristocratic Creoles could meet to eat, drink, and do business, which included selling cotton, slaves, and land. Its rotunda served as a chamber of commerce, board of brokers, and cotton exchange all in one, and it competed fiercely with the auction market at the Saint Charles. From noon to 3:00 p.m., auctions were conducted in English, French, Spanish, prompting visitors to declare it a veritable Tower of Babel.

The arrival of the Saint Louis Hotel caused some shuffling of the personalities who operated New Orleans' exchanges. When the building housing his Exchange was demolished to make way for the Creole hotel, John Hewlett moved across Canal Street and set up shop in the American sector, where he took over the former Bishop's Hotel and renamed it Hewlett's Exchange. Hewlett's place at the Saint Louis Hotel was taken by Philip Alvarez, who had managed the Exchange way back when it was owned by Pierre Maspero and presumably had continued working there under Hewlett. Alvarez leased the hotel's ballroom to host society balls and other events for the city's social season. One New Orleans writer described him as "universally popular" and noted that he had made the Saint Louis Hotel "the favorite resort of all the leading politicians, planters, and merchants of the city." Alvarez's "genial assistant," as one writer called him, was a man named Joseph Santini, and after Alvarez died in 1850, Santini branched out and started operating two of the most successful saloons in the antebellum city, the Jewel and the Parlor. The latter was described by the *New Orleans Times* as "par excellence the preference of our up-town citizens, where the very best wines and liquors are served in the most accommodating manner." Santini's real fame, though, came in the realm of the cocktail, and he is credited with creating at least two famous New Orleans concoctions, the crusta and his own variation of the pousse-café.

Jerry Thomas, the famed nineteenth-century bartender and author of the first published bartender's manual, inaccurately identified "Santina" as "the celebrated Spanish caterer." (Like Alvarez, Santini was a native of Italy.) The name of the crusta comes from its sugared rim, but its most notable feature is that the entire glass is lined with the rind of an entire lemon. That garnish that will challenge your knife skills but is well worth it if you can pull it off, for it makes a grandly impressive presentation.

The Crusta

SERVES 1

1 whole lemon (for peel)

Superfine sugar

2 fluid ounces brandy (preferably Cognac)

1 teaspoon simple syrup (page 6)

1 teaspoon orange curaçao or Grand Marnier

2 teaspoons lemon juice

2 dashes bitters

Take a collins glass or a fancy wineglass, rub a slice of lemon around the rim, and dip it in superfine sugar. With a sharp paring knife, trim the tip off of one end of the lemon and pare the peel off of one half of it, similar to the way you would an apple, so that you have a large, single piece of peel. Lay the peel flat and shave off any white pith remaining, then insert the peel into the glass so that it curves around the inside of the glass.

Combine the remaining ingredients in a mixing glass with ice, stir well, and strain into the waiting glass.

Jerry Thomas also credited Joseph Santini with formulating a concoction he called Santina's pousse-café, which calls for equal parts of Cognac brandy, maraschino liqueur, and curaçao mixed well and served in a small wineglass.

Sazerac Brandy with a Dash of Peychaud's

The cocktail was one of the most popular drinks in New Orleans during the antebellum period, as were punch and the flip and the pousse-café. But more than anything, people were drinking brandy—Cognac brandy, preferably. Somewhere around 1850, a man named Sewell T. Taylor opened a wholesale and retail wines and liquors business. His stock included fine brandies, dozens of wines, and liquors that included Holland gin, Jamaica and Saint Croix rum, and even a little "old rye whiskey." Of most interest to us, though, is that he stocked Sazerac de Forge et Fils, a noted brand of Cognac—and quite old vintages of it too. *The Times-Picayune* called Taylor "perhaps the only wine dealer in the South who can boast of having such a large supply of the celebrated Sazerac brandies, of the vintages of 1795, 1798, 1802, and 1805!"

While Sazerac was emerging as the New Orleans brandy of choice, a new name was eclipsing Stoughton's and Boker's as the city's preferred brand of bitters. Antoine Amédée Peychaud was born into a distinguished French family from Haiti. It is unclear exactly when he arrived in New Orleans, but in 1832, F. P. Ducongé announced in an advertisement in the *New Orleans Bee* that he was taking "Anthony Peychaud" into partnership. Two years later, Peychaud purchased a drug and apothecary store at 123 Royal Street, and he advertised that he would have "constantly on hand a complete assortment of Drugs, Medicines, Chemical Preparations, Surgical Instruments, &c." By 1842, he had two assistant druggists working for him, and the slave schedules in the 1860 census show Peychaud owning three slaves, a man and a woman in their sixties and a seventeen-year-old girl.

Sometime in the 1850s, Peychaud formulated his own recipe for bitters. In 1857, he placed an ad in the *Bee* declaring that his "American Aromatic Bitter Cordial" would restore the appetite and prevent dyspepsia "for infant and aged alike." The last paragraph of the ad is most interesting: "This cordial has been introduced into general use in the Sazerac House, and other principal coffeehouses in this city, as far superior to Boker's Bitters, so celebrated throughout the United States; and there can be no doubt that all who have tasted the AMERICAN CORDIAL, give it the preference over all other bitters in use." Later ads continued to plug the product for both medicinal and mixological purposes. They were touted as a cure for "chills and fever . . . cold, cough, headache" along with dyspepsia and ennui. At the same time, the ads noted that all who look for American Aromatic Bitters "find it in every hotel, barroom, and indeed in every place of public entertainment in the Union."

Those bitters eventually made their way into a cocktail called the Sazerac, but, as we will see, that didn't happen for several more decades.

8

The Mint Julep

For this chapter, it's finally time to mix up a proper mint julep. No, put down that bottle of bourbon. You won't be needing it. Instead, reach for your best bottle of brandy. Or more realistically, reach for your car keys and head to the liquor store and buy a good bottle of Cognac, which is something few Southerners keep on hand these days.

To do this properly, you really need to make your julep on a hot summer day, and before you mix it, spend at least an hour outside so you can get good and heated up. Bring the ingredients and mixing equipment outside onto your porch or patio, too, away from any air conditioning. To fully appreciate a proper julep, you need to make it in the heat and enjoy it there too.

Antebellum Mint Julep

SERVES 1

1 tablespoon pulverized sugar (see notes on old-style and superfine sugar, pages 32 and 111)

2½ tablespoons water

6 to 8 sprigs fresh mint (note, that's whole sprigs of mint, not individual leaves, though you can get by with 3 or 4 sprigs if you're running short)

3 ounces Cognac

Crushed ice

Assorted berries (such as strawberries, raspberries, blackberries) and 1 orange slice, for garnish

In a large tumbler or silver julep cup, combine sugar and water and mix well with a spoon. Add 3 or 4 sprigs of mint and press them firmly with a spoon or muddler until the flavor is extracted. (Note: You're pressing, not muddling here—the idea is to extract the flavor from the mint leaves but not leave smashed bits of leaf in the syrup.) Remove the mint, then pour the Cognac into the tumbler and fill it to the top with crushed ice. Take 3 or 4 sprigs of fresh mint (or spruce up and reuse the ones you just pressed in the syrup) and arrange them atop the glass like a bouquet of flowers, stems downward in the ice. Arrange the berries and orange slice among the mint leaves in an attractive fashion. Insert a long straw (a stainless steel or silver one is ideal, if you have one on hand) into the ice. Sip, your nose nestled among the mint, and savor the cool nectar within.

Adapted from Jerry Thomas, *How to Mix Drinks* (1862)

Mint Juleps: The Myth

Pick up a novel titled *Mint Juleps, Mayhem, and Murder*, and you can probably guess in which part of the country it's going to be set. Few cocktails are as closely associated with a particular region as the mint julep is with the South. "Wherever there is a mint julep, there is a bit of the Old South," declared Richard Barksdale Harwell, who wrote a short monograph on the history of the beverage in question, establishing the tone of most scholarship on juleps to date. Marketers love the idea of mint juleps too. Celebration Tours of New Orleans, for instance, touts its South Louisiana plantation tour by promising, "You'll feel like sipping a mint julep on the veranda of these antebellum mansions as you gaze into Louisiana's rich past!"

The funny thing is, no one drinks mint juleps in the South these days, not even on the veranda. You don't walk into a bar and see them on the cocktail list, and no one invites you over to their house for drinks and offers to stir up a couple of juleps. Unless, of course, it's that one particular weekend in May when a little horse race known as the Kentucky Derby is running. Over the course of two days at Churchill Downs, more than 120,000 mint juleps are served, which I suspect exceeds the total number of juleps served anywhere else in the South during the entire rest of the year. Today's image of the mint julep has been permanently altered by all that horse-racing hoopla and by generations of Kentuckians insisting that a true mint julep must be made with bourbon. Historically speaking, this isn't at all the case. In fact, there are at least two things that we know for certain about mint juleps: they did not originate in Kentucky, and they were not originally made with whiskey.

Unfortunately, the mint julep has become an entrenched part of the pernicious moonlight-and-magnolia myth of the Old South: genteel planters in spotless white suits, sipping mint juleps on verandas, served by smiling, deferential slaves. That association has become so strong that modern Southerners of a more progressive bent recoil instinctively against drinking juleps because of all the associated baggage. In his cocktail history *Straight Up or on the Rocks*, William Grimes notes that the julep "scarcely exists today except as a strained evocation of the Old South." He suggests that the reason for this is that "it was always a slow, complicated drink, requiring a servant class to make" and claims that today it is little more than a caricature of Southern leisure.

The real story is quite different and a good bit more complex. Plantations and slavery certainly enter into the mix, but cities—including cities in the North—play a far larger role than you might expect. Juleps were indeed made by a servant class, but even there, the relationship is a little tricky, for mint juleps ended up being the means by which a few members of that servant class, against almost unimaginable odds, were able to achieve a degree of fame, independence, and even prosperity.

A Morning Antifogmatic

Like the bitters that define the drink known as a cocktail, the julep derives from the medicinal realm. The word evolved from the Persian *gulab*, which means "rosewater" and became *julab* in Arabic and *julep* in French. In English, its usage dates back to the 1400s, when it was a term for a syrup used to compound medicine. By the end of the American Revolution, the term *julep* was applied to a similar compound used for daily imbibing purposes, and all evidence points to Virginia as the place where this practice got its start.

Thomas Anburey, the British military officer who had so much to say about peach brandy, also noted that Tidewater planters left the management of their plantations to overseers and the work to their slaves, freeing themselves to booze it up all day. Such a man, Anburey reported, would rise at eight o'clock and drink "what he calls a julep, which is a large glass of rum, sweetened with sugar." After riding his land to inspect his crops and stock, he returned to the house around ten for a breakfast of ham, hominy, toast, and cider. Around noon he began drinking toddy, dined at two, then after a short nap arose again to drink toddy until bedtime. All this time, Anburey noted, "he is neither drunk nor sober, but in a state of stupefaction." That mode of living was broken only to travel to the courthouse on court days or to go to a horse race or cockfight, where which he would proceed to get "so egregiously drunk, that his wife sends a couple of negroes to conduct him safe home."

All-day drinking was not just for the rich. *The American Museum* in 1787 described the routine of the typical Virginian "of the lower and many of the middling classes" by saying he rises at six o'clock and "drinks a Julip made of rum, water, and sugar, but very strong." If you think that sounds an awful lot like a toddy, you're right. Somewhere along the line, though, a little fragrant mint slipped into the cup. Around 1800, one visitor to

Virginia described a young man who, upon first awakening, called for a julep, which he explained as "a dram of spirituous liquor that has mint steeped in it, taken by Virginians of a morning." Just as a cocktail was a toddy flavored with a shade of bitters, so was a julep a toddy flavored with mint. The liquor used was up to the imbiber, and in the early days, rum and brandy were the usual choices.

These sorts of libations were frequently dubbed antifogmatics. "In the Southern states," American author Samuel Goodrich explained, "where the ague is so common and troublesome a malady, where fogs are frequent, and dews heavy, it has grown the custom to fortify the body from attacks of the disease, by means of juleps, or what are called antifogmatics." They were sometimes called mint slings too. The *Alexandria Gazette* noted in 1815 that a group of Virginia politicians "met at the usual hour of the morning, to take their regular antifogmatics alias Mint Sling."

That was the first stage of the julep's history: a morning tipple indulged in by men of a drinking sort. Yes, it was drunk on plantations by slaveholders, but it wasn't something sipped slowly in the afternoon while idling on the veranda, and they weren't served over ice in silver cups by liveried retainers. No, the julep was almost medicinal, stirred up and knocked back in the bedroom first thing in the morning—a dram to stave off the pain from the prior day's drinking and numb the imbiber against the ever-present threat of disease and discomfort in an era before antibiotics and analgesics.

A Hailstorm Strikes

About one-third of the way through the nineteenth century, a new ingredient found its way into the julep cup, and it transformed the morning dram of bilious planters into a national sensation for the fashionable classes. That ingredient was ice.

As one might expect, Southern icehouses first appeared in the upper parts of the region, which had colder winters and were closer to sources of frozen water. Charles Love maintained an icehouse in Alexandria in the 1790s, where he sold ice for sixpence a pound, and James Lownes operated one in Richmond through at least 1801. A lot of plantations in northern Virginia started adding icehouses by the early 1800s too. Thomas Jefferson, for instance, studied the design of European icehouses when traveling in Italy and France, and in 1802, he had one constructed at Monticello. It was a stone-walled cylinder that extended sixteen feet underground with six feet of walls aboveground and a three-and-one-half-foot-wide door on the northwest side. In March 1803, Jefferson had it filled with 62 wagonloads of ice harvested from the nearby Rivanna River. Though water from the melting ice had to be drawn out each week, the store lasted until well into the summer. It was used to make ice cream, to chill wine, and to keep meat fresh during the hot summer months.

The farther South you went, the less common icehouses were on plantations, since the winters were rarely cold enough to freeze over ponds and rivers. But a thriving ice trade developed rather early in the coastal cities, where ice could be brought in on ships from up north. Charleston had one of the first icehouses in the region, and as soon as they had access to a supply of ice, the city's residents found two primary uses for it: making ice cream and chilling alcoholic drinks. In May of 1798, hotelier Jeremiah Jessop advertised in the Charleston *City Gazette* that he had constructed an icehouse "at a considerable expense," and he was using the ice to make ice cream. From a location next to the national bank on Broad Street, he would provide "cooling and nourishing refreshment" to the ladies and gentlemen of Charleston, and families could buy ice to take home too. Jessop also sold "ice punch," which we can only assume was the traditional alcoholic punch served over ice.

The venture didn't last long. In October of 1800, Jessop announced that he was closing his icehouse, which he claimed to be the "first and only construction that ever could keep ice all year in a warm climate." He put it up for sale, along with the related furniture, fixtures, and—confirming our suspicion about that ice punch—his "stock of liquors." It's not clear whether Jessop found a buyer, and it took awhile longer for entrepreneurs to figure out how to make a going concern out of selling such a perishable product.

The man who first made it big in the Southern ice trade was Frederic Tudor, the son of a wealthy Boston lawyer. After a visit to the Caribbean, Tudor concluded that he could make a fortune supplying the islands with ice from Massachusetts ponds. The first few years were a disaster, with his profits literally melting away en route, and Tudor ended up deep in debt trying to finance additional shipments and experiment with various methods of insulation and icehouse construction. Securing funding from a Boston merchant, Tudor began building an icehouse on Fitzsimmons Wharf in Charleston similar in design to one he had built in Havana, and in the spring of 1817 he filled it with his first shipload from Boston. Tudor's ice sold for eight and one-half cents a pound in quantities from one pound to five hundred. To take it home, customers wrapped their ice in blankets, which they could buy at the icehouse for one dollar each.

In 1819, Tudor extended his ice trade to Savannah and then to New Orleans the following year, but he by no means had a monopoly in the market. By 1819, Richard Salmon was operating an icehouse in New Orleans based on a subscription model, collecting money up front from local citizens and using it to secure the shipments as well as buy needed supplies such as tongs and pails. Once the ice arrived, the subscriber would exchange his or her ticket for the subscribed amount of ice. Salmon's first shipment arrived at the beginning of July, and within two weeks, he had sold so much that he was signing up subscribers for a second shipment to ensure a sufficient supply for all comers. In 1827, a third competitor named Phillip Meyer arrived on the scene with what he called a floating icehouse, which was docked opposite the customhouse and sold ice at retail for three cents less than anywhere else in the city.

Over time, icehouses grew in size and sophistication, making ice cheaper and more widely available. In 1828, Phineas Pierce invested $15,000 to build a new icehouse in Charleston. It could hold the cargoes of four ships, and Pierce priced his product at one penny a pound, which he noted was the same rate that ice was sold for in the North and one-fifth of the price in Norfolk. Pierce also advertised that he would pack ice for shipping to the country at no extra charge, and it does seem that while ice at this point was rare in the interior parts of the South, it was not totally unavailable. In 1815, an estate in the Greenville district of South Carolina was advertised for sale, and its description included an icehouse at a nearby ironworks that "keeps that luxury well through the hot season." In the early 1820s, Little Man's Garden, a confectionery in Augusta, featured an icehouse with a fifteen- to eighteen-ton capacity, and in 1827, an L. Kennedy announced the opening of another icehouse in Augusta. This was a seasonal business, opening in May, and patrons who wished to "use it through the season" could buy tickets in advance.

Sometime around 1830, bartenders discovered that a generous amount of crushed ice had a transformative effect on the old mint julep preparation. They christened this frosty innovation with its own special name, one that has almost been lost to history: the hailstorm julep.

In 1832, John H. B. Latrobe, a Baltimore lawyer, recorded in his journal his visit to White Sulphur Springs in western Virginia, which is now the exclusive Greenbrier Resort in West Virginia, where he encountered for the first time "a hailstorm, that is to say, a mint julep made with a hailstorm around it." The drink was made just like an ordinary julep, except that the glass was "well filled with a quantity of ice chopped in small pieces, which is then put in shape of a fillet around the outside of the tumbler." Latrobe described the effect of that ice by saying that it "forms an external icy application to your lower lip as you drink it, while the ice within the glass presses against your upper lip." Latrobe's journal makes Virginia a good candidate for the birthplace of the iced julep, but Charles Augustus Murray, a Brit who toured the United States between 1834 and 1836, noted that "some Carolinians will assert that it can only be found in perfection at Charleston."

MINT JULEP.

A mint julep, 1862.

We live in an era when everything is air conditioned and our beverages are kept chilled in a refrigerator then served over ice. It's hard to comprehend today the effect that a hailstorm julep must have had on an imbiber sipping one for the first time in the antebellum South. Imagine going weeks or even months with nothing around you below eighty degrees: not the air in your house nor the liquids you drink nor the food that you eat. Imagine the thrill of lifting that glass, feeling the cold chill on your hand, lowering your nose into the fragrant aroma of mint, then drawing that icy liquid between your lips into your dry waiting mouth. Little wonder that Latrobe declared, "It is nectar, they say, in this part of the country."

The hailstorm julep and other iced drinks transformed the trade of Southern bartenders. Ice arrived from the icehouse in giant blocks, so tongs, picks, shavers, and scoops became standard tools of the trade, as did canvas bags and wooden mallets used to smash ice into the fine pieces that went into a julep. Straws became a standard utensil, too, which imbibers thrust through the big dome of ice to get at the chilled nectar below. When Captain Frederick Marryat, a British Naval officer and novelist, described the essential ingredients of the antebellum bar, he started his list with "pure crystal ice" and "large bunches of mint."

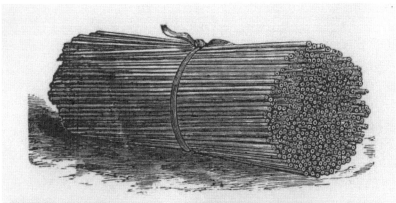

BUNDLE OF STRAWS USED IN SIPPING COBBLERS JULEPS, &c.

Juleps and cobblers made straws and essential part of the bartender's kit, 1878.

The Julep Becomes a Hit

It didn't take long for folks outside the South to discover the glories of the hailstorm julep. The famed Orsamus Willard, who kept the lobby bar at the City Hotel, has been credited with introducing juleps to New York City in the mid-1830s. Willard was said to have a photographic memory and could remember guests even twenty years after their first visit. He was also said to never leave the hotel and, in fact, to not even own a hat. Willard, incidentally, was also credited with sparking a peach brandy punch craze in the early 1830s, so perhaps he had a thing for importing Southern drinking customs. Indeed, the descriptions of these early Gotham juleps indicate that peach brandy was the liquor of choice for making a hailstorm julep. Rivaling Willard in his fame for julep making was Cato Alexander, a free

African-American man who kept an inn and tavern on the main road out of New York City. It was located about four miles north of the city at the time, which today would be somewhere around Fifty-Second Street. The Irish stage actor Tyrone Power, who was the great-grandfather of the famous Hollywood movie star of the same name, visited the United States in the 1830s, and he described Alexander as "foremost among cullers of mint, whether for julep or hail-storm." When they went north of town for a carriage ride, fashionable white New Yorkers stopped off at Cato Alexander's, as Power put it, "to give their horses breath, and wash the dust out of their throats with some of Cato's many excellent compounds." In 1838, a correspondent for London's *New Sporting Magazine* published a series of sketches of carriage racing in New York, which included a description of the requisite juleps at Alexander's, which he noted as being made with "ice, pounded small, a tumbler full; peach brandy, water iced, a wine-glass full of each; and tender budding heads of mint sprinkled upon all."

Perhaps more than any other antebellum beverage, mint juleps had a tendency to inspire its imbibers to flights of poetry. Charles Augustus Murray, a British author who toured America in the late 1830s, declared juleps "a beverage approaching more nearly to nectar than any that I had ever tasted or imagined." Captain Frederick Marryat insisted that "it is, with the thermometer at 100 degrees, one of the most delightful and insinuating potations that was ever invented." In 1845, Charles Fenno Hoffman, one of the Knickerbocker group of New York poets, composed a celebratory ode entitled "The Mint Julep." The beverage, the poem relates, was created on Olympus by the gods of old during a night of revelry when they managed to tap out Bacchus's supply of wine. All the gods contributed to the cause: Pomona offering peaches, Hybla giving honey, and Flora adding the mint. But, Hoffman declares in the poem's final lines, "JULEPS the drink of immortals became / when Jove himself added a handful of hail."

Mint juleps even jumped the pond and became a sensation in England. William Heyward Trapier, a South Carolina planter, introduced juleps to Oxford University when he visited New College in 1845. When asked by his hosts what he would like to drink, Trapier requested a mint julep. To his surprise, no one had ever heard of it. Trapier made do with some other libation, but before departing the college he wrote out the recipe and also left a small sum of money to endow a mint julep fund. The interest was to pay for a round of juleps for everyone dining in the hall on the anniversary of his visit, which was on June 1. The only condition was that a place must be set for him each year. Trapier later sent along a five-and-one-half-inch tall silver cup, a gift to the college "for the use of the Junior fellows." Julep Day became an annual event at New College, and the cup is still in the school's possession.

The Great Julep Makers of the South

It's time to turn our attention to the Southern men who gained fame for their julep-making skills. The old myths do have one part right: African-Americans did indeed mix and serve a lot of the mint juleps drunk by white Southerners. But they weren't often serving them on the verandas of big plantation houses out in the country. The mint julep was a city concoction, one of the fancy drinks associated with the great hotel bars of Southern cities. Many of the men running the show behind those bars were African-Americans, most of them slaves, and they figured out how to use bartending as a way to earn fame, gain some degree of autonomy, and—in some cases—even achieve their own freedom.

In Richmond, Virginia, the two great julep makers were John Dabney and Jim Cook, both of whom were born into slavery. Few traces remain of Jim Cook's early years, but John Dabney was owned by Cara Williamson DeJarnette, who hired him out as a young man to her relative William Williamson to be trained as a jockey. After Dabney grew too big to ride racehorses, he started working as a bartender at the Richmond hotel that Williamson managed. At some point in the 1850s, Dabney began working on his own in Richmond, under the illegal but widely practiced system of self-hire, wherein a slave would hire himself out to an employer, pay a stipend back to his owner, and keep any additional earnings for himself.

In the late 1850s, John Dabney and Jim Cook hired themselves out to John T. Ballard at the Ballard House hotel, where they earned a reputation citywide for their culinary and bartending talents. Their specialties were turtle soup and mint juleps, and both men seem to have known a thing or two about the art of public relations too. It became their habit, whenever they put on a big to-do, to provide a few samples of the fare for the press. In 1859, for instance, the two men staged a turtle soup feast at the Ballard House's newly remodeled barroom, and they sent a tray with a large bowl of soup and three mint juleps to the editorial room of the *Richmond Whig*. The editors, in turn, published a glowing endorsement of their handiwork, declaring "no two compounds intended for the regalement of the inner

The Ballard House hotel in Richmond, home of celebrated julep-makers John Dabney and Jim Cook.

man, deserved a higher rank." Trays of mint juleps appeared quite regularly at the offices of the *Whig* and the *Dispatch* until well into the 1860s.

John Dabney and Jim Cook elevated the julep to a fine art. In their hands it was not just a sipping beverage but an elaborate showpiece adorned with flowers and fruit. One account of a Dabney julep described a giant silver cup topped with a one-foot-tall pyramid of ice, and its sides were encrusted in ice, too, molded into shapes and figures. "Sticking to the ice in artistic designs," the reporter noted, "are . . . grapes, sliced peaches, bananas, strawberries, raspberries, blackberries, and raisins, roses, carnations, and violets." It was a multiserving drink, and imbibers inserted silver straws through the ice to sip the ice-cold liquor contained within.

Edward, Prince of Wales—Queen Victoria's son and the future King Edward VII—discovered the glories of the hailstorm julep on his four-month tour of America in 1860, which included a stop in Richmond. Later accounts have credited John Dabney as the maker of the future king's julep, but newspaper stories from the period make clear that it was actually Jim Cook. The prince, it is worth noting, was a month shy of his nineteenth birthday and had just completed his first year at Oxford. He and his entourage were staying at the Exchange Hotel, which shared its restaurant with the Ballard House. Having heard that "Richmond boasts the possession of the best compounder of cooling drinks in the world," the prince undertook to try one.

Jim Cook went to Edward's quarters, taking with him a large tumbler of a pint and a half capacity, in which he mixed "the cooling ingredients requisite in due proportions." Next, he took an obelisk-shaped mold, filled it with thinly shaved ice, and compressed it into a solid mass. "The base being accordingly rounded," the newspapers reported, "was fitted into the tumbler, and decorated with a bouquet of flowers at its summit. Then the glass itself was surrounded with ice, formed into an ornamental shape." Finally, Cook took several silver straws and inserted them through the covering pyramid of ice before presenting the tumbler to the prince.

The royal took a sip and "started back in astonishment at the luscious taste of the liquid." He asked how Cook had assembled such a remarkable concoction, and as the bartender explained his methods, the prince continued sipping until the julep was all gone. He promptly ordered another and was assisted in consuming it by the Duke of Newcastle, Earl St. Germaine, and Major General Bruce. Enthralled, the prince requested that a third julep be prepared the next morning before his party left the hotel. "This," the newspapers reported, "proved Mr. Cook's masterpiece." He constructed a massive julep, furnished with a total of thirteen straws, "out of which an equal number of the Royal party pulled at one and the same time." To express his gratitude, the prince sent Jim Cook twenty dollars in gold coins.

Instead of spending the money, Jim Cook was said to have kept those twenty dollars in coins as a keepsake for the rest of his life, which is plausible since he and John Dabney seem to have profited quite handsomely as self-hired bartenders and caterers. Dabney used the money he earned along with the connections he had gained among the white elite of Richmond to position himself as advantageously as he could in a slave-holding society. In 1856, he married Elizabeth Foster, though since they both were enslaved, their marriage was not officially recognized by the state. A few years later, he learned that his wife's owner was planning to sell her outside of Richmond, and he took his savings from bartending and enlisted the aid of white acquaintances to purchase Foster from her owner and then set her free. On the eve of the Civil War, Dabney negotiated with Cara DeJarnette a purchase price of $2,000 for his own freedom, to be paid in installments as he earned the money. Before he finished the payments, though, he was freed by a different means: the 1863 Emancipation Proclamation and the subsequent Union occupation of Richmond.

Men like Cook and Dabney helped popularize the hailstorm julep among the fancy drinks crowd, but before the Civil War it seems to have been a phenomenon of the coastal cities and summer resorts, which had abundant supplies of ice from which to craft such chilled concoctions. As the nineteenth century progressed, more and more rural plantations added icehouses, and over time, as construction techniques and methods of insulation improved, they were able to keep ice through the summer. But that ice seemed to have been used primarily to store food, not to chop up and put in drinks. Mary Anderson, for instance, who was born a slave on a plantation in Wake County, North Carolina, remembered that ice was gathered from the pond in the winter and stored in an icehouse that was a hole dug ten feet into the ground with a frame building constructed over it. "There was a still on the plantation," Anderson recalled, "and barrels of brandy were stored in the ice house, also pickles, preserves, and cider."

That doesn't mean that no one ever enjoyed a frosty julep on a plantation, though it may not necessarily have been sipped on a porch. When English journalist William Howard Russell visited a Louisiana sugar plantation in June 1861, just a few months after the start of the Civil War, he was awakened by a slave named Joe who offered him a mint julep made with "brandy, sugar, and peppermint beneath a mountain of ice—an obligatory panacea for all the evils of climate." When Russell finally refused the third julep he was brought, Joe warned him that "you had better take this, because it'll be the last he make before breakfast." Though there are plenty accounts of room-temperature juleps being consumed in such places, this is the only instance I have been able to find of a hailstorm-style julep being served on an actual plantation.

The mint julep is closely associated with Kentucky today, but before the Civil War it was a city slicker's drink, not something you found in the rolling horse country of the Bluegrass State. In 1855, the *Alexandria Gazette* printed an anecdote about a "broad backed Kentuckian" who traveled to New Orleans for the first time. "Whiskey, brandy, and plain drinks he knew," the *Gazette* reported, but "as to the compounded and flavored liquors he was a know-nothing." Relaxing in the Saint Charles Hotel, he noticed "a score of fashionables" drinking glasses of a cooling beverage. Intrigued, he asked the waiter for one of what they were having, and as soon as he finished the glass, he asked what it was. "Why you ordered a julep," the waiter said.

"Don't forget it," the Kentuckian declared. "Keep bringing 'em."

⸭ ⸭ ⸭

By the time of the Civil War, the julep had evolved from a regional Southern specialty to a standard of the urban American bartender's repertoire. In the process, it had taken on a multiflavored set of variations, becoming a preparation that could be applied to any number of different liquors. Jerry Thomas included the julep in *How to Mix Drinks*, his seminal American bartender's guide, noting that it is "an American beverage, and in the Southern states is more popular than any other." He provided recipes for five varieties: mint, brandy, gin, whiskey, and pineapple. The basic mint julep is made with mint, sugar, Cognac brandy, and shaved ice that's decorated with berries and slices of orange and topped with a dash of Jamaican rum. (That's the version, slightly adapted, that opens this chapter.) In the whiskey variety, Thomas instructs, omit all fruits.

And that's where we'll leave it for now. After the Civil War, the julep went through several more transformations to become the classic whiskey preparation that we know today. And the paths of Jim Cook and John Dabney, whom we'll leave compounding juleps in Richmond, take some interesting turns as well. We'll get to those parts of the story in due time.

9

Madeira and the Creation
of Connoisseurship

Mint juleps are fine for the sporting set, but if you want to get a real taste for the high end of Southern drinking, stop by the Charleston Grill in downtown Charleston, South Carolina, and plunk down thirty-five dollars for a flight of old Madeira. You'll get three small glasses, each containing one and one-half ounces of vintage wine of successive ages, the oldest dating all the way back to the 1920s.

What does a ninety-five-year-old wine taste like? It's slightly sweet with rich, multilayered spice notes—a complexity suitable for a beverage with such a complex legacy—and a taste of an age that is long past. You're not just sipping old wine. You're sipping history.

An Ever Rarer Wine

The American Revolution interrupted the Madeira wine trade, but it resumed in earnest once the hostilities ended. The island's exporters had built up a backlog of wine that had been aging for several years, and American consumers discovered they really liked the flavor of those old wines and demanded more. Thanks to their stiff foundation of brandy, fortified Madeiras continued to improve with each passing year. Aging muted the harsh taste and yeasty aroma and imparted a mellow, nutty flavor and a paler color. By 1793, Madeira exporters were regularly shipping wines that were eight or ten years old; by 1815, fifteen-year-old wines were not uncommon.

During the eighteenth century, producers and consumers had discovered the salubrious effects that heat and rocking had on Madeira wine in transit. In the nineteenth century, producers began devising ways to simulate the effect without having to ship the wine halfway around the world. They used stoves, ovens, and hothouses to replicate the heat of ship's holds. Some even immersed pipes of wine in piles of dung for the same purpose.

By 1800, exporters in Funchal, the island's capital city, had found that artificial agitation produced as acceptable an end product as did a long ship voyage, and they installed steam-powered machines to continuously rock the wine in its barrels.

Within a few decades, dung heaps were abandoned and Madeira producers settled on the less fragrant but more effective practice of using estufas—warming rooms heated by stoves. A wine suitable to American connoisseurs could be created in half the time without its ever leaving the island, a hugely profitable savings. Consumers reported that the oven-heated wines had the same body and color and were generally more consistent and reliable than those subjected to the less controlled conditions of ship holds. While some of the romance of a Madeira's making "three trips around the Horn" may have been lost, a more reliable luxury product was assured.

By the early 1800s, an appreciation of good wines was essential for any Southern man aspiring to gentry status. Laying out a spread of wines for guests became part of the code of hospitality among wealthy planters and merchants. A host would bring out a variety of fine old wines in succession, each a little better than the one that preceded it. Expounding upon the details of the wines was a critical part of the conversation at the table. Whether host or guest, talking knowledgeably about wines and being able to distinguish between different varieties and grades was essential to establishing oneself in polite society.

It was around this time that wine drinking began to develop its own language. In part, that was a natural outgrowth of the expanding wine trade, for buyers and sellers needed terms to distinguish one wine from another. But the terminology was also adopted by consumers to be used in the prolonged tableside discussions of wines—their color, their taste, their smoothness and body. Basic color descriptions like red and white were extended by terms like pale, straw, amber, and ruby. Flavors were granted terms of their own, like honeyed, flowery, or peppery. It was all part of the social rules of wine drinking, and it helped separate the connoisseurs—literally, in French, "those who know"—from the rubes who couldn't tell a Malmsey from a Sercial.

Having the right glassware and other paraphernalia and knowing the proper way to store and serve wine was an essential part of connoisseurship too. How a host managed the serving of wine in the dining room was almost as important as the quality of the wine itself. The glassware became smaller, for tiny glasses were more appropriate for savoring a few ounces of a fine vintage instead of swilling plonk by the pint. Guests were expected to know how to hold a glass properly and when and how to sip its contents. A host had to know from whom to order wine, how to store it in a cellar or attic, and how to improve it, for a proper gentleman received his wine shipments in pipes and casks and would fine, rack, and bottle it himself.

Madeira, in short, created the entire concept of wine connoisseurship in America, establishing the patterns and conventions that would be adopted by generations of wine snoots that followed. That mode of connoisseurship was driven by Southerners—elite rice planters in particular—but over the course of the nineteenth century it spread northward and westward and was adopted by any American wanting to seem a person of wealth, sophistication, and taste.

One of the first great connoisseurs of Madeira was Colonel William W. Alston of Charleston, often known as King Billy. Alston inherited Clifton and Fairfield plantations from his father and, as their production increased, he used the income to purchase additional tracts, including True Blue and Rose Hill plantations. After his first wife died, Alston married Mary Brewton Motte and paid £7,000 sterling to her mother and aunt, the daughters of Miles Brewton, to purchase the Miles Brewton House, the most splendid residence in Charleston. Alston embodied the conspicuous consumption of the newly wealthy planter classes, purchasing an extensive wardrobe and grand carriages for his new bride, commissioning portraits from Edward Savage and Samuel F. B. Morse, and creating an elaborate formal English garden.

What better way for such a man to display his newly amassed wealth than with a collection of fine Madeira? King Billy did just that, and, as was the practice in Charleston, he built not an extensive wine cellar but a wine attic. Madeira did better when held high in the heat above the house than in the relative cool below it. Probate records contain the first record of a Charlestonian storing his Madeira in a cask loft in 1773, and the practice really took off in the years just after the Revolution. In the top of the Miles Brewton House, Alston had built a special louvered attic that could hold 1,200 bottles. He marked changes to inventory in chalk on the walls. Dinners at the Alston residence were long, drawn-out, rambunctious affairs, and King Billy maintained the pre-Revolution practice of locking the doors and allowing no one to leave until the sun came up the next morning. In 1792, Alston's marks recorded 468 bottles of Madeira and other fine wines being consumed, much of it likely used during the celebration of the tercentennial of Columbus's first voyage to the New World.

Alston's friend, John Rutledge, built a similar wine attic, and the fashion spread to other planters in the South Carolina Lowcountry. The "attic caves" spread southward from Charleston to Savannah and northward to Richmond too. A large wine collection said a lot about a gentleman—or, at least, a gentleman hoped it did. It showed that he was a man of means, secure enough financially to be able to purchase not only the wines themselves but also to have the physical location and equipment required to store them. It also showed that he had the sophistication to know the proper way to purchase and care for wine and the leisure time necessary to devote to such a pastime. Being invited to visit a host's wine cellar or wine garret told a guest that he was particularly esteemed, allowing him access to the host's most private room.

In the colonial era, Madeira had been the most popular wine among all classes of Southern drinkers. As the nineteenth century advanced, it became increasingly the wine of the elite alone. Once the new American states were freed from British trade restrictions, wines from Spain and France were no longer subject to prejudicial duties and they became much more affordable. In the 1770s, Madeiran wines had accounted for more than half of all wine imported into America. By 1805, they constituted only 8 percent. Madeira was falling out of favor in Britain, too, thanks in part to the many adulterated versions that were launched on the market to simulate long-aged wines, and discerning Britons turned their attention to sherry. By the 1840s, Madeira was producing between fifteen thousand and eighteen thousand pipes of wine per year, and most of it went to the United States and the East and West Indies.

This was the era of the Madeira party, a gathering of gentlemen for a late afternoon of fine food, conversation, and—most importantly— good wine, over which each detail was laboriously noted. There was much commentary on the wines. Guests would be invited to come to a gentleman's house after their dinners, which in Charleston was the largest meal of the day, customarily taken around 3:00 p.m. A mahogany table would be set with finger bowls, four pipe-stem glasses per guests, and trays of olives and parched ground nuts (that is, roasted peanuts). Guests would sample a half dozen or more bottles of Madeira, tasting and commenting on wines for an hour or longer.

In the world of connoisseurship today, wines are identified by the variety of grape from which they are made—Chardonnay, Pinot Noir, Riesling—or by the region in which they are produced—Burgundy, Barolo, Côtes du Rhône. In the nineteenth-century South, the names of Madeira wines reflected their provenance. They might be named after the ships that brought them to America, the family who purchased them, the places they had traveled before arriving, or even notable events or famous people with which they had been associated. The Blake family of Charleston owned the Earthquake Wine, known as such because it was brought to Charleston in 1755, the year of the great Lisbon earthquake, which killed tens of thousands of Portuguese and destroyed almost the entire capital city. Robert F. W. Allston's cellars included three dozen bottles of the Enterprise Madeira, named for the ship on which it arrived.

The Domestic Wine Industry

One of the reasons that Madeira became the great Southern wine was because Southerners had consistently failed to create a domestic wine of their own. In the early nineteenth century, though, in the spirit of innovation and patriotism that characterized the era, ambitious men turned their energies once more to winemaking. Thomas Jefferson was a major promoter of this effort, and the Scuppernong wine of North Carolina caught his notice. Wealthy planters along the Albemarle Sound in North Carolina had begun to cultivate vineyards of muscadines and scuppernongs, and in 1817, General John Cocke sent Jefferson some wine made from those North Carolina grapes. Not long after, Jefferson planted fifteen scuppernong vines in his vineyard at Monticello, though he was never successful in getting them to produce. Jefferson praised North Carolina for taking the lead in the cultivation of domestic wine grapes and claimed that the state's scuppernong wine "would be distinguished on the best tables of Europe for its fine aroma, and chrystalline transparence."

By the early nineteenth century, the ravages of cotton farming had so exhausted the soils in the Carolinas that many farmers had started moving on to the newly opened lands of Alabama and Mississippi, seeking more fertile soil. As their residents departed, the governments of the old cotton states looked around for alternative cash crops, and they returned to the old Southern dream of producing wine. Starting in 1800, the governments of North and South Carolina made periodic efforts to promote grape growing, including importing cuttings from Europe and distributing them to farmers. Over the next two decades, Carolina farmers experimented, with various degrees of success, with crossbreeding hybrid varieties that could stand up to the heat and pests of the region.

French-born Nicholas Herbemont of South Carolina had the most success of any of these aspiring winemakers. He began growing grapes in 1811 on his Palmyra farm, and he wrote frequently of his efforts in agricultural journals and newspapers. He tried importing French vines but soon concluded that native grapes offered the best opportunity for domestic winemaking. In 1830, he wrote, "My chief object is to shew the capability of our Sand-hills and light dry soils generally, to produce Wine of excellent quality." His best wines came from a grape he that ambitiously called Madeira; others started calling it Herbemont's Madeira and later just Herbemont. It was a Southern grape, sensitive to cold and needing a long growing season, but in the right conditions it would produce a fruit with a good balance of sugar and acid—that is, a grape that was well suited for winemaking.

As the name he gave his grape suggests, Herbemont's goal was to make a wine that could take the place of imported Madeira. By 1830, he was claiming that the quality of his wine so closely resembled Madeira's "as to be easily mistaken for it." William J. Grayson and some other South Carolina legislators sampled Herbemont's wine, and while Grayson himself found it "very pleasant." he reported that his "more experienced colleagues, adepts in Old Madeira and Sherry," disagreed, holding it in "very slender estimation" though admitting it was "a good wine to keep."

Southern wine was not destined to eclipse Madeira, but it did manage to find a place for itself in the domestic market. In 1845, Henry Durell wrote that "the best wine of this country is grown in North Carolina; it possesses the mildness and flavor of Muscat, without its cloying sweetness." The South also contributed the most successful wine grape of the nineteenth century: the Catawba. The variety was introduced to the public by a vintner from York, Pennsylvania, who had gotten cuttings that originated in North Carolina as a spontaneous field cross between native vines and transplanted European ones. It was the first native hybrid grape to make a good, drinkable domestic wine, and it quickly spread across the United States.

Nicholas Longworth of Cincinnati, America's leading winemaker, embraced the Catawba and with it transformed the banks of the Ohio River into the so-called Rhineland of America. Longworth hoped to make a dry table wine from the native grape and establish a domestic wine industry, but Americans still preferred their wines sweet and didn't take much to the Catawba variety. Longworth kept at it, enlisting the aid of a Frenchman to learn traditional Champagne methods, and in the 1840s, Longworth developed a native sparkling wine that was a hit. By 1852, he was producing seventy-five thousand bottles a year and distributing them nationally. Plenty of wine made from Catawba grapes—as well as scuppernongs and another hybrid known as the Isabella—were produced in the South, too, especially in North Carolina. With three thousand acres in production in 1860, Ohio dominated American domestic wine production, but North Carolina had three hundred acres of vineyards, South Carolina two hundred, and Georgia one hundred. Together, these states were producing some 200,000 gallons of wine per year. In 1859, one plantation in Warren County, North Carolina, in addition to what was consumed locally, shipped 495 gallons of wine to New Orleans, where it sold for four dollars per gallon.

Southern wine never achieved a level of quality that would impress even the most open-minded connoisseur of fine Madeira, but it did become a sort of workhorse wine of the South, beloved by many. In 1931, William M. Robinson Jr., writing an essay on Prohibition, looked back on the glory days of drinking in the South, and he noted, "What Southerner past forty does not recall the excellence of the Catawba wine of North Carolina, the scuppernong and muscadine wines of South Carolina, and the peach brandy of Georgia!" If you travel through the Carolinas today, you can find lots of small vineyards producing muscadine wine—a product that seems cloyingly sweet to palates trained on dry European and California varieties. Catawba wine, I'm afraid, is now lost to history.

10

The Whiskey Boom

As we shift from wine back to whiskey, a cobbler might help smooth the transition. It was originally a wine formulation, made with sherry or Champagne or even domestic Catawba, but as they did with many of their favorite libations, Southerners started subbing in whiskey. Shake one up and see if the substitution works (I think it does). Careful, though: it's a pretty stiff drink, and if you aren't up to drinking in antebellum quantities, you may want to halve the recipe or share it with a friend.

Whiskey Cobbler

SERVES 1 OR 2

1 tablespoon superfine sugar (see note below)

1 teaspoon water

4 ounces rye whiskey

2 orange slices, ½ inch thick

Cracked ice and shaved ice

Put the sugar and water in the bottom of a cocktail shaker and stir until the sugar is dissolved. Add the whiskey, orange slices, and cracked ice (cut the orange slices in half if needed to fit in the shaker). Shake thoroughly, allowing the cracked ice to muddle the orange as you do. Fill a large bar glass with shaved ice and strain the cobbler into it. Serve with a straw.

A Note on Superfine Sugar: Superfine sugar is known as caster sugar or bakers' sugar, but it is not the same as powdered or confectioners' sugar, which generally contains starch. To make your own, simply put regular granulated white sugar in a food processor and pulse for about 1 minute until it's ground almost to a powder.

Whiskey Distilling Goes Commercial

During the first half of the nineteenth century, whiskey distilling became established as a large-scale commercial enterprise, and it was a curious time for Southern drinking. The making of this grain-based spirit, which had gotten started largely out of necessity, evolved into a craft in which master distillers, through a combination of technology, knowledge, and skill, transformed a harsh, wild spirit into something smooth and flavorful. The same distilling advances also allowed sharp operators to churn out barrel after barrel of cheap, shoddy booze and disguise it just enough to foist upon a gullible market. And thus Southerners witnessed whiskey getting better and worse simultaneously, and they found themselves deluged with an increasing volume of both kinds.

In the early days of the whiskey trade, distilleries were small-scale, almost casual operations. It took a full day of work to produce just ten gallons of whiskey. In a week, a typical distillery might produce all of two barrels. Most were not even full-time operations, just side businesses that earned millers and farmers a few extra dollars. A handful of enterprising men, though, aspired to make whiskey on a much larger scale and, they hoped, to get rich in the process. One of the first such operations was the Hope Distillery, which opened in Louisville, Kentucky, in the summer of 1817. Reportedly bankrolled at $100,000 with money from Yankee investors, the distillery boasted a forty-five-horsepower steam engine and a mechanized grain processing station that did the work of ten men. Its three copper pot stills were imported from England and produced between 1,200 and 1,500 gallons of raw spirits per day, more than one hundred times the output of a typical farmer-distiller. Despite its impressive volume, the distillery went belly-up after just five years. Some whiskey historians have theorized that agrarian America simply wasn't ready for big distilleries or, in a more romantic vein, that whiskey drinkers rejected so-called factory whiskey in favor of the old handcrafted kind. I would suggest a more prosaic explanation. The Panic of 1819 plunged the United States into an economic depression that lasted until 1823, and many otherwise healthy enterprises went bust. But the sense of ambition and scale that drove the creation of the Hope Distillery was widespread during this early era of manufacturing, and others soon tried their hands at making whiskey not by the barrel but by the wagonload.

They got a little help in that effort from protectionist taxes. British factories were flooding American markets with inexpensive manufactured goods at the same time that plummeting agricultural prices were hurting the export market for American crops. In 1816, Congress passed a tariff act that was intended not just to raise revenue for the government but also to protect domestic industry and agriculture from foreign competition.

It imposed stiff duties on foreign brandy and rum because, politicians reasoned, driving up the price of imported spirits would in turn boost sales of cheaper domestically produced whiskey. That, ultimately, would raise the price of domestic wheat and corn and put more money in the pockets of farmers.

Protectionist sentiments peaked in 1828, and in the decades that followed, the tariffs on most goods were gradually reduced, but those on imported spirits and beer were actually increased. The idea was to raise the revenue necessary for running the government by taxing luxury goods that were consumed mostly by the rich, like silk, lace, fine wines, and brandy. The so-called Black Tariff of 1842 was particularly harsh on brandy, which formerly was taxed at 20 percent of its wholesale price but became subject to a duty of one dollar per gallon. Most French brandy at this time was selling for between 90 cents and $1.30 per gallon, so the tariff effectively doubled the price. Duties on other imported spirits were set at 60 to 90 cents per gallon. By comparison, domestic whiskey could be had at wholesale for 20 cents a gallon—making it one-third of the price of competing imports, if not even cheaper.

As whiskey production and whiskey quality increased and imported brandy grew progressively more expensive, what started out as the home-made tipple of mountaineers began to take on an air of respectability. And Southerners began to drink a whole lot more of it. Alcohol historian W. J. Rorabaugh determined that annual per capita liquor drinking increased from 3.7 gallons at the time of the Revolution to more than 5 gallons by 1830—almost three times today's consumption rate.

But you didn't need charts and statistics to detect this surge in antebellum drinking: you could see it in people's faces. In an 1826 travelogue, the American journalist Anne Royall described a journey she made from Nashville, Tennessee, to Alexandria, Virginia. Her party passed by the courthouse in Fairfax, Virginia, while court was in session, and she noted many "gentlemanly looking men on horseback, reeling in the saddle, their red faces and bloated bodies proving them to be old veterans of the bottle." She claimed to have found only a single carriage driver during her entire trip who did not drink while behind the reins. The one who conducted her through Fairfax carried a bottle in his box and, as soon as it was empty, would leave the stage in the middle of the road and disappear to find a nearby grogshop, which might take as long as a half hour. In the late 1820s, the British novelist Frances Trollope captured her travel experiences in *Domestic Manners of the Americans.* She noted that the Potomac area of Maryland and Virginia was as different from the new cities and states on the western side of the Appalachians as Amsterdam was from Saint Petersburg, but they had one thing in common: whiskey, she wrote, "flows everywhere at the same fatally cheap rate of twenty cents" per gallon, and "its hideous effects are visible on the countenance of every man you meet."

The Rise of Old Monongahela and Old Bourbon

As Southerners started drinking more whiskey, they began to notice that not all of it tasted the same. Where it was distilled made a big difference, and the best kind came from the counties along the Monongahela River in Pennsylvania. In an 1808 advertisement in the *Scioto Gazette* in Chillicothe, Ohio, a man named John Sherer announced he had just returned to town with a load of "Monongahela whiskey" that he was selling "at a very low rate." Within a decade, such whiskey was being advertised for sale in cities as far away as New Orleans, Boston, and Saint Louis. The market was also learning that the longer whiskey spent resting in barrels the better it tasted, and by the 1820s, Old Monongahela was firmly established as the most desirable type. It's not clear exactly how old a whiskey needed to be to be classified as Old Monongahela, but it was measured in years, not months. In 1823, the Wine and Liquor Store on East Bay Street in Charleston announced that it had received "a few gallons" of Monongahela whiskey, "warranted seven years old" and "a delicious flavored Liquor."

That delicious flavor came from the oak sides of the barrels in which the whiskey was stored. The liquid expanded into the wood as the surrounding temperature rose, and it contracted back out as the temperature fell. The oak filtered away the harsh congeners and imparted an array of flavors— vanilla, tannin, tobacco, leather. Instead of the clear white of raw rye spirits straight off the still, aged rye whiskey was tinged a rich amber color.

To reach the Southern cities on the Eastern Seaboard, most of the whiskey from the Monongahela region traveled eastward through Pennsylvania along the National Road and ended up in the hands of merchants in Boston, Philadelphia, or Baltimore, who then sent it southward on ships. At this early stage, whiskey was sold primarily in bulk— in barrels, pipes, or casks—not in bottles with labels or brand names. In fact, the names of the actual distillers were rarely even mentioned on the barrels or in retailers' advertisements. It was the region that produced the whiskey, not the distillery, that mattered.

About a decade after Monongahela rye established itself in the market, Kentucky whiskey began to make a name for itself too. As distilling became a more formal commercial enterprise in the Bluegrass State, a crowd of small operators entered the market. Many lasted only a few years, but a fair number lived on until well after the Civil War, and a few of the family names can still be found on the market today. Johannes Jacob Beam, for instance, moved from Maryland to the frontier of Kentucky and started selling whiskey around 1795, and his son David M. Beam took over the stills at the Old Tub Distillery around 1820. Around 1800, Elijah Pepper launched a distillery in Versailles, and in 1817 built a new operation on Glenn's Creek near Millville, which is where a very influential figure in early Kentucky whiskey history got his start. Dr. James C. Crow, a Scottish-born physician and chemist, introduced the use of saccharometers and thermometers, and he stressed quality over quantity, making only two and a half gallons of whiskey per bushel of grain. Crow helped improve the mashing process and ensured it could produce a more consistently high-quality whiskey. James Crow never owned a distillery of his own, but he worked at the Elijah Pepper distillery until just a few years prior to his death in 1855. Fifteen years later, Pepper's grandson launched the Old Crow brand of whiskey to market, named in honor of the whiskey innovator.

The story of J. W. Dant is typical of how many Kentucky distillers got started in the trade. In 1836, at the age of sixteen, Dant began making whiskey on his farm in Marion County. Before long, he was producing more than he could sell locally, so he hired a wagon to take him and several barrels of bourbon to the Beech Fork River. Once there, he built a raft, loaded his whiskey aboard, and floated down the Beech Fork to the Rolling Fork and down the Rolling Fork to the Salt River and down the Salt to the Ohio and down the Ohio to the Mississippi and finally down the Mississippi all the way to New Orleans, where he sold the whiskey. Then, Dant walked back home to Marion County. He did the exact same thing for his second shipment, though on his third trip he bought a mule to ride back in style.

It wasn't just the use of corn in place of rye as the primary grain that separated Kentucky distillers from their kinfolk over the mountains in Pennsylvania. The Kentuckians adopted the sour mash process, which refers not to the flavor of the mash itself but rather to the practice of conditioning a new batch by adding in a little spent mash from the previous run. That step introduces yeast into the mash and is similar to the way bakers use a yeast-laden starter when making sourdough bread. The process seems to have been widely in use by the 1810s, for in his 1818 book *The Distiller*, Harrison Hall describes "mashing with pot ale" and notes that it was common in Tennessee and Kentucky. Yeast ferments better in an acidic environment, so by adding back a portion from their previous run, distillers were able to increase the acidity of the mash and make the fermentation more reliable. It also had an added advantage of letting them extend the amount of whiskey they could distill from the same amount of grain. The sweet mash approach, which used all new grain, would produce about two gallons of whiskey from a bushel of grain, whereas sour mash could produce three.

A Substitute for Brandy and Rum

Around the 1820s, whiskey distillers began adopting what would become the most important innovation for improving their products: aging the raw spirits in oak barrels whose insides had been thoroughly charred. Akin to charcoal filtering, using charred barrels enhances the filtering effect during aging and helps mellow the whiskey over time. It also creates a layer of caramelized sugars from the sap in the oak, which imparts additional caramel and vanilla flavors and gives the spirits a darker amber-red hue.

A truckload of tales purport to explain how the practice of charring barrels came about. Most of them involve lucky cheapskates. According to one account, a cooper was heating barrel shooks over a fire to make them more pliable and accidentally burned them, but he used them anyway and by blind chance discovered that the spirits aged in them had a much-improved flavor. Another tale involves a distiller who tried to save a few bucks by putting his whiskey in barrels that had previously been used to store fish. He scorched the vessels thoroughly to get the fishy taste out and discovered by happy accident the salubrious effects on the whiskey.

Like most origin stories involving lucky accidents, this one is a myth. Coopers and distillers had been heating and seasoning barrels with smoke and fire for quite a long time, and the effect of carbon—be it in the form of charcoal or the charred sides of a wooden barrel—was well known. During the 1820s, numerous articles in scientific journals explored the effectiveness of storing drinking water for sailors in charred barrels, which would keep it "perfectly sweet" for three years or more. It didn't take some clumsy cheapskate trying to destink a fish barrel to discover that charcoal could alter the taste of whiskey. Instead, it seems, the practice of charring came about quite deliberately as a way to imitate the color and flavor of the more prized and therefore more expensive imported brandy. In his 1824 farmer's and mechanic's guide, Dr. M. Parker provided a slate of options for "colouring liquors," including adding parched wheat, burned sugar, or dried peaches to a barrel of whiskey. He also notes that "if the inside of a new barrel be charred or burned black, it will add much to the flavor, and will also give a good color to the liquor." In 1826, a Lexington grocer wrote to distiller John Corlis of Bourbon County, from whom he had been purchasing whiskey, to place another order. "It is suggested to me," he added, "that if the barrels should be burnt upon the inside, say, only one-sixteenth of an inch, that it will much improve."

Pennsylvania rye and Kentucky bourbon whiskey, it seems, got a whole lot better because their makers were trying to create a spirit that could be passed off as French brandy or Jamaican rum. One anonymous Kentucky writer explicitly endorsed the counterfeiting of spirits. Through clarifying techniques like charcoal filtering, "the native oil of the grain" could be extracted from the whiskey and the manufacturer could then add the essence of other spirits and "make it what we please." If Kentucky distillers would focus their energies on making spirits of the best quality, he argued, "the product of our distilleries will not only be drank under its proper name of whiskey, but pass throughout the world as genuine Cogniac, Geneva and Jamaica spirits." This advice wasn't presented in some secretive underground tract, either. It was advanced in a straightforward essay presented to the Kentucky Institute in Lexington as a proposal to "promote the wealth and prosperity of the Western country."

This line of thinking was echoed in commercial distiller manuals. Harrison Hall argued that when whiskey was made properly—double distilled and aged one year—men "will drink it without being able to say what it is, and may finally prefer it to French brandy." Samuel McHarry devoted many pages of his guide to explaining how to make rye whiskey or apple brandy pass as good French brandy or Jamaican rum. One could filter it through ground maple charcoal, burned brick dust, and three layers of flannel to filter out the oils and other impurities so that it would have "scarcely any taste or smell of whiskey." One could then add one-fourth to one-third French brandy (if imitating brandy) or Jamaican spirit (if imitating rum). To color the whiskey, another writer advised, one could boil a pint of water, a pint of whiskey, and three pounds of sugar until the mixture turned almost black, then dilute it with more whiskey and water and stir in a half pound of pulverized cinnamon. Four ounces of this mixture would be sufficient to give "a fine colour" to thirty gallons of white whiskey.

Using charred barrels offered an effect similar to these more convoluted tricks, and the adoption of the practice was a key turning point in the history of whiskey. It may have started out as a dodge for passing off American whiskey as something better, but it ended up creating a spirit that was a desirable product in and of itself. Time in charred barrels came to be the defining characteristic of good whiskey and, later, was even codified in the laws governing what could be marketed as rye and bourbon.

Bourbon Gets Its Name (and an Imitator)

The question of how bourbon whiskey came to be called bourbon has been the subject of considerable debate, thanks to the confusing geographical history of the Bluegrass State. Before the American Revolution, the land that became Kentucky was part of Virginia's western Fincastle County. After 1776, Fincastle was carved up into several units, one of which was called Bourbon County. Shortly after Kentucky was admitted to the Union in 1792, the massive Bourbon County was subdivided into thirty-three separate counties. Just to keep things from being too simple, one of those new counties kept the name Bourbon.

These repeated divisions have thrown historians for a loop. Though there were scads of distilleries in the old Bourbon County, by the time Kentucky whiskey took on the name bourbon the large county had long been split apart, and there were almost no distilleries operating in the one that retained the name Bourbon. This fact has inspired commentators to seek out alternative explanations. In *Kentucky Bourbon Whiskey: An American Heritage*, Mike Veach speculates that the name might have come from "river travelers drinking the aged whiskey of New Orleans on Bourbon Street and starting to ask for that 'Bourbon Street whiskey.'" Others have pointed to the fact that early Kentucky whiskey was competing with fine imported French brandy and that adopting the name Bourbon after the French royal family would have given it more appeal to those prone to prefer spirits from France.

These theories get us past the paucity of distilleries in the actual Bourbon County, but the evidence makes it clear that in the 1820s, at least, when people advertised "Bourbon whiskey" for sale, they were talking about whiskey from a specific place. In August 1824, S. & H. P. Postlethwaite of Natchez advertised in the *Mississippi State Gazette* that they were offering for sale "100 Barrels Superior Bourbon County Whiskey." In 1825, another Natchez newspaper, the *Ariel*, printed an ad for two hundred barrels of superior-quality "Bourbon county, Ky. Whiskey." A year later, an ad in the same paper offered "50 Barrels Old Bourbon County Whiskey." The dealers may have latched onto the Bourbon County name because of the appealing French connotations, and perhaps they took some liberties and lumped all thirty-three of the new counties under their former name of Bourbon. But it seems clear than Bourbon whiskey gets its name from Bourbon County, Kentucky, and not from Bourbon Street nor the old French monarchy.

WHISKEY FOR SALE. 200 barrels superior quality Bourbon county, Ky. Whiskey.
50 bbls. FLOUR, Ohio brand.   10 do. SUGAR.
50 pairs Negro Shoes, (stitch downs)
Barrel Pork, Bacon, Lard, Butter, Candles, Soap, &c.
for sale by   STURGUS & MILLER.
Natchez, Nov. 14.   17t4

FOR SALE 50 barrels Old Bourbon County Whiskey, 10 Boxes best Cavendish Tobacco, 2000 lbs Bacon, 1 new Wagon for plantation use, for sale by   J. W. TREMBLY.
Natchez Landing, Jan. 25, 1826   27 3t

Advertisements offer "Bourbon County whiskey", 1825 and 1826.

Though there are scattered references to Bourbon County whiskey in newspapers in the 1820s and 1830s, it wasn't until the 1840s that the name really caught on. It did so primarily in the states along the Mississippi River, including Louisiana, Arkansas, and Mississippi. Though plenty of Monongahela and other varieties of rye whiskey were advertised in Atlantic coast cities like Charleston and Savannah, Bourbon whiskey didn't arrive there in any appreciable volume until the eve of the Civil War.

At the same time that Old Bourbon was earning a reputation for itself in the market, a new type of whiskey was appearing, and the hub of its production was Cincinnati, Ohio. As one commentator explained in 1849, Cincinnati was the center of "the largest district in which corn is raised with facilities to convert it into some convenient shape for export, either by feeding it to hogs or cattle, grinding it into meal, or distilling it into whiskey." By the 1850s, Cincinnati was the largest whiskey-producing city in the country, churning out some nine million gallons per year. The city became the center of the practice known as rectifying, which took raw, high-proof common whiskey distilled in the country and ran it through massive charcoal filters to remove the fusel oil, a substance produced during fermentation that imparts a rank, hot, solventlike taste and odor (the word *fusel* is taken from the German for "bad liquor"). From there, the remaining spirits were sweetened and colored with burned sugar, prune juice, or cherry juice. The really sharp operators diluted their whiskey with water and added things like black pepper or pellitory, a pungent herb, to give it more bite so the spirits wouldn't seem watered down. Manufacturers in Cincinnati took to calling their product Patent Bourbon, suggesting that through proprietary processes they were transforming cheap whiskey into something resembling the fine aged, dark-colored spirits produced by Kentucky's best distillers.

An entire subgenre of publications cropped up that provided detailed instructions on how to create counterfeit whiskey. An 1860 volume modestly entitled *600 Miscellaneous Valuable Receipts, Worth Their Weight in Gold* offered the following formula for "How to Imitate Old Bourbon Whiskey": "Take 30 gallons pure rectified whiskey, 6 gallons pure Bourbon whiskey, 3 half-pints simple syrup, 1½ ounces sweet spirits of nitre; mix them all together, and colour with sugar colouring." The "sell it fast and get the hell out of town" part, one supposes, was too obvious to print. Some drinkers could tell the difference. By 1860, the term *copper whiskey* was being used to denote whiskey made on a small scale using copper stills that could produce only two or three barrels of high-quality whiskey at a time. Most Southerners, unfortunately, had to settle for the cheaper stuff made in large distilleries using massive iron stills. They showed their esteem for such products by giving them names like prison whiskey, rifle whiskey, and rotgut, though they tossed it back all the same.

Drinking and Slavery During the Antebellum Era

There was a tremendous tension among white Southerners when it came to the drinking habits of African-American slaves. On the one hand, whiskey and brandy were still widely considered necessities of agricultural life, both a stimulant for work and a medicine used to treat any number of illnesses. At the same time, alcohol in the hands of slaves posed a threat to white control. As sectionalist tensions increased and slaveholders became more and more worried about losing control, they began to pass stricter and stricter laws attempting to limit alcohol consumption by African-Americans.

In 1831, the South Carolina legislature passed an act that forbade any free person of color or slave from using a still or other vessel "on his own account" and from being involved in the selling of spirituous liquors of any kind. An offense was a misdemeanor punishable by up to fifty lashes on the bare back. Owners were forbidden to allow their slaves to be employed in liquor distilling or selling. In 1858, the Virginia legislature tightened its limits on the sale of alcohol to slaves and imposed restrictions on free blacks, too, prohibiting the sale of wine or ardent spirits to African-Americans regardless of whether they were free or enslaved.

Slave owners did not necessarily want to eliminate alcohol consumption by slaves altogether, but they wanted to ensure that they had tight control on when and where it was consumed. Early on Christmas morning on coastal South Carolina plantations, the slaves gathered at the main house to receive allotments of rum or whiskey, tobacco, extra rations, and small gifts. The slave narratives captured in the 1930s by the New Deal–era Works Progress Administration (WPA) provide fleeting glimpses of the role alcohol played in the lives of enslaved African-Americans. Many record masters providing whiskey either by the dram or the bottle on certain holidays. Minnie Davis of Georgia remembered that they were given whiskey on two occasions: Christmas morning and New Year's Day. She also noted, "They couldn't risk giving slaves much whiskey because it made them mean, and then they would fight the white folks. They had to be very careful about things like that in order to keep down uprisings." Abraham Harris remembered that the owner of the plantation where he was enslaved kept a big orchard with apples and peach trees, and when the fruit was ripe he would send it down to the still to be made into brandy. When the kegs and barrels arrived back, the owner would call the slaves up to the back gallery of the house to get themselves a dram.

Other voices from the era paint a quite different picture of alcohol consumption among slaves, viewing it not as a potential threat to white control but as an instrument through which whites maintained their power. In his famous 1845 autobiography, Frederick Douglass labeled the practice of giving slaves alcohol at Christmas "one of the grossest frauds committed upon the down-trodden slave." In Maryland, where Douglass was born and lived before escaping to freedom, the period between Christmas and New Year's Day was treated as a holiday, and slaves were not expected to work. Douglass related that his sober and industrious peers engaged in productive work for themselves, like making brooms and baskets or hunting game. But the majority occupied their time with merriments such as games, wrestling, footraces, music, dancing, and, especially, drinking whiskey, which is exactly what the slaveholders wanted. Owners, Douglass explained, treated slaves who did not get drunk at Christmas with disdain and contempt. He recounted slaveholders placing bets on slaves to see who could drink the most whiskey and undertaking other deceits to make them drink to excess, so that at the end of the holidays "we staggered up from the filth of our wallowing, took a long breath, and marched to the field—feeling, on the whole, rather glad to go, from what our master had deceived us into a belief was freedom, back to the arms of slavery." Douglass was not alone in this interpretation of the role of alcohol in the lives of Southern African-Americans. In an 1846 temperance address, Henry Highland Garnet declared that masters deliberately plied slaves with alcohol because it "stupefies the mind" and made it difficult for them to plot resistance.

White elites wanted to be the ones determining when and how their enslaved workers were able to drink, but if there's one thing the history of drinking in the South shows, it's that, despite the best efforts of those in power to prevent it, those who want strong drink will figure out how to get it. As the new colonists had been two centuries before, African-Americans in the South were quite resourceful in making their own alcohol. In Africa, there was a long tradition of making a fermented beverage from the fruit of the ebony tree, a cousin of the American persimmon, and those of African descent knew just what to do with the plentiful persimmon trees dotting the South. West Turner of Louisiana recalled that they made persimmon beer by sticking the fruit in a keg "with two or three gallons of water and sweet potato peelings and some hunks of corn bread and left it there until it began to work." Millie Evans of Arkansas described a similar recipe, putting persimmons in a keg of water, adding two cups of cornmeal, and letting it sour for three days. The seeds of the locust tree were used to make a similar beer. Charlie Hudson of Georgia remembered that at Christmastime they would go "from house to house looking for locust and persimmon beer" as well as little balls of gingerbread.

But whiskey, not home brew, is the alcoholic beverage mentioned more often than any other in the WPA slave narratives, having replaced rum as the cheapest spirit on the market. Its availability and attitudes toward its consumption seem to have differed widely from state to state and even from plantation to plantation. In 1820s and 1830s, numerous letters from Virginia planters mention whiskey allotments at harvesttime. Emma Blalock of North Carolina remembered that slaves "could get plenty of whiskey" and that "most everybody drank it but you hardly ever seed a man drunk." In her part of the state, slaves were given whiskey as part of their rations and could drink it as they saw fit, though they were at risk of being whipped if they consumed to excess.

Many in the South, both white and black, were happy to supply alcohol to slaves if they could earn a little money doing it. John Andrew Jackson, a runaway slave from South Carolina, recalled that his master operated a liquor store where he sold alcohol to whites during the day and, at night, traded whiskey to slaves in exchange for cotton. He made a handsome profit, selling a gallon of whiskey worth one dollar in exchange for fourteen dollars' worth of cotton. Jackson noted that "this method of getting rich is very common among the slaveholders of South Carolina." Many times it was the slaves themselves who were the distillers and liquor dealers. Rebecca Hooks of Florida recalled that her father made corn whiskey during his time off, which he sold to purchase things his family needed, like books. Fannie Dorum of Arkansas remembered that, though the plantation owner kept brandy in the storehouse, it wasn't given to the slaves. Instead, "my Daddy used to make it and buy it from the white folks and slip and sell it to the colored folks."

Define Horry, a driver at Brookgreen Plantation on the South Carolina coast, regularly stole rice from the plantation's barn, pounded it himself with a makeshift mortar in the woods, and hid it in a sack in the prow of the boat that he and Brookgreen's owner, John Joshua Ward, would take into Georgetown on Saturdays to buy provisions. While in town, Horry would sell the rice and use the money to buy a jug of liquor, which he took back to the plantation. Another Georgetown planter, Dr. Andrew Hassell, sent a note to Colonel Daniel W. Jordan, taking him to task for giving whiskey to Hassell's slave Isaac, whom Hassell claimed had never been intemperate for fourteen years. Jordan replied that he was not in the habit of offering liquor to Hassell's servants, but that after Isaac had offered some service, Jordan had given him about two tablespoons of whiskey out of politeness. He maintained that Isaac was not at all drunk, but added, "It is not difficult for negroes to get whiskey if they want it."

Some Southerners were beginning to worry about alcohol use not just by slaves but by the population more generally, especially as cheap whiskey became more widely available. In the wake of the religious fervor of the Great Awakening, a new temperance movement was beginning to emerge in the South and in the country at large. The first Southern temperance societies were founded in the early 1820s. Driven primarily by evangelical Christians, the movement enjoyed rapid growth out of the gate, surging from 10 societies in 1828 to 339 in 1831. The movement even managed to get a few laws passed to regulate drinking. Most of these measures were aimed at controlling the retail sale of liquor by the drink, especially in barrooms and saloons. In 1831, the Tennessee General Assembly passed a measure requiring the licensing of saloons, and they replaced it seven years later with the so-called Quart Law, which prohibited the sale of liquor in containers smaller than a quart.

Enthusiasm began to wane in the 1830s, though. What had begun as a temperance movement—that is, a movement encouraging moderation in drinking and the avoidance of hard liquor—increasingly started moving toward teetotalism, a shorthand for "T-Total Abstinence," and divisions appeared in the ranks. The Georgia State Temperance Society ended up dissolving over whether to advocate teetotalism or moderation. Even among Southern evangelicals, there was no unanimity on the subject. Isham Peacock, a Baptist minister from Georgia, was known to carry a hollowed-out cane filled with whiskey. Nearing one hundred years old, he frequently took a nip from the cane in front of his congregation to prove one could drink whiskey regularly without getting drunk. The Hard-Shell or Primitive wing of the Baptist church, which focused on personal piety and morality, wanted no truck with modern innovations like Sunday schools and Bible societies, and they lumped temperance organizations into that category, too, deeming them to be "unscriptural."

But the biggest dampening effect was white Southerners' growing fear of abolitionism, since many of those active in the Northern Prohibition movement also advocated the end of slavery. In 1829, the *National Philanthropist*, the country's first temperance newspaper, merged with abolition firebrand William Lloyd Garrison's *Investigator*, linking those two Yankee reform efforts in the minds of many Southerners. In the 1840s and 1850s, temperance movements gained momentum in the Northern states.

Championed by Neal Dow, the so-called Maine Law was passed in 1846, making that state the first in the country to go dry. Vermont followed in 1852, as did New Hampshire and Massachusetts in 1855. Southerners, however, had largely abandoned the cause. By this point, the storm clouds of secession and war were looming on the horizon, and those forces did far more than social reformers ever could to disrupt drinking in the South.

The Civil War

There are several scurrilous recipes floating around the Internet and other unsavory places for a cocktail called The Rhett Butler. Some versions blend Southern Comfort with orange liqueur or curaçao and various citrus juices; others mix bourbon whiskey with ginger ale. All are gross anachronisms. Here's something Rhett Butler might have actually used to toast the fate of the Confederacy as he was profiting handsomely off blockade-running (if, of course, he wasn't a fictional character).

The Real Rhett Butler

SERVES 1

2 ounces Cognac

½ ounce simple syrup
(page 6)

2 dashes Fee Brothers
black walnut bitters

1 large chuck of ice

1 tablespoon Madeira

Combine the Cognac, simple syrup, and bitters in a mixing glass with ice. Stir well. Strain into a rocks glass over one large chunk of ice. Pour the Madeira over the top as a float.

The End of Madeira

In 1852, the grapes in Madeira's vineyards were attacked by *Oidium tuckeri*, a powdery mildew, and by the end of the decade it had destroyed three-quarters of the island's vines. Many of the best vineyards were converted to sugar, cotton, and tobacco, and wine production collapsed from its high mark of twenty-five thousand pipes a year to just six hundred. With no new vintages to replenish them, the island's reserves were rapidly depleted. By 1860, the *San Francisco Bulletin* reported, only four hundred pipes of wine remained on the island.

The collapse of Madeira wine foreshadowed the fate of its most loyal consumers—the aristocracy of Southern planters, whose entire world was about to be torn violently asunder. Attics filled with fine Madeira were physical representations of their owners' extraordinary wealth, a tangible badge of sophistication and taste. Over the course of just four years, those attics would be emptied, their contents smashed, consumed by ruffians, or vanished seemingly into thin air. After all was said and done, a few surviving cases of dusty Madeira bottles were among the last remnants of their once-prodigious wealth.

A Crisis of Grain

In late 1860s, decades of sectionalist tensions over the institution of slavery finally came to a head. In the wake of Abraham Lincoln's election as president, seven Southern states, starting with South Carolina on Christmas Eve 1860, declared they had seceded from the United States, and in February they established themselves as the Confederate States of America. At 4:30 a.m. on April 12, Confederate cannons began launching shells at Fort Sumter in the middle of Charleston Harbor. The American Civil War had begun.

Despite the fact that its economy was agriculturally based, the South was almost immediately confronted by food shortages. The dominance of cotton had made the region increasingly dependent upon grain imported from the Midwest. Once that supply was cut off, the South struggled to feed itself. Newspaper editors urged planters to reduce cotton acreage and replace it with grain, and both the Confederate government and state governments passed laws encouraging the growing of grain instead of cotton.

Grain, of course, was used to make more than just bread, and the shortages began cutting into the supply of whiskey too. Within two months of the shelling of Fort Sumter, the price of a gallon of whiskey jumped from twenty-five to fifty-five cents. With the whiskey traffic from Cincinnati and other Northern distilling centers halted, Southern distillers cranked up production. In February 1862, the *Richmond Examiner* observed that "Whiskey distilleries are growing up in every part of the State and monopolizing all the grain in their districts." In Georgia, the *Macon Telegraph* lodged a similar complaint, noting that "the whole State swarms with whiskey stills." Within weeks, a commodity that was sold before the outbreak of war for a quarter per gallon had risen to six dollars.

Governor Joseph E. Brown of Georgia declared that in the richest grain-growing section of the state there were as many as seventy distilleries in a single county, consuming more grain each day than the local population was eating. As of the 15th of March, 1862, the governor ordered all distillers in the state to cease operation. He also ordered military officers to suppress the use of intoxicating liquors by those under their command and to seize and destroy any liquor brought near the army for sale. The governor of South Carolina similarly prohibited the distillation of spirits from any type of grain, excepting only those distilleries licensed to sell spirits to the state or Confederate governments. In North Carolina, the legislature opted to reduce distilling through taxation, imposing a levy of thirty cents per gallon on alcohol manufacturing, the first in the state's history. One by one, municipal governments in cities like Norfolk, Wilmington, and Columbia banned all sales of spirituous liquors within their limits, and the directors of railroads determined to allow no liquor to be transported upon their trains.

But the military needed alcohol. Brandy and whiskey were primary ingredients in the manufacture of medicines, and it took one gallon of spirits along with the bark of dogwood, poplar, or willow trees to make sixty-four doses of quinine substitute, an essential drug due to the high incidence of malaria in the South. Alcohol was used as a general stimulant, given in small doses to strengthen patients suffering from fever and/or in shock after being wounded. Whiskey was part of the daily rations for sailors in the Confederate navy, and it was supplied to army troops "under circumstances of great exposure and protracted fatigue."

Increasingly, the states' efforts to restrict alcohol production put them in direct conflict with the Confederate government in Richmond. In September 1862, the Confederate War Department put out calls in Georgia newspapers for contractors to supply it with 250,000 barrels of whiskey to be delivered via rail and requested that Governor Brown exempt it from his ban on liquor shipments. Brown insisted that the demand for bread in both the army and at home was far greater than the need for whiskey, and he denied the request. In North Carolina, Governor Zebulon Vance was incensed when the War Department began contracting with farmers in his state to produce medicinal alcohol. Virginia was the last state to join the prohibition ranks, outlawing the distillation of spirituous liquors in March of 1863. In October, it took a direct slap at the Confederate government, passing an act that made it illegal for any Virginian to fulfill a contract with the Confederate government to manufacture ardent spirits.

The Confederate government, though, went right on issuing contracts to individuals to produce whiskey, paying two to three dollars per gallon for the finished product and granting those contractors the power to impress grain if needed. Many contractors took advantage of their government licenses to produce more liquor than was called for in their contracts, selling the excess on the private market at inflated wartime rates. The really sharp operators hit upon an even more profitable dodge. The government contract called for whiskey to be "at proof," which is to say 50 percent alcohol. By diluting their contracted whiskey to be below proof, it would be condemned by the government and returned to the distillers. Those distillers could then turn right around and sell it on the open market, where it would draw not three bucks a gallon but anywhere between twenty-five and eighty.

Confederate officials soon grew weary of such shenanigans. In January 1864, Surgeon General S. P. Moore wrote to Secretary of War James Seddon to inform him that the Medical Department had purchased a distillery in Salisbury, North Carolina, "for the purpose of dispensing with the system of contracting for alcoholic stimulants." Much of the whiskey manufactured by contractors, Moore reported, was of inferior quality, and a large quantity "has been sold to private parties when it should have been delivered to the Government." The distillery at Salisbury eventually turned out as much as five hundred gallons per day. When Governor Vance learned of the operation, he dashed off a fiery letter to Secretary Seddon, reiterating that North Carolina law forbade any kind of distillation with grain and that it would "be my duty to interpose the arm of civil law to prevent and punish this violation thereof unless you order it to cease." But his threats don't seem to have materialized into action. After heated negotiations with the governor of South Carolina, the Confederate navy built its own distillery in that state to produce whiskey for their exclusive use, and the army soon followed suit.

Soldiers and Drinking

Excessive drinking became a more pronounced problem during the long period of inactivity that followed the battle of First Battle of Bull Run in July 1861. "Drunkenness became so common as to scarcely excite remark," one chaplain recorded, noting that many formerly temperate soldiers "fell into the delusion that drinking was excusable, if not necessary, in the army." Military leaders did what they could counteract that notion. In December 1861, General Braxton Bragg issued an order prohibiting liquor sales within a five-mile radius of Pensacola. A few months later, the

Confederate War Department issued a general order that commanders use every means in their power to suppress drunkenness. The order stated that drunkenness was "the cause of nearly every evil from which we suffer." General Bragg put it even more sharply: "We have lost more valuable lives at the hands of whiskey sellers than the balls of our enemies."

That statement ceased to be true as the battles became bloodier, but drunkenness remained a persistent problem on both sides throughout the war. When troops passed through Nashville, Chattanooga, and Memphis, they bought up as much whiskey, apple brandy, and gin as they could get their hands on, got tight as drums, and picked fights with each other in the streets. Drunken soldiers were a common sight on the streets of Richmond and New Orleans too. The *Richmond Examiner* decried the fact that at night one could see "hundreds of good looking young men wearing the uniform of their country's service, embruted by liquor, converted into bar room vagabonds."

Richmond was transformed by the war, thanks to its new role as the capital city of the Confederacy as well as the constant stream of officers and enlisted men who came to the city on leave. Its population effectively tripled, and there was a severe shortage of both short-term and permanent housing. Dozens of new cafés and saloons opened to cater to officers and troops on leave, as did gambling dens and cockfight pits. Soldiers on leave drank on the streets, got into brawls, and broke into saloons on Sundays. One soldier smashed a plate glass window at the American Hotel with his fist to win a bet. Periodic whiskey shortages swept the town, and robberies and theft were rampant. There were frequent fires, many set intentionally, and vandals even broke into the House of Representatives, where they smashed a clock and stole furniture.

On March 1, 1862, President Jefferson Davis suspended the writ of habeas corpus and declared martial law in Richmond. One of his first acts under military rule was to close all distilleries and liquor-selling establishments and outlaw all sales of alcohol in the city. The *Richmond Examiner* endorsed the move, hoping that "every barrel and jug of whiskey now stored in Richmond may in three days be emptied in the gutters." Those jugs ended up getting emptied all right, but not necessarily into the gutters. A steady stream of men was arrested for violating the liquor ban and sentenced via court-martial, including bartender Jim Cook, "the celebrated toddy mixer," who in June 1862 was arrested on suspicion of dispensing alcohol and put into the prison known as Castle Godwin.

He must have been released fairly quickly, for he was arrested again in November along with John Dabney after a search of their restaurant turned up evidence of liquor sales. Such actions did little to stop the flow. "Whiskey and brandy are brought into town in large quantities every day," the *Examiner* complained in November, "and sold at fifty cents a drink." As 1863 opened, under pressure from local attorneys, the War Department ended courts-martial for violators of the liquor ban and Richmond was once again a wide-open town.

Away from towns and cities, soldiers came up with any number of creative ways to get their hands on booze. Confederate pickets traded tobacco for Northern whiskey. Some soldiers were sent stocks of liquor by family members, and they not only drank it themselves but also sold it by the bottle and by the drink. A common sight at camps was a peddler lingering with a canteen full of whiskey and a thimble as a jigger, selling shots for as much as two dollars a pop. Members of one Mississippi company hollowed out a watermelon and filled it with a half gallon of bootleg liquor, hid it on the floor of their tent, and tapped it with a long straw, allowing them to lay flat on the ground and suck a dose or two at a time.

Theft of medical alcohol was a constant problem, especially considering how short the supply was. Soldiers would tap casks of whiskey en route to field hospitals, refilling them with water. On holidays, the commissary would often issue rations of whiskey to the troops, but usually in such small quantities and of such poor quality that it provoked as much complaining as celebration. One soldier wrote home to his sister that the whiskey his company was served on Christmas was "such villainous stuff that only the old soakers could stomach it." But most soldiers made do with it as best they could. On Christmas Day at Bowling Green, Kentucky, in 1861, one sergeant reported that some of his men "got drunk and cut up generally and was put under guard." Following multiple rounds of eggnog on Christmas in Murfreesboro, Tennessee, "Captains, Lieutenants, and privates was drunk and very troublesome."

Drinking on the Home Front

At first, there was plenty of drinking on the home front too. Despite government bans, distillers in the mountainous regions kept right on making brandy and whiskey for the simple reason that it was the most profitable thing they could produce. They sold it to their neighbors and to soldiers stationed in the area, ensuring a thriving black market for liquor. Plenty of whiskey was advertised for sale in Macon and Augusta newspapers throughout 1862, though the prices were sky-high. In February 1863, the *Macon Telegraph* reported that a commission merchant had sold eleven barrels of whiskey for $8,000, or more than $700 each.

The bloody Battle of Gettysburg, the turning point of the war, was fought in July 1863, and by this point the liquor supply in most Southern towns was tapped out. In August, the *Columbus Daily Enquirer* reported that rogues were concocting counterfeit whiskey out of unaged apple brandy, diluting it with water and vitriol (that is, copper sulfate), and even soaking the raw flesh of wild game in it for weeks to impart a softer, richer taste. By the end of 1863, whiskey was selling for thirty-five dollars a gallon. "Genuine Catawba Brandy" was advertised in many Southern newspapers through the end of 1862, but by 1863 it could be found only in New Orleans, which had fallen to the Union in April 1862.

Not all Southerners were cut off from the good stuff, though. In the summer of 1863, as drinkers in inland areas were choking down adulterated spirits or paying extortionate rates for rare decent whiskey, newspapers in Charleston, South Carolina, brimmed with advertisements for brandy, rye, bourbon, and any number of other fine liquors. How was that possible? Early in the war, it turns out, the Union blockade was pretty ineffectual, allowing Confederate runners to bring supplies into thousands of miles of coastline dotted with bays, inlets, and rivers. Southern cotton still flowed to the mills of England and France, and in return came rifles, gunpowder, and military supplies. They were made in England and shipped to the Caribbean, transferred to light, fast blockade-runners, many of which had been built in English shipyards and designed specifically to outrun Union warships. From Nassau or Bermuda, they sailed fast to Wilmington, Charleston, or Savannah, their owners carrying a letter of marque from the Confederate government, then loaded up with cotton and tobacco for the outbound trip.

The manifests for blockade-runners leaving Bermudan ports included exactly the types of military supplies one would expect to see—five hundred bags of saltpeter, five hundred barrels of gunpowder, fifty bales of cartridge paper, telegraph wire, hoop iron, and preserved beef. And then there were other necessities like the following, which left the port of Saint George's, Bermuda, on September 26, 1862: "48 hogsheads brandy, 21½ casks brandy, 63 cases brandy, 10 casks wine, 673 cases wine, 6¼ quarts whiskey,

14 hogsheads spirits." On February 6, 1864, Jefferson Davis signed a law prohibiting the importation of a long list of luxuries that included distilled spirits, beer, and wine, but shipmasters knew that a few bottles of fine Champagne had a salubrious effect on port officials, making them suddenly occupied elsewhere while dockworkers brought in a few dozen barrels and crates of fine clarets, Cognacs, and Champagnes. Those illicit imports didn't come cheap. During the first year of the war, brandy sold for thirty-six dollars a case (or three dollars a bottle). By the opening of 1864, it was selling for $175.

Planters' Madeira: Gone with the Wind

As General William T. Sherman began his deadly march through the South in 1864, it was clear that the Confederates were on the ropes. Wealthy white Southerners like Robert F. W. Allston feared that their prized Madeira collections would be looted by soldiers and freed slaves. Allston was already sixty years old when the Civil War began, and his offer to serve in the field was refused, so he remained behind in Georgetown, South Carolina, managing his plantations and assisting with his sons' and nephews' properties. He believed that Chicora Wood, being just twenty miles from the mouth of Winyah Bay, was exposed to invaders from federal gunboats, so he had his slaves ship most of his old Madeira to Loch Adele, another of his plantations just over the North Carolina line. There, the bottles were packed into hogsheads and rolled into the lake.

Allston didn't live to see the Yankees arrive, for he died of pneumonia on April 7, 1864. The following month, General Sherman's forces left Chattanooga and began their approach to Atlanta, which fell in September. Sherman reached the sea at Savannah just before Christmas 1864 and the following March turned his eyes toward the Carolinas. At Chicora Wood, Allston's widow, Adele, and her family set about hiding every treasure they had. Once the silver was secured in the nearby woods, they turned their minds to the cache of old Madeira that remained in the storeroom. They took an old piano box, which had been doing service as a grain bin, and packed the bottles in it with hay. Nelson, a trusted slave, and Allston's sixteen-year-old son, Charlie, then dug a hole in the middle of the road leading to the plantation, carefully collecting the dirt on bedsheets so no telltale yellow clay from the layer beneath the topsoil would be left on the surface after they finished. They lowered the box into the hole with ropes and refilled the hole, removing the excess dirt and leveling the surface with rakes and then wagon wheels so there was not a trace of anything unusual. They left just two dozen bottles of wine in the storeroom to tide over the family while they waited.

Chicora Wood, home of the Allston Family.

The news for the Confederacy grew worse with each passing day. One evening at dusk two horseman galloped up to the house, members of the Charleston Light Dragoons, who were serving as Confederate scouts. General Wade Hampton, they informed the Allstons, was removing all his troops from the state. They implored Mrs. Allston that, if she had any wine or whiskey left, "do not let a drop of it be found in the house." Mrs. Allston promised she wouldn't. She fed the two soldiers a good supper and let them have two hours of sleep, then in the middle of the night they mounted their horses and galloped away. As the two dragoons disappeared into the darkness, the women could hear shots being fired on the public road a quarter of a mile away. "They were gone," Elizabeth Pringle, Mrs. Allston's daughter, later recalled. "Our last friends and protectors."

The next morning they learned that the shots they had heard were not from Union soldiers but rather from local African-Americans, who were shooting the fattest of the Allstons' hogs. Mrs. Allston promptly had the last two demijohns of rye whiskey poured into a nearby stream. Elizabeth Pringle took the remaining bottles of wine up to the attic, where she lifted the floorboards, which were not nailed down, and hid the bottles beneath them, each resting on the ceiling laths below. Nelson, one of their last two slaves remaining, insisted on packing a bag of provisions and leaving, claiming, "I know too much" and that he didn't know what he might say if a Yankee put a pistol to his head. The next day, Daddy Aleck, the last slave—and the last male adult on the plantation—also left, explaining he was taking the horses into the swamp so he could save them from the Yankees.

Again the women waited, dining sumptuously on the fine smoked turkeys and hams that they had saved to welcome the men of the family home from the war, a party they now knew was never going to occur. When Yankee soldiers finally appeared at the door, they searched the house top to bottom for wine and whiskey. They tramped across the attic, opening every box and trunk but never thinking to lift the rattling boards beneath their feet. Out in the backyard, several soldiers ran ramrods into the ground, looking for anything that might be buried, but they neglected to try the front drive and thus missed the big piano box. Finally, in sober frustration, the soldiers departed. After four days, the noises out on the highway faded away, and the Allstons knew that Sherman's army had passed.

Soldiers searching for buried valuables.

Up at Loch Adele, Union soldiers under General Kilpatrick were luckier in their search. They cut the dam and drained the lake, uncovering the casks of Madeira that had been hidden beneath the surface. They invested some of the stash in getting stinking drunk then sent the rest off in wagons. A few weeks later, Allston and Pringle took the oath of loyalty to the Union. The house at Chicora Wood had been stripped of its furniture and valuables, including the mahogany trim and staircase banisters. Over time, with the help of occupying federal troops, the family recovered enough of their furniture to furnish the house and, we can assume (though Pringle's memoir is silent on this point), retrieved the piano box full of wine that was buried under the drive.

In the wake of the war, Adele Allston assumed control of her late husband's affairs. Heavy debts had been incurred against the Allston estate, and Adele struggled unsuccessfully to save the family lands. She leased out some of the plantations while trying to direct her son Benjamin to manage the others, and she herself ran a school for girls from her Charleston home, but it was to no avail. The whole of her husband's estate was sold at auction in 1869, with the exception of Chicora Wood and a tract of timberland. Adele Allston made her home at Chicora Wood, planted a few acres of rice, and remained there until her death in 1886.

The Allstons were just one of many families whose wealth disappeared along with their Madeira collections. Charles Manigault had secured 1,200 bottles at his Marshlands plantation outside of Charleston. After the Union army occupied the city in February 1865, Manigault and his family were stunned when, as he put it, "every one of our house & yard Negroes immediately left us." Manigault managed to obtain permission to drive through the Union fortifications out to Marshlands, where he discovered that "our own and neighbouring Negroes," along with soldiers from both sides of the line, had already made off with tables, bedsteads, and most of the bottles of his finest wine. Of the original store of 1,200 bottles, only 400 remained. For the next decade, they were used sparingly for toasts at the end of meals and parties.

The war had all but destroyed the source of wealth that had allowed Southern elites to amass huge collections of prized Madeira wine. Like the plantation lands on which it was once enjoyed, much of that wine moved into the hands of a new set of wealthy elites, and their money came not from large-scale agriculture but from new industrial ventures like factories, railroads, and shipping. In Charleston, Charles Manigault and his son,

Gabriel, eked out a small income selling consignments of their prized Madeira to Northern wine merchants. By the time Charles died in 1874, only 120 bottles remained. Gabriel sold them for five dollars per bottle, and they ended up being served as "the Manigault Madeira" at Delmonico's restaurant in New York City.

A bottle of old Madeira remained the beverage of choice for special occasions within Charleston's old money families, but case by case and bottle by bottle their cellars were being depleted. And there was no more fine Madeira on its way to replace the dusty old bottles. In the 1870s, some Madeiran winemakers replanted their vineyards with American grape varieties that were resistant to the mold and pests that once ravaged them, and the island slowly rebuilt its wine industry. Throughout the twentieth century, though, its products languished, suffering under a reputation as cheap cooking wine. If the general public—or even the many lovers of fine wine, for that matter—had even heard of Madeira at all, they knew it primarily as an ingredient in sauce madère.

The Fate of the Julep Makers

Before we end, we need to return to those two famous Richmond mixologists, John Dabney and Jim Cook, for their experiences during the closing days of the war say much about the contradictory nature of their positions and the process of myth making that unfolded over the decades that followed.

In January 1864, Jim Cook was temporarily ensconced at a saloon called Oak Hall. General John Hunt Morgan, who had escaped from a Union prison camp just a few months before, was in Richmond for a visit, and Cook sent him a letter along with "a small token" that consisted of "dishes of viands, rare as exotics in a desert, and liquors of unsurpassed brands." The letter, which was written in third person, expressed Cook's admiration for the general and his recent exploits. "As a slave," it notes, "he bids General Morgan speed in his good and righteous work." Such sentiments were perfectly in line with Cook's other methods, like sending complimentary turtle soup and juleps to white newspaper editors, for he knew which side his bread was buttered on.

But what did he really think? His subsequent actions may speak louder than notes to Confederate generals. In September 1864, just a few weeks after Atlanta fell to General Sherman, the Richmond newspapers reported that Jim Cook, julep maker to the Prince of Wales, "has deserted old Virginia and gone over to the Yankees." He was reportedly making a living by delivering speeches on street corners in Washington, DC, telling of life in the South. On September 29, Union forces, including African-American soldiers in the Ninth United States Colored Troops, made a drive north from the James River in a bid to take Richmond. They were repulsed by the Confederates at Fort Gilmer and several other strongholds along New Market Road. A few days later, the *Richmond Examiner* reported, "persons who knew this once-celebrated Richmond barkeeper, who went over to the enemy some several months since, report that they saw his dead body on the field after the assault on Fort Gilmour." Cook was reportedly stripped naked but had been recognized by his features.

The reports of Cook's death turned out to be false. Union troops entered Richmond in April 1865, and by summer, Jim Cook was back in the city mixing juleps. In September, he hosted one of his famous free turtle soup lunches, this time at the Franklin House Hotel, where he presided over the bar. Cook's brother, Fields, emerged as one of the leaders of Richmond's African-American community as they struggled to secure the civil rights and judicial protections promised by Emancipation. Fields Cook had gained his own freedom by 1850, and he was in the hospitality trade himself before and during the Civil War, including managing the bar and restaurant at the Ballard House in 1865. After the war ended, he became a Baptist minister and led protests against abuses to freed people at the hands of the municipal police force and federal troops. A tireless Republican activist and committed advocate of racial equality, Fields Cook represented Richmond in Virginia's first convention of African-Americans, and he was one of five African-American men appointed to the grand jury that indicted Jefferson Davis for treason.

Fields Cook's feelings toward his work as a restaurateur and caterer can be glimpsed in an incident from 1873. The *Richmond News* and the *Alexandria Gazette* had run the same short piece retelling how Jim Cook had served juleps to the Prince of Wales, and it noted that his brother Fields had been "lead waiter" at Ballard's Exchange Hotel. Fields Cook dashed off a curt note to both papers declaring, "I never served a day in my life under John P. Ballard, and the only transaction of any prominence between him and myself was that I at one time leased a portion of the Ballard House, for which he paid me $2,000 to relinquish my claim."

Fields Cook moved to Alexandria in 1870, and he remained politically active in that city until his death in 1897. What happened to his brother, Jim, is a little less certain. Just a few weeks after announcing his free turtle lunch at the Franklin House in 1865, Jim Cook was arrested and charged with stealing money from the hotel's proprietor. He was released after the proprietor's son and other witnesses gave him good character references, and he seems to have left town soon after. It's possible that he ended up in Burkeville, Virginia. In 1867, a *New York Times* correspondent filed a dispatch on traveling south by rail, and he mentioned that in tiny Burkeville, a "littery dumping place," the restaurant at the depot was run by "a gentleman of color, who rejoices in the name of Jim Cook" and offered a well-patronized bar. Cook had a placard posted behind a bar advertising: "The celebrated new drink by JIM COOK - Squint you foolishness." When asked by the reporter the origin of the unusual name, Cook replied cryptically that he "wanted to get it right." The scribbler passed on sampling the concoction, since he had already paid seventy-five cents for a sandwich and cup of coffee and didn't feel up to further expenditures. Not much else is known, except that by 1873 Jim Cook had died.

John Dabney's story ended quite differently, and his fame as a julep maker continued for many decades after the Civil War. In September 1865, Dabney opened his own restaurant and saloon in Richmond, which he called Dabney's House. In the years that followed, he and his wife secured credit and bought and sold real estate, and they moved the restaurant to several different locations during the 1870s. All along, he continued spending the summers working the resorts in western Virginia.

As previously noted, Dabney was in the process of purchasing his own freedom when the war began, and he continued to make payments using Confederate dollars, though that currency was rapidly devaluing. Finally, his owner, Cara DeJarnette, asked that he suspend payments until the war ended or money became more reliable. Following the war, DeJarnette, like many former slaveholding families, was left destitute, and when Dabney heard of her plight, he reportedly went to visit her and gave her the balance of the payments even though he had no legal obligation to do so.

Dabney's repayment of that debt became a much-repeated story, and each teller drew a different lesson from the tale. An 1866 version in the *Richmond Enquirer* casts the incident as reflecting the individual character of John Dabney, who, when told by friends that he had no need to pay off the balance, replied, "I owe [her] the money honestly, and I intend to pay it." Such actions, the paper concluded, "evinces regard for honor which would ennoble any man, and John will stand (and deservedly) higher than any in the estimation of any Richmond gentleman." In 1868, the *Weekly Freedman's Press*, an African-American newspaper, used the story as a lesson in equality. "It is only another proof," the editors wrote, "that a man of honor will act honorably, whether his skin is bleached or tanned."

By the time the 1890s had rolled around, the moonlight-and-magnolia myth-making machine was in full gear. John Dabney was still making a living as a caterer and bartender, spending his summers working at the Old Sweet Springs resort in western Virginia. In 1894, the *Charleston News and Courier* reported that Northern visitors to the springs "are talking still of the old uncle down there, who is so entirely a picturesque figure of the past, a type of the negro in ante-bellum days." Dabney was still wowing guests with his colossal fruit-laden juleps, and he seems to have added to his repertoire a "happy faculty for reminiscences of 'befo' de wah.'" which made him the most popular person at the resort. The article interpreted Dabney's debt payments to be "as fine an instance of the honor and affection of the higher slave as adorns history's pages anywhere. . . . It was his kind who during the war stayed at home and faithfully cared for and protected women and children when the men were fighting at the front."

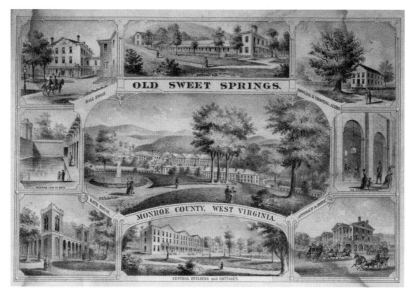

Old Sweet Springs, where John Dabney practiced his craft after the Civil War.

Southern Spirits

Unlike Fields Cook, John Dabney did not respond to such newspaper accounts with his own interpretation of the story. But the writings of his son, Wendell P. Dabney, offer glimpses of what the man might really have thought. Wendell attended Oberlin College and, after working as a musician and a teacher, moved to Cincinnati, where he held various positions in city government and founded *The Union*, an influential African-American newspaper and publishing company that he used as a platform to speak out against injustice and crusade against segregation and discrimination. He later wrote that his father instilled in him a respect for religion as a means of overcoming racial injustice as well as the idea that Republicans (the more progressive party at the time) helped blacks and Democrats did not. John Dabney had earned a reputation for being courteous and polite to his customers. In fact, before the war, a group of Dabney's customers had presented him with two silver goblets engraved with the words "Presented to John Dabney by the citizens of Richmond" to express "their appreciation of his courteous behavior and uniform politeness." At the same time, his son recalled that John Dabney was quite hot-tempered, and he could sometimes even be violent. He remembered his father telling him, "White folks are awfully wicked." He also cautioned: "If you do everything white folks want you to do, you will go either to the penitentiary or the gallows."

Above all, the great julep maker advised his son, "Never let a white man know how much you really do know about anything except hard work."

By the Light of the Moon: The Rise of Illegal Whiskey Distilling During the Reconstruction Era

For this chapter, you need to get your hands on a little moonshine, which isn't nearly as hard as it used to be. In just the past few years, white whiskey—raw spirits distilled from corn, the unaged distillate that several years in charred new oak barrels transforms into bourbon—has started popping up everywhere. There's a practical reason for that. Following the path blazed by craft breweries, a new wave of entrepreneurs is now opening craft distilleries. These are capital-intensive operations, and bourbon and rye whiskey require years of barrel aging before they are ready for market. White whiskey is an expedient way for fledgling distillers to get some product out and bring in a little revenue while waiting for the good stuff to age. If you want to sample a little moonshine, you no longer have to know a guy whose cousin knows a guy.

For the most authentic experience, pour the whiskey from the bottle into a stoneware jug or a tin cup. No ice, no mixers. Just tip it back and take a good slug. If beneath the alcohol burn, you find the flavor a bit cloyingly sweet, that's the corn talking. That stubborn corn flavor makes it tough to come up with a passable moonshine cocktail, especially if you try to use it like rye or bourbon or any other aged spirit. Instead, try approaching it like you would that other hot-as-fire white liquor that people drink when they want to tie one on: tequila. Their raw bites are different in flavor, but they're raw bites nonetheless, and the same ingredients that complement and transform the natural flavors of tequila—like lime juice and orange liqueur—work pretty well with white whiskey too.

Moonshine Margarita

SERVES 1

1½ ounces white whiskey

1 ounce Cointreau

1 ounce freshly squeezed
lime juice

1 lime slice

Shake the whiskey, Cointreau, and lime juice in a cocktail shaker filled with ice until well mixed, about 10 seconds. Pour into a rocks glass filled with ice. Garnish with a slice of lime.

Dodging the Tax Man

Before the Civil War, there was no such thing as illegal whiskey. Most of the whiskey consumed in the South was made by small producers using pot stills, wooden mash tubs, and other rudimentary equipment, and much of it was made by farmers or millers who sold it to their neighbors as an informal side business. They didn't need a license or a permit and didn't need to worry about taxes.

The Civil War changed all that. In 1862, the United States Congress, in need of revenue to service the war debts they were racking up, began taxing all domestically distilled spirits at twenty cents per gallon and established the Bureau of Internal Revenue to collect them. As war debts continued to mount, the whiskey excise was raised in several big leaps, going first to sixty cents, then a dollar and half, and finally hitting two dollars per gallon at the beginning of 1865. At that rate, the excise amounted to an astonishing ten times the cost of manufacturing whiskey, which before the Civil War had sold for as little as twenty-five cents per gallon. Those who wanted to stay on the right side of the law had to get big fast or be squeezed out of the market. Not surprisingly, a lot of small producers decided the best course was to just dodge the tax man, continuing on in the business as small-scale—and now illegal—producers.

Southern distillers didn't have to worry about the new federal excise taxes as long as their states were still in rebellion. In 1867, though, the first Reconstruction Act divided the South into military districts, and as federal commanders restored political order, they put a renewed emphasis on tax collection. State liquor laws had tended to rely on local sheriffs for enforcement, but the Bureau of Internal Revenue dispatched its own team of marshals and district attorneys, many of whom were former Union soldiers. These interlopers immediately rubbed many Southerners the wrong way. In May 1867, Major General Daniel E. Sickles, commander of the Second Military District in North Carolina, reported that Internal Revenue officers were "frequently treated with disrespect and sometimes menaced with violence" and that local juries routinely failed to convict violators of the liquor law.

As they had almost a century earlier during the Whiskey Rebellion, Southern highlanders proved fiercely resistant to taxes on their whiskey. Conservative politicians and newspaper editors, intent on returning control of the region to white Southerners, did everything they could to fan the flames. Editorials decried the oppressive liquor taxation, which was keeping poor citizens from distilling their own liquor and was creating a monopoly for wealthy Yankee capitalists. Corruption, they insisted, was rife in the internal revenue system, and there was much excoriation of "whiskey rings" as the fruits of corrupt radicalism and carpetbaggers. Such talk touched a particular nerve in the mountainous whiskey-making districts of the Carolinas, Georgia, and Tennessee, and Southern politicians exploited it for all it was worth, using it to drive a wedge between the mountaineers, who had tended to be more pro-Union in their sympathies before the war, and the now-dominant Republican Party.

The North Georgia Moonshine War

It was only a matter of time before violence broke out. On March 12, 1868, a party of men fired on the camp of E. R. Hampton and six federal soldiers, who earlier that day had confiscated a still and twenty-five gallons of brandy in Macon County, North Carolina. In 1871, a distiller named Thompson in McDowell County, North Carolina, took a shot at revenue agent W. H. Deaver, but his rifle misfired. Deaver shot back and killed Thompson. A year later, agent C. C. Vest was killed in a shootout in Union County, Georgia, and in 1874 a distiller named William R. Dills fired upon federal agent N. H. Burns in Swain County, North Carolina, killing him instantly. A mountain jury acquitted Dills, a verdict that shocked Judge Robert Dick, who felt it was "a clear case of murder." Such leniency had become common in local courts, so many district attorneys started moving illegal whiskey cases to federal courts, which increased their odds of conviction but only strengthened residents' belief that they were being persecuted by a callous federal government.

In these early days of the whiskey wars, the United States Army was tasked with supporting the enforcement of tax law—a duty they wanted no part of but reluctantly executed. Directed by a revenue agent with tips on illicit distilleries, patrols left their camps and rode into the countryside on horseback under the cover of darkness. They were usually guided by a local civilian incentivized by cash rewards of up to $300. They dismounted a safe distance from the suspected still and moved in quickly to try to catch the distillers at work. The liquor was poured out, and the stills were either broken up at the site or carted away to be sold as scrap.

In 1876, gubernatorial candidates Zebulon Vance of North Carolina and Wade Hampton of South Carolina made opposition to liquor law enforcement a central plank in their campaign platforms along with unseating Republican governors and "redeeming" conservative white control of the statehouses. Congressional candidates played up the tax issue, too, portraying the laws as devices of oppression by the Northern conquerors and revenue collectors as carpetbaggers and thieves. The federal government, though, was determined to collect its much-needed revenue. The Grant administration ordered an increase in the use of US Army troops for supporting and protecting revenue officers, which put the soldiers in the middle of increasingly hostile confrontations.

In January 1876, Deputy US Marshal Charles Blacker and four soldiers went out in search of the still belonging to John Emory in Gilmer County in the north Georgia mountains. They discovered the stillhouse and four men inside, whom they placed under arrest. What happened next depends upon whom you believe. According to the official army report, John Emory and another man approached the still and were challenged by Private William O'Grady. Emory drew a pistol and fired, and O'Grady fired back, killing Emory instantly. Emory's friends had a different version of the story: that Emory had merely come to see what was going on, and O'Grady shot him down in cold blood.

The justice of the peace for Gilmer County promptly issued an arrest warrant for the soldiers, who were detained in Atlanta and charged with murder. They were to be tried in the local county court, but before the trial began, President Grant issued a writ of habeas corpus and transferred the case to the US Federal Circuit Court in Atlanta. The soldiers were acquitted, and the verdict provoked howls of outrage among the residents of Gilmer County.

During the year that followed, revenue agents supported by troops from Fort McPherson in Atlanta conducted regular raids throughout north Georgia, increasing the resentment of local residents. Things boiled over in

February 1877. Deputy Marshal Blacker, the same revenue man involved in the John Emory killing, and a party of troops commanded by Lieutenant Augustine McIntyre of the Second US Infantry were led by two guides into a so-called dark district on the border of Gilmer and Fannin Counties. The mission was to arrest Ayers Jones, an infamous blockader who lived on Frog Mountain. (Blockader was what illegal distillers in Georgia and the Carolinas tended to call themselves, aligning themselves with the Civil War–era blockade-runners.)

The party proceeded to Jones's house, where they found only women and children inside. Blacker, McIntyre, and another soldier stayed in the house while the rest of the troops went to look for Jones and his still. Suddenly, Jones and an armed band of mountaineers burst into the house and opened fire. The federal men fled through the rear door, returning fire as they went. All escaped but Lieutenant McIntyre, who was mortally wounded. Blacker and his men fled into the woods, and when they returned around daybreak to retrieve McIntyre's body they were chased away by a hail of bullets fired by armed men hidden behind rocks near the house. Later that day, Lieutenant James Ulio and a party of twenty or more soldiers were sent in. They, too, were shot at by the mountaineers, but they returned fire and killed three of their assailants, then recovered McIntyre's corpse and carried it away on horseback.

In the wake of the shooting, the citizens of Gilmer and Fannin Counties staged a series of mass meetings to vent their outrage. Deputy marshals were accused of going through the upper counties of Georgia with blank warrants, lying, spying, and even murdering. Ayers Jones and several men were arrested, but a local jury quickly acquitted them, agreeing that Lieutenant McIntyre had invaded a private home and insulted women and children under their own roof. The governor of Georgia appointed a commission to investigate McIntyre's killing, and their report concluded that all the troubles that occurred had been caused not by resistance to the laws but rather "by the character of the officials employed to execute them, and the manner in which they had discharged that duty." The commission defended Ayers Jones's killing of Lieutenant McIntyre as "the act of a maddened man, who approached his home, expecting to find every thing quiet, but found it occupied by strangers to him, and hearing his wife and children being cursed and abused, resorted to the only means in his power to protect them."

How the Blockaders Operated

A decade of avoiding federal taxation had transformed what was once a small-scale industry operating openly on rural farms into a covert illegal enterprise. The mountains of the Carolinas, Tennessee, Virginia, West Virginia, and Kentucky formed the country's primary blockading region, and distillers moved their operations into more and more remote regions. Some even constructed them on cliffs above a river or large creek, pumping water up from the stream below. In Kentucky, many distilleries were hidden away in subterranean caverns.

A typical wildcat rig consisted of a small copper still, a couple of worms, and one or two barrels in which the mash was fermented. A stillhouse might be a solid log cabin with a single door and few if any windows, or it could be a simple lean-to made out of logs and brush. It needed to be near a running stream of water, which would be conveyed by wooden troughs to the still. Corn whiskey is the liquor most closely associated with bootleg distillers, but they made plenty of brandy from apples and peaches too. The meal or fruit for the mash was carried in under the cover of night, and it was allowed to ferment in tubs or open barrels for four to six days. The spirits were usually passed through the stills twice, but most the primitive rigs were unable to strip out all the congeners and impurities. The high wines might be poured through everything from a charcoal filter to a blanket or felt hat to filter it, but aging was unheard of. Some bootleggers might color their product with cherry juice or burned sugar to give it the brown color of aged whiskey, but appearance was about all they could achieve. The odor and raw harsh bite of the liquor couldn't be masked.

The finished whiskey or brandy was carried away and hidden in a cave or hollow log. Often, it was put in kegs and lowered down the sides of the mountain on sleds, for the stills were generally located far from any road. During this period, illicit whiskey was pretty much a local commodity, sold and consumed in the same area where it was distilled. Regular customers would know to go to a certain tree, place an empty jug or bottle at the base along with their payment, and make a predetermined signal, such as to hallo three times. The thirsty man would leave for a few minutes and then return to the tree to find his payment gone and his vessel filled. In an economy where cash was scarce, that payment often took the form of barter, and many distillers would swap a gallon of whiskey for three bushels of cornmeal.

The stills up in the hills supplied nearby towns too. The whiskey was put in five- or ten-gallon kegs, and a keg was placed in each end of a long bag and thrown across the back of a horse or mule for the trip into town. Kegs and barrels were also carted in by wagon, hidden beneath a load of corn stalks or quilts and blankets. They were often sold directly from the wagons to consumers and to country storekeepers, who would in turn sell the whiskey in smaller quantities to their customers.

"Illicit distillation of liquors—Southern mode of making whisky," 1867.

As outlaw distillers moved their operations deeper into the remote mountains, they also created increasingly elaborate systems to evade arrest. During a run, blockaders staked pickets around the approaches to the area where their stills were hidden. If intruders were spotted, the pickets would blow horns or fire guns to warn those working the stills. They kept watchdogs that would bark loudly at the approach of strangers. Revenue officers started avoiding roads, clambering over rugged bluffs and ridges to try to reach stills undetected. They paid local tipsters to guide them to the stills, and they examined rivulets of water for traces of still slop, sniffed the air for the scent of beer (the fermented mash that fed the stills), and looked for the glimmer of fires at night. Some agents posed as clock peddlers or roaming tinkers in order to scout out an area and track down stills. Others found hunting and fishing to be effective decoys, roaming the hillsides with rods and rifles.

"It was a desolate, lonely business," recalled George Atkinson, a revenue man who recorded his experiences in an 1881 book. "Away up there in the Cumberland mountains, where the sun rarely ever shone, where the water poured over the cliffs, and the nights were rendered hideous by the sepulchral voices of the 'hoot owls.'" When revenuers did manage to find a still, they chopped it to pieces with axes. When they found the blockaders at work, they arrested them and took them into town for trial. And as soon as they were released from jail, the distillers rebuilt their rigs and went right back to work.

Lewis Redmond, King of the Outlaws

On March 1, 1876, Alfred Duckworth, a US Deputy Marshal, obtained a warrant for the arrest of twenty-one year-old Lewis Richard Redmond, a young blockader from Transylvania County in mountainous western North Carolina. The two men had been friends during boyhood, so Duckworth easily recognized Redmond when he came across Redmond and a friend in a wagon on the road near the East Fork community. Duckworth drew his pistol and announced that he was placing Redmond under arrest. Redmond, who was unarmed, said he would go peacefully, but as soon as Duckworth lowered his gun, Redmond grabbed a derringer from his companion and shot Duckworth point-blank in the throat. Duckworth died soon after, and Redmond fled into Pickens County in western South Carolina. Thus began the saga of Lewis Richard Redmond, the undisputed King of the Outlaws. During the era of the moonshine wars, there was no figure more notorious nor more romanticized. He became the very embodiment of the complex passions, motives, and myths that came to surround illegal liquor in the nineteenth century.

Redmond had family ties in Pickens County and a network of friends to draw upon. He surrounded himself with a gang of "desperate men" and turned himself into more of an illicit whiskey dealer than an actual distiller, buying the products of local distillers and selling it in adjoining counties. On January 11, 1877, after ten months on the lam, Redmond was apprehended by three deputy revenue collectors named Barton, Gray, and Hendrix. As they were transporting him to the jailhouse, Redmond escaped, took a position of ambush on the side of the road, and fired into the party as they pursued him, wounding Barton and Hendrix. Redmond fled the scene, and nine days later he gathered a band of twenty ruffians and surrounded Barton's house near the town of Easley. The outlaw forced Barton's wife to accompany him into town and cash a check for $105. Redmond took the cash, stole Barton's best horse, and made his escape.

This episode brought Lewis Redmond to the attention of the man who would become his fiercest adversary, Green Berry Raum. An Illinois-born lawyer, Raum was the campaign manager for Senator Stephen A. Douglas and served as an officer in the Union army during the Civil War, rising to the rank of brigadier general. After the war, he became the president of the Cairo and Vincennes Railroad and was elected to Congress for one term in 1866. Ten years later, President Grant appointed him Commissioner of Internal Revenue.

It was the height of the whiskey wars, and Raum was determined to turn the tide in favor of the federal government. It was bad enough that Lewis Redmond was a fugitive from justice for murdering a US Marshal. Now he had shot and wounded two of Raum's own revenue collectors. Raum deployed more federal agents to western South Carolina to search for Redmond, and this force conducted raids throughout the spring of 1877. They captured several of the outlaw's associates, but Redmond himself eluded them. Many of the residents of Pickens County helped shield Redmond, since they viewed him as an unreconstructed Confederate standing up to an unjust federal government. This image was burnished by the editors of the *Pickens Sentinel* and the *Charleston News and Courier*, who published dramatic accounts of the Barton incident that were highly sympathetic to Redmond.

By 1878, the moonshine wars had shifted from north Georgia to the Upstate of South Carolina. Raum doubled down on his efforts to suppress illegal distillers, and he shifted his bureau's tactics too. In the past, agents had used a guerrilla warfare–like approach to combating moonshiners, ordering raids once a year in a particular area and attempting to surprise moonshiners at work so that they could destroy their stills. This had proven to be quite ineffective, as illicit distillers went right back home after the revenuers left, rebuilt their stills, and fired them back up. Under Raum's leadership, the revenuers adopted more of a conventional warfare approach. They organized a movement to cover a whole territory and hold the ground after it had been taken. Revenue agents who destroyed illicit distilleries often found themselves arrested by the local sheriff and tried in county courts on trespassing charges, so Raum arranged to have all such indictments transferred to federal courts to ensure fair trials. In many cases, no one representing the state would even appear at the federal trial and the charges were dismissed.

These renewed raids gained a lot of attention in national newspapers, and readers from across the South became fascinated with the new breed of Southern rebels known as moonshiners, since they practiced their illegal arts by the light of the moon. Sensational pieces in Northern magazines like *Harper's Weekly* and *Appleton's Journal* portrayed Appalachia as a beautiful, unconquered region and the mountaineers who lived there as naturally wild, stubborn individualists living far from civilization and bitterly resistant to change. Illegal liquor distilling was depicted as part and parcel of their way of life, a peculiarity of the mountain South. A new American myth of the lawless but romantic mountaineer was being crafted.

No one embodied those myths more than Lewis Redmond, who was still on the loose in Upstate South Carolina. After the Barton incident, Redmond kept a low profile for over a year. Then, on March 9, 1878, a special deputy arrested three illegal distillers and tossed them in the Pickens County jail. In broad daylight, Lewis Redmond and an armed band of thirty men on horseback surrounded the courthouse and forced the sheriff to surrender the keys so they could free their compatriots. Three months later, four revenue men seeking Redmond went to the house of Amos Ladd, the friend who had been accompanying Redmond when he shot Alfred Duckworth and first became a fugitive. Ladd drew his rifle and aimed it at one of the officers, and the officers opened fire, killing Ladd. The officers promptly surrendered themselves to the authorities in Greenville, and the local press declared it a case of cold-blooded murder on the officers' part. The *Pickens Sentinel* branded it "one of the most fiendish, cold blooded murders ever committed in this County." The Greenville *Enterprise and Mountaineer* decried the "reign of terror" of the revenuers and declared the killing "unjustifiable on any ground whatever." The four federal agents were indicted on charges of first-degree murder, jailed, and refused bail.

Up to this point, Redmond's name was known only in the Upstate of South Carolina, but the Ladd incident thrust him onto the national stage as a folk hero. He was interviewed in his mountain retreat by C. McKinley of the *Charleston News and Courier*, who filed a glowingly sympathetic portrait. He described Redmond as "one of the handsomest men I ever saw" and "a man of striking beauty, not more than twenty-three years of age, of slender build, and mild manners." Like a dime novel hero, Redmond was not only loyally supporting his three sisters, one of whom was crippled, but he sprang up in out-of-the-way places to rescue women from runaway horses and save children from mountain torrents, all while dashingly dressed in a green hunting suit.

McKinley allowed the fugitive to tell his own story of how he became an outlaw. It all started, Redmond said, when his father was seventy-eight years old and his mother was confined to bed by palsy. One Sunday morning without warning, revenue officers burst into the Redmond home looking for Lewis, who was off at a spring. The officers seized Redmond's father and took him to a nearby church, where they interrupted the service and captured several other men. Redmond's mother, badly frightened by the experience, died just a few days after. His father was taken to Asheville, where, made ill by the journey and exposure, he died a few weeks later. As for the Alfred Duckworth killing, Redmond maintained it was self-defense. He had known Duckworth since they were children, Redmond told the admiring reporter, and Duckworth had it in for him. Newly appointed as a deputy marshal, he was determined to take Redmond "warrant or no warrant, or would kill [him] in the attempt." Duckworth took a warrant for a different man and substituted Redmond's name when he read it aloud. When Duckworth drew his pistols on him, Redmond grabbed the derringer from his companion and shot Duckworth first.

Federal officials, of course, had a slightly different version of these events. Their accounts, which were published widely in Northern newspapers, described Redmond as a desperate criminal. The *New York Herald* wrote of him, "He is handsome, carries a silver-mounted rifle, and a brace of navy revolvers—just the figure for a Bowery drama or blood-curdling novel." It also noted that it was widely said that Redmond was "a vulgar thief and general ruffian." Far from a moonshine-running Robin Hood, he and his band would break into the homes of "colored men" and rob them of their few valuables. Northern newspapers of a Republican bent decried the *News and Courier*'s interview as romantic propaganda with a political agenda of fomenting resistance against federal authority.

By August, word came that Redmond was willing to surrender, provided he stood trial only for the murder of Alfred Duckworth and received a suspended sentence for all other charges. Raum responded with a long letter enumerating Redmond's many crimes and insisting that the outlaw be captured and tried on all charges. But Raum did authorize his commissioner to accept guilty pleas in exchange for suspended sentences for all other illegal distillers. Hundreds of wildcat distillers leaped at the deal. Once their crimes were cleared, many of them licensed their stills and began operating legitimately. By September, things seemed to be calming down, and revenue collectors were allowed to go about their jobs unmolested. The number of registered stills in South Carolina leaped from 7 in 1876 to 109 in 1879.

That September, Lewis Redmond married Adeline Ladd, the sister of his late comrade Amos. The ceremony occurred at midnight at Redmond's hideout deep in the Blue Ridge Mountains, and the marriage notice sent to the *Pickens Sentinel* was rumored to have been accompanied by a flask of mountain dew. Though still a hunted man, Lewis Redmond managed to stay at least one step ahead of Green B. Raum and his revenue men. At some point, Redmond slipped away to Swain County in western North Carolina, where he took up farming and apparently lived openly but quietly in the community.

The Tennessee Front

South Carolina wasn't the only place where moonshiners were battling Raum's collectors. In August 1878, the *New York Tribune* declared that an "Illicit Whiskey War" was being waged in Tennessee too. At the heart of the action was a larger-than-life revenue agent named James M. Davis. Standing six foot two inches tall, with broad shoulders, jet-black hair, and curly chin whiskers, he had signed on with the Bureau of Internal Revenue in his early twenties. During his first ten days in office, he destroyed twenty-seven illegal stills and arrested fifteen moonshiners. Over the course of his career, it was estimated he arrested more than three thousand men, killing two and wounding twelve in the process. He operated most frequently in the Cumberland Mountains midway between Nashville and Knoxville, where the harsh terrain provided plenty of prime spots for hiding illegal stills.

This region was home to Campbell Morgan, the "the grand sachem of the moonshiners of the Cumberland mountains." Morgan's distillery was hidden away in a deep hollow surrounded on all sides by densely wooded hills. With double-lined doors and a porthole on each of the four thick walls, the structure did double duty as a fortress, and no revenue officer seemed willing to confront Morgan in his fortified lair. No officer, that is, except James M. Davis. In February 1878, a raiding party led by

Davis found Morgan at work in his distillery. As they drew within one hundred yards, Morgan spied them and cried out "halt." The officers kept approaching, and Morgan thrust a gun out of one of the portholes and began shooting. Davis and his men returned fire, and their balls shattered Morgan's pistol. Undaunted, Morgan grabbed another gun and continued to fire. Finally, one of Davis's shots struck Morgan in the right shoulder, and the moonshiner shouted that he was surrendering. Morgan, one newspaper reported, threw down his weapons, then ran to Davis, wrapped his wounded arms around the lawman's neck, and, calling him "honey," begged Davis not to let his men kill him. Morgan was taken into custody, and the revenue men destroyed his stills.

CAPT. JAMES M. DAVIS.

Legendary lawman James M. Davis.

That wasn't the end of the conflict between Davis and Campbell Morgan. In August of the same year, in the middle of a raiding expedition, Davis and eleven other men put up for the night at the home of James Peek, a 102-year-old man who lived about nine miles north of Cookeville. When a couple of Davis's men went out to feed horses, a rifle shot rang out from the woods surrounding the house, and Special Deputy Collector J. M. Phillips fell to the ground wounded. The rest of the revenue party rushed outside to assist their comrades and found themselves besieged by twenty to thirty heavily armed wildcat distillers. For forty-five minutes, they traded fire, killing one of the moonshiners and wounding several more, before the revenue party retreated to an unfinished log building nearby. Davis sent two men flying on horseback to Nashville to get reinforcements, and the rest holed up for the night.

When morning broke, the revenuers found themselves surrounded by upward of one hundred men, with Campbell Brown as their leader. The lawmen had no water and little food, and their attackers kept them pinned down in the log house all day with a periodic volley of bullets. Late the next afternoon, a party of citizens from Livingston, the county seat, arrived to intervene. They were allowed to pass through the moonshiners' lines and check on the conditions of the wounded revenuers, then went to Campbell Morgan to negotiate an honorable peace. Morgan's initial offer was that if the officers would petition the president of the United States and the federal court to pardon all their offenses, they would let the captives go. The officers responded that they couldn't control the actions of the federal court, that they had plenty of ammunition, and that reinforcements were on the way.

A worried Morgan began to backpedal. He told the delegation that he had heard that Davis intended to kill him upon sight and that the whole siege was nothing more than self-defense. If the government had a warrant to serve, he offered, as long as someone other than Davis served it, he would give himself up and end the confrontation. The revenuers agreed, and Morgan and his men filed away into the woods. The revenuers, accompanied by a band of citizens, made their way to Cookeville by sundown.

The showdown was widely covered in the national press. The *Daily Inter Ocean* of Chicago labeled it "War in Tennessee" and linked it to the Lewis Redmond escapade, saying the illicit distillers had been "encouraged by the condition of things in South Carolina." Campbell Morgan remained on the loose throughout the fall, despite an intense round of federal raiding in Overton, Putnam, and Jackson Counties that resulted in the arrest of ninety other moonshiners. Finally, in April 1879, Attorney General Charles Devens offered amnesty to those who participated in the Peek fight. On April 26, Campbell Morgan came to the US Circuit Court in Nashville and surrendered. There, he shook hands with Special Deputy Collector Davis, and the two men resolved to bury past animosities. Morgan accepted the amnesty and returned to his home in peace.

In a remarkable twist, not long after he was pardoned, Morgan applied for and received a job as a revenue officer himself. He served under James M. Davis, and the two men became friends. Together, Davis and Morgan went after Bill Berong, the notorious King of the Moonshiners in north Georgia. Berong and his sons had as many as three distilleries running at full capacity at one time on four hundred acres of remote mountain land. In November 1879, a party of revenue men had managed to slip through the mountain pass to Berong's home and place the infamous moonshiner under arrest. Before they could leave, though, they found themselves surrounded by armed men and were forced to relinquish their prisoner. Two months later, when revenuers led a party of forty well-armed men toward Berong's mountain home in a second attempt to capture the outlaw, friendly mountaineers warned the party that Berong had gathered seventy-five men, armed to the teeth, who would fight to the death to defend the King of the Moonshiners. The daunted revenuers turned back.

In May of 1880, an exasperated Commissioner Raum asked James M. Davis and Campbell Morgan to capture Berong once and for all. They took a train to Atlanta then proceeded by horseback up into the mountains. Under the cover of night, they concealed themselves outside Berong's house and waited. At dawn, two men came down from the hills and entered the house. Davis and Morgan closed in and captured them, and they turned out to be two of Berong's sons. As the story was later told in the newspapers, Berong's daughter first tried to scare Davis into flight by warning him that an armed band of men was about to sweep down from the hills. That failing, she burst into tears and pled with Davis not to break up her home. Davis is said to have responded with sympathy and persuasiveness, convincing the daughter and sons of the error of their ways. The sons induced their father to surrender peacefully to Davis.

Far from a fierce warrior, Berong turned out to be a tiny, wizened old man. When brought before the US Commissioner in Blairsville, he pled that he was "guilty, if I am hung for it," then promised that "I am finished with this blockading business." That fearsome "band of moonshiners" that had surrounded and repulsed forces of twenty and then forty revenuers, Berong revealed, had consisted solely of his three sons.

Davis continued his career as a revenuer, and the work became increasingly violent. He was wounded in a fight with the notorious Welch

A moonshine distillery.

brothers in December 1880. The following year, Davis killed John Welch in a fight that left Davis with a bullet in the thigh and a skull broken in two places. In March 1882, as Davis was traveling with a raiding party from Beersheba Springs to McMinnville, he was fired upon by unknown persons concealed in the bushes along the road. Davis fell from his horse, but he rose up to fight, only to be shot again repeatedly. James M. Davis, just thirty-four years old, died from his wounds.

The Tide Turns Against the Moonshiners

In the 1878 elections, the conservative Democrats won both houses of the United States Congress, and lo and behold, the liquor taxes that they had once found so tyrannical suddenly seemed far more reasonable. After all, they were the largest single source of revenue for the government. Raum's new enforcement tactics had improved the standing of his federal revenue agents, and farmers were growing tired of their workers getting drunk on cheap illegal booze. The South's shattered economy was starting to see new flickers of growth, too, and nascent milling and manufacturing industries were starting up in the western Carolinas and eastern Tennessee. An increasing number of rural residents gave up farming to move to growing cities like Greenville and Chattanooga, and they began to see illegal alcohol as an impediment to commercial prosperity and moonshiners as the instigators of crime and violence.

When moonshiners murdered a deputy marshal in Pickens County, South Carolina, in 1881, no one sprang to their defense. The *Charleston News and Courier*, which had so romanticized Lewis Redmond just a few years earlier, condemned the murderers as "men with little property and no education, who openly and defiantly violated the law for their own personal gain." Governor Wade Hampton recognized that supporting moonshining, tacitly or otherwise, was becoming a political liability, and he declared he would no longer tolerate violations of revenue laws. That same year, revenue agent George W. Atkinson declared that "moonshining is on the wane." Thanks to the vigorous policies of Commissioner Raum, Atkinson believed, "it is now only a matter of time, and a very brief period at that, for them to be entirely suppressed—to be literally wiped out forever."

Atkinson was a bit too optimistic. For almost another century, moonshiners supplied alcohol to a great many residents of the South, and revenuers kept trying to track them down and put them out of business. But as the romanticism faded and the public opinion started to turn against them, the violators of liquor laws learned to be much more discreet in their activities.

The story of Lewis Redmond isn't quite finished, though. He was laying low in North Carolina, but the federal government was still on the hunt. In April 1881, revenue officers surrounded Redmond's house in Swain County, and when his dogs began to bark, Redmond grabbed a gun and stepped outside. The officers shouted for him to halt, but Redmond raised his gun, and the officers opened fire. Redmond was struck by at least six bullets. He was taken to Asheville, where a doctor tended his wounds, and in August, federal authorities transferred him to Greenville, South Carolina, to be tried. Crowds gathered at railway stations along the way to cheer Redmond as his train passed through, and he was received in Greenville with a hero's welcome. More than five hundred people visited him in jail, bringing gifts of food, cigars, and whiskey. "Disgusting as it must appear to sensible people," the *New York Times* sniffed, "Redmond is at this time the most popular man in South Carolina." Redmond pled guilty to conspiracy and violating internal revenue laws and was sentenced to ten years in the federal penitentiary at Auburn, New York.

Though the public sentiment toward moonshiners in general had cooled, Lewis Redmond still had folk hero status. Greenville residents signed a petition demanding that Redmond be transferred from New York to the state penitentiary in Columbia, and the request was granted in April 1884. In May, after serving twenty-two months, Redmond was granted a full pardon by President Chester A. Arthur. Walking on crutches and wheezing from the shot still lodged in his windpipe, Redmond left the penitentiary in Columbia and was seen off at the train station by a crowd that included former Governor Wade Hampton and his successor, Hugh S. Thompson, who presented the former outlaw with refreshments for his trip home to Pickens County.

In a final twist to his long, curious story, the century's most famous moonshiner ended up going legit. After farming for a little while, Redmond moved to the town of Walhalla to work as a superintendent for Henry D. Biemann's government distillery. For several years, he produced and marketed "Redmond's Hand-Mashed Corn Whiskey." Redmond seems to have known that it was not the formula for his whiskey but his well-known name that had the real brand power. In 1890, the *New York Herald* reported that the former outlaw was selling the right to paste his name and image on the side of whiskey barrels for seventy-five cents a barrel.

If you believe the stories told by his family and the press, the former outlaw remained law-abiding for the rest of his life. In its 1906 obituary for Redmond, the *Keowee Courier* declared that, after his pardon, Redmond had "settled into a sober, quiet life and has since been a changed man." As an illustration of the "big, warm, tender heart beneath the rough exterior of Redmond's character," the author recalled seeing Redmond at the local train depot, hugging his deaf daughter, tears running down his face, as her mother left to take her to the Cedar Springs, an institution for deaf and blind children.

But Redmond's postpardon life was hardly free from violence. One Saturday night in June 1890 in the town of Walhalla, Redmond was out "riding with two women of dissolute character" when he stopped to go into a barbershop for a shave. While Redmond was occupied, James Smith, the son of a wealthy lumberman, came along and took the women with him. A furious Redmond pursued Smith and stabbed him in the chest. Redmond claimed afterward that he was too drunk to remember anything that happened. He was arrested by the sheriff and charged with assault and battery with intent to kill.

Lewis Redmond, the King of the Outlaws, died of pneumonia in 1906.

The Golden Age of Whiskey

We have plenty of whiskey cocktails to look forward to, but for this chapter let's not adulterate the brown water with any sweetness or flavorings. Instead, get yourself two bottles: one bottled in bond rye, one bottled in bond bourbon. Rittenhouse is a good choice for the rye, and Old Grand-Dad or Old Fitzgerald would do well for the bourbon. If you want to really go all out, seek out Col. E. H. Taylor Jr. straight rye and Col. E. H. Taylor Jr. small-batch bourbon.

Take two rocks glasses and pour an ounce of rye into one and an ounce of bourbon in the other. Brace yourself for the burn, since no matter which brand you choose, with a bottled in bond whiskey, it's guaranteed to be 100 proof. Sniff the aroma of each, then take a sip and let it roll back over your tongue. Beneath the alcohol bite, savor the sweet vanilla, and oaky notes and the smoothness of the finish.

Now that you've done that, feel free to add a few drops of water or an ice cube to each glass. You can use the rest of the bottles for the whiskey cocktails that come later, but take a sip neat every now and again in memory of Colonel E. H. Taylor Jr. That strong, clean flavor of pure aged whiskey didn't come easy.

Whiskey Comes of Age

In the years following the Civil War, whiskey distilling became a large-scale modern business. The story of rye and bourbon between the Civil War and Prohibition is that of a maturing and industrializing business that was trying to balance scale and quality of product simultaneously. Innovations in distilling and transportation made inexpensive whiskey more widely available than ever before. At the same time, a combination of factors made imported brandy more and more expensive and domestic fruit brandies not economically viable. As a result, the postwar years saw the crowding out of brandy and the emergence of whiskey as the preeminent spirit in the South.

Fierce battles were waged against adulteration and bogus whiskey during the last half of the nineteenth century, creating a period that might well be termed the golden age of bourbon and rye whiskey. It was the era when advertising and modern marketing were born, and whiskey led the way in establishing the importance of name brands and mass marketing. The industry also began to consolidate, as large companies coalesced from smaller operations. Much of this activity occurred in the states along the northern edge of the South—Kentucky, Pennsylvania, and Maryland—but it had a transformative effect on what was available to drink in the South and, therefore, what Southerners drank.

Barrels, Bottles, and Brands:
The Marketing and Distribution of Whiskey

Before the Civil War, whiskey was a generic commodity, and one type was distinguished from another not by who made or packaged it, but simply by its place of origin, like Old Monongahela and Old Bourbon. A handful of distillers, like Dr. James Crow and Jacob Spears, had achieved sufficient reputation for their talents to be able to trade upon their names, and pioneers like S. J. Pike, the creator of Magnolia Whiskey, had started promoting and selling their goods under trademarked names. Actual whiskey brands, however, were rare until after the Civil War.

Advertisement for Old Crow whiskey, circa 1870.

The legal system had much to do with that. Trademarks had been protected under common law since the colonial era, but the enforcement of such measures at the state level was scattershot at best. The first

United States trademark law passed in 1870, and it allowed companies to nationally register the brands under which they sold their goods, which helped consumers more easily identify the source of what they were purchasing. Whiskey brands, in fact, were at the center of many early landmark legal decisions and played an instrumental role in shaping American trademark law.

As these cases show, all sorts of shenanigans were rife in the rough-and-tumble years of the whiskey trade. Take M. J. Cole and Co. of Boston, for instance, which struck a deal with a western distillery, M. Murphy and Co., to become the exclusive distributor of Murphy's products in New England. Cole decided to market the spirits under the name Paul Jones whiskey, and to do so he had a literal brand created—a tool used to sear the name and logo into the wood of the whiskey barrels. That logo proudly declared the barrel's contents to be "Paris, Kentucky, Bourbon."

The Paul Jones brand sold well in the Boston market, but Cole soon learned that his supplier was selling whiskey in the South and West under the same Paul Jones name. Cole sued Murphy for trademark infringement, but the "Paris, Kentucky, Bourbon" brand on his barrels tripped up the case. Paul Jones whiskey, it turns out, had never come within a hundred miles of Paris, Kentucky, for M. Murphy and Co. distilled the liquor in Cincinnati. According to the testimony of Mr. Cole, the two firms had figured that if they slapped the name Kentucky on the barrels, the brand "would take better with the trade." The court ruled that the device "had its inception in fraud" and therefore was not a legitimate trademark. M. J. Cole and Co. lost the suit, and M. Murphy and Co. was free to continue selling faux-Kentucky whiskey under the Paul Jones brand wherever it pleased.

Around 1870, another applicant from Boston, John E. Cassidy, sought to trademark Chestnut Hill Bourbon as a brand for his whiskey. Questioned whether the name might confuse purchasers and create "a wrong idea of origin," Cassidy responded that "the word 'Bourbon' is used to designate all whiskeys made from corn in contradiction to those made entirely of rye and known as 'rye-whiskey." The trademark application was rejected, but Cassidy was actually on to something. Bourbon, a term used originally to identify the place of origin of a particular type of superior whiskey, was already on its way to becoming a generic trade term.

Early trademark records make plain how widespread phony whiskey labeling was. Adams and Taylor of Boston trademarked whiskeys named G. O. Blake's Bourbon Co, Ky., Daniel Boone, Paris, Ky., and Kentucky

Pioneer. Brady and Co. of Washington, DC, registered Brady's Kentucky Whiskey. In Cincinnati, Capel and Roebuck sold Bone's Old Kentucky Bourbon and the Hoffheimer Brothers trademarked Fairfax Old Bourbon. Using such subterfuge in labeling your whiskey might prevent you from enforcing your trademark, but slapping patent falsehoods on your barrels was still perfectly legal.

At the same time that they were starting to trademark the names of their spirits, whiskey sellers were also changing the way they packaged their products for sale. The old decorative glass whiskey flasks of the antebellum years, which were designed not to identify a particular product or brand but just to look pretty, gave way to molded cylindrical bottles with the seller's trademark and brand name embossed on the sides. Those sellers, in most cases, were not the firms that actually made the bottle's contents. The names of most distillers were separated from the end consumers by one or more intermediaries. The whiskey makers sold their spirits to distributors, who in turn went out and promoted it to consumers.

Some of these distributors had exclusive arrangements with distilleries, but more often, a producer would work out wholesale arrangements with a network of agents in various cities or regions, and each agent would have the exclusive rights to sell that brand in their territory. One distiller's whiskey was often packaged and sold under many different names. Drugstores bottled rye and bourbon, too, selling them at retail just as they did medicine. Grocery stores tended to handle whiskey in bulk, buying it by the barrel and packaging it as jug goods or case goods—that is, whiskey put in earthenware jugs or glass containers. The vessels bore the names and addresses of the merchants, impressed or stenciled on their sides, and their capacity ranged from one pint to three gallons. Many bars carried their own house-labeled whiskey too.

As distillers started establishing brands, they wanted their names—not those of retailers or generic designs—to appear on the bottles that the end consumers saw. Some started shipping labels along with their barrels, with names like Old Crow Hand Made Sour Mash Bourbon Whiskey, for retailers to use when they bottled the whiskey for resale. Before 1900, advertising for spirits was unsophisticated at best. Newspaper ads tended to be straightforward announcements of names and prices. To promote their brand names, liquor marketers instead focused their attention on novelties, such as calendars, bar glasses, matchboxes, and pocket diaries, to be given out to the trade.

In the years just after the Civil War, whiskey drummers fanned out across the South to drum up business on behalf of wholesale liquor merchants. Traveling by train and wagon on months-long swings through their territories, these roving salesmen spent lavishly, treating customers in bars to win loyalty for their brand. They tended to be ambitious and charismatic young men, quick with the joke and the sample bottle. Their main goal was to get a store owner or barkeeper to place an order for a barrel or more. For some of the more disreputable drummers, making that sale at the expense of the competition was just fine too. A common trick was to slip a nail into a competitor's whiskey barrel while visiting a bar, since the iron from the nail would turn the whiskey a repellant black.

One Dallas merchant, fatigued with drummers constantly calling on his store, came up with a novel way of handling them. "When . . . a whiskey drummer comes in and begins to talk business," he explained to a fellow merchant, "I buy a dozen barrels of whiskey from him. I never argue with the drummers. I just buy whatever they want to sell."

"But what do you do with all the goods?" the other merchant asked.

"I cancel the order as soon as the drummer leaves the store. I have regularly printed blanks which my clerks fill out, and they are mailed to his house at once."

The Brandy Bust and the Industrialization of Whiskey

At the same time that whiskey producers were learning the art of branding and marketing their products, their main competitor at the high end of the market—imported French brandy—was getting kicked in the teeth. Before the Civil War, no Southern gentleman of any self-worth would be caught drinking low, common whiskey. That changed rapidly in the 1870s, and it was all thanks to a little bug.

The phylloxera, a tiny aphidlike insect, had arrived in France as early as 1865. By 1872, the Cognac-producing Charente region was officially declared infected, and dry summers in 1873 and 1875 only encouraged the bug's spread. The tiny louse destroyed the roots and leaves of the grapevines, leaving them fit only to burn. In some areas, the harvests of the late 1870s didn't produce a single grape. Production of new brandy in and around Cognac dropped from 225 million gallons in 1875 to just 17 million two years later.

Like good whiskey, Cognac is aged in barrels for years before being ready to bottle and sell, so producers still had large stocks on hand. But since there was no new brandy backfilling their supply, they began raising prices and limiting releases to conserve their stocks. And then a funny thing happened—or, rather, didn't happen. Instead of a Cognac shortage, plenty of Cognac remained available on the market, at least in name. The rising prices had prompted a horde of schemers to devise imitations, blending grain and beet spirits flavored with a little actual brandy and adding all sorts of additives to simulate the flavor and color of the real stuff. By the early 1880s, American newspapers were complaining that almost all of the imported brandy was falsified and adulterated. The good name of Cognac was ruined. For their juleps and smashes, Southern drinkers summarily abandoned French brandy in favor of domestic whiskey, which had steadily been improving in quality. By 1900, the Cognac region's vineyards were replanted with phylloxera-resistant hybrids (grafted from American rootstock), but it took until 1970 before sales of Cognac brandy reached prephylloxera levels.

Apple and peach brandy were on the ropes, too, thanks in large part to the federal excise tax. Apple brandy, the *Alexandria Gazette* reported in 1874, "used to be one of the staples of Southside Virginia" but had been growing scarcer with each passing year because "not many country people care to subject themselves to the expense and trouble of passing through the custom house mill." The same was the case with peach brandy. "The stringent excise taxes of recent years have caused most persons to abandon its manufacture," one writer noted in 1886. Some stills would lurch back into production in years when there was a bumper crop of peaches or apples, but in general, Southern peach and apple brandy faded away amid the more lucrative whiskey trade. In 1899, ninety-seven million taxable gallons of spirits were produced in the United States. Of these, just 210,000 gallons were apple brandy and less than 41,000 gallons were peach.

For most of the nineteenth century, much of what Southerners drank had been produced close to their homes, for thousands of small distilleries—what we today might call artisanal or microdistilleries—dotted the South. One such distillery was that of Henry D. Biemann in Walhalla, a town in the far west portion of South Carolina, which was profiled by the *Charleston News and Courier* in 1886. It was a medium operation that mashed 40 barrels of corn and produced 120 gallons of spirits each day, which amounted to an annual output of just over 37,000 gallons, on which

Biemann paid $33,000 in federal taxes. Biemann employed twenty hands, and he used the spent mash to raise and fatten livestock, selling as many as three hundred cattle and four hundred hogs each year. Distilleries like Biemann's were not producing aged whiskey but rather unaged corn spirits, making them essentially the same way as the moonshiners did, but doing so out in the open and paying the required taxes. Biemann's distillery, the *News and Courier* noted, is run "on the old-fashioned plan," or, to be more plain, "on the moonshine style." For a time, Biemann even employed Lewis Redmond, the notorious outlaw moonshiner who had gone legit.

By this point, corn whiskey had eclipsed fruit brandy as the cheap, locally made spirit, but forces were at work that would make it increasingly difficult for small distilleries like Biemann's to survive. Federal tax policy tilted the field in favor of distillers with deep pockets, since they had to pay the tax as soon as their whiskey was produced but, as barrel-aging became the standard, they had to wait several years before selling it. As taxes increased, they were not made retroactive, meaning that any liquor produced before the new tax went into effect would be subject to the old rate. As soon as Congress passed a new tax bill, distillers would crank up their stills and even erect entire new factories to produce as much liquor as possible before the higher rate took effect, leaving them with warehouses filled with huge inventories that allowed them to undercut the market.

Even more threatening to the small distiller were the remarkable innovations in distilling technology during the Gilded Age. In an old-fashioned pot still, the boiling alcohol simply rose to the top of the chamber and was drawn out. The new stills consisted of tall metal columns, inside of which were a series of perforated metal plates. The vapors from the boiling beer would rise up through the plates, which would strip impurities away and result in a purer distillate. Unlike pot stills, which had to be cleaned after each run to remove the solids from the mash, the new stills could be multicolumned and run continuously, with wash constantly being fed into the still and alcohol constantly being drawn off. The new stills didn't need the solids removed from the mash since the rising steam kept them from drying and scorching—they just fell to the bottom of the columns with the rest of the spent beer. Where a pot still yielded spirits that were 40 to 50 percent alcohol, the new column stills could achieve more than 90 percent. As distillers built ever larger stills, some of which might rise four stories in height, they could churn out more finished alcohol in a day than old pot stills could over the course of several weeks.

The stills themselves weren't the only innovations. The old style of malt, a crude product generally made from corn, was replaced by high-quality commercial malt made from barley. Fermenters grew in size, and more machinery was introduced to assist in the distilling process. Copper-lined fermentation tanks were easier to clean and made for more consistent fermentation. New steel roller mills made grinding grains more efficient. As output grew, so did inventory, requiring more barrels and larger warehouses. Distillers needed more grain, so they began establishing complex supply chains to import it from out of state. The pig and cattle pens surrounding the distilleries grew, too, since there was more and more slop to feed an ever-growing number of animals, turning the large distilleries into major livestock operations.

As whiskey making evolved into an industrial, marketing-driven business, many of the smaller producers didn't survive. Those older firms that did make the transition, such as D. M. Beam and Company and J. W. Dant, tended to have been the most established before the war and had deep pockets. Increasingly, entrepreneurs from other trades like banking and manufacturing—men who were well versed in finance, promotion, and distribution—started entering the business, seeing the enormous potential of bringing industrial methods to distilling. Some were intent on making their fortune through reputation, by producing and selling a consistently high-quality brand. Far too many others were interested only in making a fast buck, and the long-running phenomenon of whiskey simultaneously getting much better and much worse continued on a larger scale than ever before.

The Rise of Baltimore and Kentucky

In this consolidating, industrializing whiskey market, the city of Baltimore took control of the Southern market for the finer grades of rye whiskey. Before the war, Baltimore had already served as a great funnel for the spirits trade, bringing in rye whiskey and brandy distilled in western Maryland and Pennsylvania and distributing it to cities all along the southern Atlantic and Gulf Coasts. By 1873, more than two hundred Baltimore firms were involved in the liquor trade, and six of them sold more than fifty thousand barrels of spirits per year. As trade increased during the postwar years, many of the city's whiskey dealers started establishing distilleries and making their products themselves.

Maryland rye became a prestigious term in the industry. It indicated a style of rye that was sweeter than the spicy Pennsylvania variety. A great limestone shield spreads eastward from Pennsylvania into western Maryland, with one narrow prong reaching all the way to Baltimore. Just as it was in the case of Kentucky bourbon, the limestone in Maryland's water was credited with having a softening effect on the whiskey made with it. In the fast and loose days of whiskey marketing, though, Maryland rye quickly became a generic term used to refer to a type of spirit, regardless of where it was distilled. Maryland Union Club rye, for instance, was produced by Samuel C. Boehm and Co. of New York City. The seal of the state of Maryland adorned the labels of Old Maryland rye, but the whiskey was actually distilled in Saint Louis.

The whiskey industry in Kentucky was undergoing dramatic changes, too. A few antebellum distillers, such as the Wathens and the Peppers, continued to prosper, but the postwar industry was dominated mostly by new names. In 1810, there had been 2,000 distilleries in operation in Kentucky. By 1888, the overall volume of whiskey produced had grown to a remarkable 4.6 million gallons, but it was produced by only 165 firms.

Kentucky distilleries had gotten a particular leg up on their competitors in the Carolinas and Georgia because of the transportation network. The Civil War left most of the Southern railroad system crippled, but the Louisville and Nashville Railroad, being based in Union-held Kentucky, had profited nicely during the war by hauling Union troops and supplies. While the railroads farther south were struggling just to restore their shattered lines and equipment, the L and N used its reserved capital to expand rapidly. The transportation routes southward into Tennessee and beyond gave Kentucky distillers a direct pipeline to ship whiskey to the Southern interior.

One big beneficiary of the L and N's success was a whiskey distilling family named Beam. Just before the Civil War, David M. Beam, who was then making whiskey at the Old Tub Distillery in Washington County, made a rather daring gamble. When he learned that the railroad was planning a branch line that would run through Bardstown in neighboring Nelson County, he up and moved the Old Tub Distillery one county over to Nelson. The L and N was completed through to Nashville in 1859, and the following year, the Springfield/Bardstown branch opened. David M. Beam was now able to ship his product by rail not just to the important whiskey hub of Louisville but also directly south to Nashville, opening a whole new market for his aged Kentucky bourbon.

But a distiller needed more than good transportation to prosper in the late nineteenth-century whiskey market. David M. Beam retired in 1892 and handed over management of the family business to his son, Jim. At this point, the distillery produced only a single line of bourbon, called Old Tub, and they did a brisk business with it in their older markets in the Deep South. But Jim Beam knew that he needed capital if his firm was to continue to grow, and he would have to look past family ties to find it. In 1898, two wealthy Chicagoans, Thomas Dennehy and Jeremiah S. Kenny, invested in the firm and became co-owners. The new concern was rechristened the Clear Springs Distillery Company of Bardstown. Beam experimented with different mash bills and strains of yeast, and the company soon brought three new brands to market: Clear Springs, Jefferson Club, and Pebbleford. In 1913, the company bought the distilling plant owned by F. G. Walker, who had declared bankruptcy, adding the Queen of Nelson and F. G. Walker brands to the Clear Springs stable, along with good distilling equipment and twenty thousand barrels worth of warehouse space. Jim Beam was a man on the rise in the Kentucky whiskey industry. He was elected president of the Kentucky Distillers Association in 1916, and the Clear Springs Distillery Company would remain one of the leading market players straight through until Prohibition.

Advertisement for Belle of Nelson whiskey, 1883.

The Golden Age of Whiskey

Colonel E. H. Taylor and the Bottled in Bond Movement

As the new century approached, the trend was toward fewer and larger distilleries, and that consolidation put many of the South's favorite whiskey brands in the hands of capitalists in New York City and Chicago. Despite its new market dominance, though, whiskey was still an unreliable and often notorious product—blended, rectified, and tarted up with any number of flavorings and adulterants to let cheap neutral spirits be passed off as fine aged whiskey. The industry needed a leader to step forward and transform it into something more respectable, and that leader was Colonel E. H. Taylor Jr.

Edmund Haynes Taylor Jr. was born in Columbia, Kentucky, in 1830. After getting his start in banking, he later entered the liquor trade, opening an office on Louisville's Whiskey Row in 1864. Taylor served as a sort of bridge between the old, pre–Civil War whiskey business and the new Gilded Age industry. He personally knew many of the pioneering distillers from the early days, including James Crow and Elijah Pepper. At the same time, he was an innovative merchandiser who helped transform whiskey distilling from the simple manufacturing business that it once was into a large-scale, marketing-driven industry.

When Oscar Pepper died (Elijah Pepper's son) in 1864, Taylor was appointed to be his estate's executor and the guardian of Pepper's son James, who was still a minor. In 1867, Taylor formed a partnership with William A. Gaines and Hiram Berry and leased the old Pepper distillery, where they made whiskey that they sold under the brand name Old Crow in honor of James Crow, whose methods and recipes they used (fermenting sour mash in small tubs and distilling it in old-fashioned copper pot stills heated over a wood fire). In the 1870s, Taylor struck out on his own and rebuilt the old Oscar Pepper distillery, operating it with his former ward, James E. Pepper, under the name E. H. Taylor Jr. Co. Over time, they introduced multiple brands of whiskey to the market, including Old Taylor, Hermitage, O.F.C. (Old Fire Copper), and Carlisle. Taylor staked his reputation of making a reliable, uniform product, but he paid a lot of attention to packaging, too, understanding the impact that first impressions had on brand and consumer preference. He insisted that brass rings be used on all his barrels and that they be polished clean and bright before being shipped to a customer. He published letters of recommendation from important customers and created prints of his distillery that he distributed far and wide.

Taylor's methodical approach blended old techniques and styles with modern marketing and financing. The new distillery he constructed on Glenn's Creek near Frankfort became known as the Old Taylor Castle, for it looked like a medieval castle complete with stone walls, towers, and crenelated battlements. The springhouse had an art nouveau design, open to the air with a roof supported by carved limestone columns. The distillery was surrounded by landscaped grounds worthy of a gentleman's estate, and picnickers would come to enjoy the waters of the spring and a complimentary taste of Taylor's whiskey. Taylor also built up one of the most celebrated herds of Hereford cattle in the country and, for good measure, served as mayor of Frankfort for seventeen years and two terms as a state senator. It was around this time that he took the lead in a national fight to save the good name of Kentucky whiskey from the depredations of the blenders and the rectifiers.

Colonel Edmund H. Taylor Jr.

In the mid-1890s, a series of congressional hearings began probing the inner workings of the whiskey trade and turned a bright light on the rampant practices of adulteration. Reports estimated that only two million gallons of whiskey each year were sold as originally distilled, while more than one hundred million gallons were blended with other ingredients. Some so-called whiskeys were nothing more than ethyl alcohol mixed with the essence of bourbon and prune juice, a formulation that could be manufactured in a matter of minutes and sold at a premium as aged "Old Bourbon" whiskey. Distillers, like Taylor, who took pride in the quality of their product were dismayed by such figures, and they were even more concerned by another sales trend. Just a few decades after whiskey had eclipsed rum and brandy as the predominant American alcoholic beverage, its sales were in decline. According to IRS records, per capita consumption of whiskey decreased each decade after the Civil War, sliding from 2.86 gallons in 1860 to 1.36 in 1900. A half century of temperance reform had helped drive that trend, but equally important was the rise of beer, whose per capita consumption had soared from 3.27 gallons in 1860 to a whopping 17.49 gallons in 1900. Distillers chalked up much of their fading fortunes to growing mistrust among the public toward the purity of whiskey.

For more than forty years, the government had cared little for what happened to a barrel of whiskey once the taxes were paid and the barrel released from the warehouse. Its contents could legally be blended, augmented, bottled, and branded in any number of adulterated forms. Distillers might sell two-year-old whiskey one month and a six-year-old the next, all under the same label. They might mix it with neutral spirits and colorings and flavorings to transform a single barrel of good whiskey into five barrels of—well, something resembling whiskey, I suppose.

Edmund H. Taylor joined forces with two prominent Kentucky politicians, Senator Joe Blackburn and Secretary of the Treasury John G. Carlisle, to promote a whiskey purity measure that became known as the Bottled-in-Bond Act, which Congress passed in 1896. The act laid out federal standards categorizing the various types of whiskey and the qualifications that each type must meet in order be sold in that category in the market. To be called rye whiskey, a spirit must have a rye content of at least 51 percent, and the remaining grains can be corn, wheat, or malted barley. Rye must be distilled at 160 proof—meaning what emerged from the still had to be 80 percent alcohol. It then had to be diluted with pure water so that it was at least

80 proof and no more than 125 proof and put into charred new white oak barrels to age. The same rules apply for bourbon, except that 51 percent of the mash must be corn. Whether rye or bourbon, to be considered straight whiskey, it must be stored at least two years in the barrel.

In order to put the federal government's official stamp of approval on so-called pure whiskey, the act created a special category of spirits called bottled in bond. To receive that designation, the liquor had to be produced by a single distiller at a single distillery in a single season (measured January through December), so there would be no blending of spirits from different producers nor from different years. The spirits had to be aged in bonded warehouses under federal government supervision for at least four years, and it had to be bottled at 100 proof in a government-supervised facility. Bottled in bond is usually associated with rye and bourbon, but it applies to other spirits, too, including corn whiskey and apple brandy. So that consumers could be confident that no monkey business had occurred after bottling, a government tax stamp—a green strip of paper with the date of distilling and date of bottling stamped on it—was glued over the top of the cork or cap.

The law took effect in 1901, but bonded whiskey caught on slowly in the market. The bottled in bond requirements flew against many of the routine practices in the trade, like blending whiskeys of different ages and from different producers. The distiller's name, furthermore, had to be displayed on each bottle's label, so wholesalers couldn't private label a bottled in bond whiskey. In 1904, the trade journal *Wine & Spirit Bulletin* noted about bonded whiskey, "Many saloonists not only do not handle it, but do not even know what it is. The average consumer has yet to be made thoroughly acquainted with it."

So distillers undertook campaigns to promote the idea of bonded whiskey, sending representatives to saloons to offer free samples and educate both barmen and patrons as to what it was. Edmund H. Taylor wrote newspaper editorials and spoke at expositions around the country to promote the guarantees that the bonded whiskey brought. Brands like Sunny Brook straight whiskey, Old Crow, Old Overholt rye, and Old Barbee bourbon advertised heavily throughout the South, promoting their bottled in bond status. Though that designation was simply a testament of the purity and not necessarily the quality of the whiskey, it soon took on that connotation. Whiskey distillers touted the federal government's seal of approval in their advertisements and even incorporated pictures of Uncle

Sam or his representative, a government man in a cap marked with the word *Inspector*.

The law ensured that whiskey bearing certain labels—straight rye whiskey, bourbon whiskey, bottled in bond—were what they claimed to be, but they did nothing to clear up what might be inside the bottles labeled just whiskey. The same advocates who successfully pushed through the Bottled-in-Bond Act continued their momentum to push for more broad-ranging federal regulation of all food and drugs, a movement that helped lead to the passage of the Pure Food and Drug Act of 1906. Whiskey was front and center in the effort.

"Never drink blended whiskey," Dr. Harvey W. Wiley, the chief chemist of the Department of Agriculture, told the members of the House Commerce Committee in February 1906. Wiley claimed that more than 85 percent of all the so-called whiskey on the market was not real (that is, straight) whiskey and that less than 2 percent had the green bottled in bond stamp. To make his point even more dramatically, he produced a bottle of ethyl alcohol, a tube of burned sugar, and a box of flavoring extracts. Within five minutes he had produced samples of four fine spirits—Scotch, bourbon, rye, and brandy—that he passed around to the committee members to sample. Their judgment on the taste wasn't recorded, but the *New York Times* did note that committee members "smacked their lips," which probably says less about the quality of imitation whiskey than it does about the palates of congressmen. They did approve the bill, though, moving it to the floor of the House for debate, where Representative A. O. Stanley of Kentucky stole Wiley's trick and blended neutral spirits with flavorings to create "fourteen-year-old whiskey" in the forum in front of Speaker Joseph G. Cannon's desk.

The Pure Food and Drug Act was signed into law by Theodore Roosevelt, and it only intensified the battle between bonded spirits producers and the rectifiers, for the executive branch now had to answer the question "what is real whiskey?" Harvey Wiley insisted that a product should be called whiskey only if it contained no additives other than water. One drop of anything else—neutral spirits, additives for coloring or flavoring—should make it "imitation whiskey." Irate rectifiers countered that neutral spirits might be a by-product of distillation, but they were nevertheless distilled from fermented grains and came out of the still spout just as pure as the primary product, only at a later stage of distillation. Plus, they insisted, the gentlemen imbibing such spirits were perfectly aware that they were blends and didn't mind the additives in the least, since they improved the color and flavor of the product.

Rounds of debate and hearings and protests followed, and it was left to Roosevelt's successor, William Howard Taft, to make the final call. He announced his decision on the day after Christmas in 1909. Blends of neutral spirits and flavorings had been sold as whiskey for almost a century, he declared, and there was no injustice done to allow producers to sell their products as whiskey so long as they clearly indicated the type of spirits from which they were made. Only true straight whiskeys could be branded as such, but any whiskey made from rectified, distilled, or neutral spirits could be sold as blended whiskey.

The so-called Taft Decision was a victory for the blenders and rectifiers, but it forced them to alter their trade practices. Countless Baltimore firms that had been selling Pure Maryland rye had to update their labels to read Maryland Whiskey—A Blend. Pure whiskey advocates like Edmund H. Taylor and Harvey Wiley hadn't gotten everything they wanted, but their efforts had set in motion a permanent transformation in what Southerners drank. Whiskey lovers could now be confident that their rye was made with rye and their bourbon was made with corn. If they wanted to know the exact place of origin, they could opt for the bottled in bond stuff with the green stamps on the cap. The rules defined during that period remain in force today.

14

The Golden Age of the Southern Cocktail

It's time to return to the Sazerac. As we discussed in chapter 7, it was by no stretch of the imagination the very first cocktail, but it is perhaps the quintessential late nineteenth-century Southern cocktail, for it embodies so many elements of drinking in the South during that period.

The Sazerac

SERVES 1

Cracked ice

1 lump sugar (or 2 cubes)

3 dashes Peychaud's bitters

1 dash Angostura bitters

1 jigger (1.5 ounces) rye whiskey

Ice cubes

1 dash absinthe or absinthe substitute (like Herbsaint)

1 strip lemon peel

Start with two heavy-bottomed, 3½-ounce bar glasses. Fill the first with cracked ice and set it aside to chill. Place the lump of sugar in the second glass and dribble a few drops of water on top of it—just enough to moisten the cube. Add both types of bitters, the rye, and several cubes of ice and stir.

Empty the ice from the first glass, dribble in a dash of absinthe, and swirl it around until it coats the sides. Pour out any excess absinthe—it's there just to flavor the glass. To serve, strain the whiskey mixture into the first glass, then twist the lemon peel over the glass and let the tiny bit of extracted oil fall into the drink. Discard peel.

This recipe was adapted from Stanley Clisby Arthur's *Famous New Orleans Drinks and How to Mix 'Em*. Arthur got the recipe from Leon Dupont, one of the expert mixers at the Sazerac House in New Orleans, home of that famous cocktail, so you've got to figure Dupont knew what he was talking about. He even provided Arthur with a couple of Sazerac strictures. Never use bourbon nor a shaker to make a Sazerac, he insisted, and dropping the lemon peel in the glass would be a "sacrilege."

I usually make a few slight alterations to Arthur's recipe. Since I rarely have lumps of sugar lying around, I typically use two cubes. To help it dissolve, I'll usually add the dashes of bitters straight on top of the cubes and mash them in with a muddler or the handle of a wooden spoon to help the sugar dissolve before adding the whiskey. Finally, after twisting the lemon peel over the top, I'll wipe it around the rim of the glass to get a little of the lemony essence on the rim. But I am always sure to throw that peel away immediately and never let it come close to falling into the glass. I wouldn't want to upset Mr. Dupont.

The Best Bartenders in the World

Before the Civil War, the South had already given the country the hailstorm julep, mastered by the great African-American caterers. After the war, New Orleans took the lead, ushering in the golden age of the Southern cocktail. No region of the country loved fancy drinks more than the South. In 1883, a San Francisco bartender who had recently arrived from back East noted that "fancy drinks are not used so much in San Francisco as they are in the cities of the East and the South." The reason, he explained, was that the West Coast was much cooler in the summer and "people don't feel the need of them." The recent pre-Prohibition cocktail revival has elevated the romantic image of the mustachioed bartenders of New York City, but nineteenth-century Gothamites knew where the real cocktail artists could be found. In 1886, an "uptown bartender" in New York declared he could determine a patron's place of origin simply by the drink he ordered. "North Carolina, Alabama, Louisiana, Tennessee and other southern states send us great fancy drinkers," he observed. "The best barkeepers in the world come from the south."

"Southerners," he continued, "are heavy on sherry cobblers, mint juleps, brandy smashes, brandy juleps, and Bourbon sours." Indeed, the great Jerry Thomas, the author of America's first bartender's guide and the patron saint of the pre-Prohibition cocktail revival, made his own tour of service through the South, with stints shaking up beverages at the Mills House hotel in Charleston in 1853 and later at the Planter's Hotel in Saint Louis, before returning to New York City in 1858.

A Survey of the Drinks of New Orleans

In 1885, the popular newspaper and magazine author Lafcadio Hearn published *La Cuisine Creole*, a collection of New Orleans recipes that includes a catalog of the city's favorite drinks. The pousse-café, which was popular before the Civil War, remained in fashion, and Hearn's book provides recipes for four variations. The crowning beverage at a fancy dinner, though, was the grand brule, which Hearn called "the grandest pousse cafe of all." When the dinner was finished and coffee served, the lights in the dining room would be turned down and the brule brought in. It was constructed by combining good French brandy, kirsch, maraschino liqueur, and a small amount of cinnamon and allspice. The bowl was placed in the center of the table, and a dozen sugar cubes were placed in a ladle then covered with brandy, which was then set alight and poured carefully over the top of the brule. As the brandy burned, the flame shed a flickering light on the faces of the diners. "The stillness that follows," Hearn noted, "gives an opportunity for thoughts that break out in ripples of laughter which pave the way for the exhilaration that ensues" once the brule was finally ladled into glasses and served.

For more ordinary New Orleans evenings (and mornings, for that matter), Hearn's book offered two dozen mixed drinks, including two gin fizzes (one with seltzer water and egg white, the other with celestine vichy and egg yolk), a Jamaica rum punch, and Ponche Romaine (a shaken blend of water, whiskey, Jamaican rum, sugar, and lemon). The transition from brandy to whiskey was well under way and the New Orleans toddy Hearn described called for a lump of sugar, tablespoon of water, one wineglass (two ounces) full of whiskey or brandy, and a lump of ice. He also included details on "Whiskey, Brandy, or Gin Cocktails New Orleans Style," which include two dashes of bitters (Boker's, Angostura, or Peychaud's), a lump of sugar, a piece of lemon peel, a tablespoon of water, and a wineglass of liquor, which is stirred on ice and strained into a cocktail glass.

Hearn's inventory provides a useful baseline for the state of the New Orleans cocktail as the nineteenth century drew to a close. Most involved sugar and water along with some combination of lemon, eggs, and bitters. A few of the city's creative mixologists took this palette of ingredients and perfected from them the cocktails that made New Orleans famous.

The Ramos Gin Fizz

The Sazerac is the cocktail that gets all the attention in New Orleans these days, but in the late nineteenth century the Ramos gin fizz was considered the city's quintessential cocktail. It was invented by Henry Charles Ramos, a son of German immigrants who got started in the beverage trade working for Eugene Krost, who pioneered the practice of selling lager beer for a nickel per glass at his Exchange Alley establishment. In the late 1870s, Ramos moved to Baton Rouge, where he operated the Capitol Saloon, a bar popular with the political denizens of the state capital. In 1888, he returned to New Orleans and opened the Imperial Cabinet, which was located just across the street from the New Orleans Cotton Exchange, and there he made a name for himself with his shaken gin concoctions.

Ramos's specialty was built upon the foundation of a gin fizz, which was quite in vogue nationwide in the 1880s. The most popular style was the so-called silver fizz, a mixture of gin, lemon, sugar, and seltzer that was shaken with an egg white to create a smooth, foamy concoction. Ramos added lime juice, a few drops of orange-flower water, and, most notably, cream, which made the drink even richer but also required much more vigorous shaking to emulsify into a smooth, finished drink. By 1895, Ramos's fizz was so popular that his saloon was commonly referred to as "the gin fizz place." That year, a story in the New Orleans *Times Democrat* described him as "the foremost mixologist of New Orleans." His Imperial Cabinet was portrayed as "an atmosphere of strangely admixtured hustling and luxury." Before the bar stood a row of well-dressed gentlemen, each languidly sipping the house's famous concoction, while behind the bar "the barkeepers leap round with the energy of crickets." The magic began as soon as a customer ordered. The barkeeper combined the ingredients from one bottle after another into a tall glass, which was then handed to one of the many so-called shaker boys standing next to them. "The delicious concoction is shaken and jouseled," the *Times-Democrat* reported, "the ice tinkling against the glass, the rich cream rising, the delicate color becoming richer." Finally, in one deft movement, the mixer removed the silver cover, and "the fizz in all its toothsome glory stands ready to be sipped in ecstasy."

Ramos's cocktail earned him fame as far away as New York, San Francisco, and Paris. During Carnival, his place swarmed with customers, but he and his barmen refused to alter the pace of cocktail shaking. Guests at hotels and in clubs would dispatch waiters bearing silver trays to place orders for a half dozen fizzes at a time in exchange for generous tips. In 1907, Ramos bought the Stag, a saloon located across from the Saint Charles Hotel, and moved his fizz-shaking operations there. During the 1915 Carnival season, he had thirty-two shaker men working behind the forty-foot bar.

The Ramos Gin Fizz

SERVES 1

1 teaspoon superfine sugar
(see note on page 111)

1 tablespoonful freshly
squeezed lemon juice

1 dash orange-flower
water

1 jigger (1½ ounces) Old
Tom gin (see note at right)

1 tablespoon heavy cream

1 egg white

Cracked ice

2 tablespoons club soda or
seltzer water

Combine all of the ingredients into a shaker. Shake five minutes. Strain into a cocktail glass and serve.

A Note on the Gin: Don't use regular London dry gin for this recipe. Ramos made his fizzes from Old Tom gin, which was a good bit sweeter than the dry gin that is omnipresent today. Fortunately, a few sweet Old Tom versions, like Hayman's, are now available on the market. Get your hands on one of these to do a Ramos gin fizz right.

Yes, you read that recipe right. Five minutes. Or at least as long as your arms can hold out. The amount of time that Ramos had his assistants shake his famous cocktail seems to have increased with each telling. In 1895, the New Orleans *Times-Democrat* reported that Ramos's assistants shook the cocktails for two minutes. By 1908, the Kansas City *Star* was reporting the duration as five minutes. In 1921, by which point Prohibition had sent Ramos gin fizzes into retirement, the *New Orleans Item* remembered them being shaken a full ten minutes. Five minutes seems like a reasonable middle ground.

Henry Charles Ramos himself offered the following advice for making a gin fizz: "Be sure to use an airtight shaker and shake and shake until there is not a bubble left but the drink is snowy white and of the consistency of good rich milk. The secret of success lies in the good care you take and your patience; and be certain to use good materials."

The Roffignac

Of all the great cocktails from pre-Prohibition New Orleans, the one that has been most thoroughly forgotten happens to have the most splendidly grandiose name: the Roffignac. It was named for a man known in New Orleans as Joseph Roffignac but whose full name was even more grandiloquent: Count Louis Philippe Joseph de Roffignac. He fled France during the Revolution and established himself as a leading merchant in New Orleans. Roffignac served as mayor of the city from 1820 to 1828, inaugurating under his watch the first paving and lighting of streets. By all accounts, he was a bon vivant and all-around great guy. He didn't invent the drink named in his honor, though, and it's unlikely that he ever tasted it, since he died in 1846, long before any trace of the cocktail appears in print. By the 1890s, though, it was one of New Orleans' signature drinks.

The Roffignac first appeared on the scene at Mannessier's Confectionery, a Royal Street shop known for its ice cream, pastries, and coffee as well as a few stronger libations. In its 1899 guide for Carnival visitors, the New Orleans weekly *Harlequin* included Mannessier's alongside the Sazerac Saloon and the Imperial Cabinet as drinking spots not to be missed, noting that "the Mannessier has a great reputation for its roffignacs."

So what kind of cocktail was it? All published recipes seem to trace back to a single version that Stanley Clisby Arthur included in his slim 1937 volume *Famous New Orleans Drinks and How to Mix 'Em.* It's just a jigger (1½ ounces) of whiskey and a pony (1 ounce) of raspberry syrup topped off with seltzer or soda water. Arthur's instructions note that you could replace the whiskey with Cognac, which was used in the original version of the drink, and instead of raspberry syrup use something called "red hembarig," which he describes as "a popular syrup when old New Orleans was young." Arthur's version isn't a bad drink, but it's really just a raspberry-tinged whiskey soda. Perhaps that old ingredient Arthur alludes to, red hembarig, would make a difference?

Arthur, it turns out, was working phonetically, and what he heard as "red hembarig" was actually "red himbeeressig," a syrup whose name combines the German word for raspberries (*Himbeer*) with the German word for vinegar (*Essig*). To modern palates, raspberry vinegar seems more suited for salad dressings than for cocktails, but it was rather common in drinks a century or more ago, coming out of the medicinal realm. Recipes for raspberry vinegar and raspberry vinegar syrup appear in any number of nineteenth-century handbooks for pharmacists and chemists, though the *National Dispensary* noted that "this syrup has no special medicinal virtues. It forms an agreeable addition to mixtures, and with water a pleasant drink for febrile affections." Back then, febrile affections meant pretty much any medical condition accompanied by a fever, so it might be safe to say that raspberry syrup is good for whatever ails you. During the Civil War, a letter writer to the *New York Times* recommended raspberry vinegar as "a grateful, cooling and wholesome drink for the fevered, sick and wounded."

But why wait until you are sick or wounded? Pharmacists and bartenders alike (and in old New Orleans, these occupations were often one and the same) knew that *Himbeeressig* made an agreeable addition to beverages, and there was plenty of raspberry vinegar syrup floating around pharmacies and soda fountains around the turn of the century. Little wonder that it made its way into a few liquor drinks, especially at Mannessier's Confectionery, an ice cream parlor that offered tempting treats for grown-ups too.

Mannessier's closed in 1914, but the Roffignac lived on at Maylie's Restaurant on Poydras Street, which by the turn of the twentieth century was considered second only to Antoine's among the city's restaurants. The Roffignac survived Prohibition and continued on as the house drink at Maylie's all the way until the restaurant closed in 1986. By then, though, it had evolved into a blend of Cognac and rye with a dose of grenadine and a splash of club soda. If you want to try one the old-school way, use Cognac and raspberry vinegar syrup made following Jerry Thomas's recipe. The preparation of the syrup will give your house a good fumigation, but once it cools and the flavors blend in the fridge overnight, it's truly remarkable: sweet and tangy and complex, the bite of the vinegar mellowed and smoothed by the raspberries and sugar. Use it to mix up a Roffignac with some Cognac and a simple syrup made with Demerara sugar, which has a darker, richer flavor, and you'll find something remarkable. Could this be the original Roffignac, a drink as mild as Coca-Cola but as potent as a Sazerac? It just might.

The Original (Perhaps) Roffignac Cocktail

SERVES 1

1½ ounces Cognac or other good brandy

⅔ ounce simple syrup (page 6)

⅓ ounce himbeeressig syrup

Club soda

Combine the Cognac and syrups in a rocks glass and stir. Fill glass with ice, top with a little club soda, and give one final stir.

Himbeeressig, or Raspberry Vinegar Syrup

MAKES ABOUT 4 CUPS

12 ounces raspberries

3 cups apple cider vinegar

4 cups sugar

Put raspberries and vinegar in a large plastic container and let them soak for eight days. Strain through a fine-mesh sieve, mashing and pressing the raspberries to extract all their juice. Put the liquid in a saucepan along with the sugar, bring to a boil over high heat, stirring to dissolve the sugar. Let it simmer a minute or two, then cool, bottle, and refrigerate. Keeps for several weeks in the refrigerator.

The Sazerac

In 1843, the *Times-Picayune* noted that "the Sunday Mercury says that if you are at a hotel, and wish to call for a beverage compounded of brandy, sugar, absinthe, bitters, and ice, called by the vulgar a cocktail, ask for une queue de chanticleer." This describes to a T what we know today as the Sazerac, but with brandy instead of rye. Such a brandy cocktail had been around for a long time, and made with premium Sazerac Cognac—the product of the French firm Sazerac de Forge et Fils and the most esteemed brand in New Orleans—it would have been natural to call it a Sazerac cocktail. No one person, it seems, actually invented the Sazerac, but there were some definite names and personalities who took the drink and made it famous, and they altered the ingredients a bit along the way.

When we left the story on the eve of the Civil War, the pharmacist Antoine Amédée Peychaud was selling his bright red bitters from his shop at 90 Royal Street. Those bitters were gaining quite a following around New Orleans, and they won a diploma and medal at the 1870 and 1871 Louisiana State Fair. Before long, "the Celebrated Peychaud's Bitters" were being sold by many different pharmacists, grocers, and liquor dealers around the city.

Enter Thomas H. Handy, Civil War veteran, liquor dealer, entrepreneur, and political hack. Handy was born around 1839 in Maryland and moved to New Orleans with his father in 1847. When the Civil War broke out, he was twenty-two years old and working as a clerk in Sewell T. Taylor's retail liquor shop on Royal Street, which was known for its stock of fine Sazerac brandy. Handy served in the Crescent Light Artillery, where he spent time as a POW and injured his leg, and by the time he returned to New Orleans, Sewell Taylor had died and his liquor business dissolved. Handy found work with another firm involved in selling Sazerac brandy, becoming a clerk for John B. Schiller at the Sazerac Coffee House, directly across the street from Taylor's old shop. In 1871, he took over the business, renamed it Thomas H. Handy and Co, and advertised his firm as "Importers of Sazerac Brandy." His stock included "old superior Sazerac Brandy and Sazerac 1805, choice Bourbon and Rye Whiskeys, from the best known distillers, held by us to mature."

Handy was also involved in city politics and a variety of speculative ventures. During the 1870s, he did stints as a member of the school board, the civil sheriff, and livestock inspector, but his biggest venture was running the Canal Street, City Park and Lake Shore Railroad Company, which was founded in 1873 to build a railroad line that ran along the west side of the Orleans canal to the Spanish Fort amusement park on Lake Pontchartrain. In 1876, the firm went bankrupt, and Handy contrived to buy it himself, paying one-third in cash and the rest through a mortgage on the railroad property.

In December 1878, Handy sold his liquor business (but not the building) to a former employee named Vincent Micas. One can only assume that Handy needed the money to make the mortgage payments on his struggling railroad. Micas quickly renamed the firm Vincent Micas and shortly thereafter announced that he had "effected arrangements" with Peychaud to become "sole proprietor of his Celebrated American Aromatic Bitter Cordial." Micas noted that Peychaud "still devotes his personal attention to their manufacture," and connoisseurs would find the product to be fully equal to its former standard. Micas also advertised himself as the "sole agent for Southern States" of Sazerac brandy.

Handy was still unable to pay the note on his street railway business, and in 1879, the company was seized and sold at auction. Handy worked briefly for Vincent Micas as an employee, but by August 1880, he had left to relaunch his firm, which he once again named Thomas H. Handy and Co. and located just a few blocks down the street from Micas's shop. There seems to have been quite a rivalry between the two men. Though Micas declared himself the sole Southern agent for Sazerac brandies, Handy claimed to be an importing agent for the famed brandies too. By 1882, Handy was also selling a product called "Handy's Aromatic Bitter Cordial" that seemed remarkably similar to Peychaud's bitters, for which Micas claimed to be the sole proprietor.

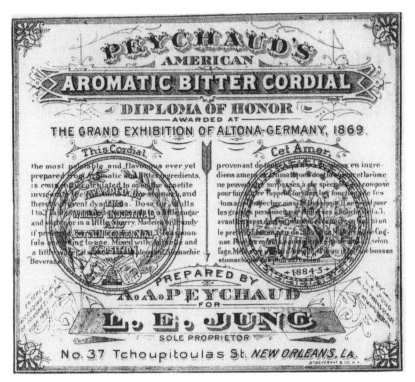

Label for Peychaud's Bitters.

In March 1882, Micas moved his "wholesale and retail liquor establishment and Sazerac bar-room" out of the building owned by his rival and into a new location two blocks away on Camp Street. Less than a month later, workmen began demolishing Handy's old building. As it turns out, Thomas H. Handy was in the process of re-creating the very saloon he once ran. In October 1882, Handy's new establishment, called once again the Sazerac House, held its grand opening in what the *Times-Picayune* described as "an entirely new building, provided with all the modern improvements." This building stood on the same spot as Handy's original saloon, running the length of the short block between Royal Street and Exchange Alley. So now, in a situation that has caused no end of confusion for cocktail historians, we have Vincent Micas running the Sazerac Barroom on Camp Street and Thomas H. Handy running the Sazerac House on Royal and Exchange in the very place where Micas once ran a business by the same name. To add to the confusion, city directories frequently identify Micas's firm as the Sazerac House too.

Peychaud passed away in 1883, and the following year Vincent Micas sold his business. Both Peychaud's bitters and Micas's barroom ended up in the hands of a firm called Baumann and Jung, who began distributing Peychaud's American Aromatic Bitter Cordial on a wide scale. A business guide published in 1885 noted, "There is hardly a bar in the South that it does not ornament. In fact, such is the universal demand for this product, that it may truthfully be said that the saloons 'can not do without it.'" One of the partners, Louis Emmanuel Jung, took over the firm in 1887 and renamed it L. E. Jung and Co. He eventually got out of the bar business, patented Peychaud's formula, and focused on selling bitters. New Orleans was finally left with just one Sazerac House, the one being run by Thomas Handy.

Label for Handy's Bitters.

After Handy died in 1893, a shadowy man named William McQuoid—who had been involved in some of Handy's railroad ventures in the past—teamed up with Handy's widow to run the Thomas H. Handy Company. The firm continued to operate the Sazerac and sell its line of bright red Handy's Aromatic Cocktail Bitters. It was those bitters that got the Handy Company involved in one of the more unusual court cases in the history of the liquor business.

The trouble started in 1894, when a man named Anthony Commander began selling a product he called Commander's Aromatic Cocktail Bitters. (The name Commander might ring a bell for fans of New Orleans fine dining, for Anthony Commander was part of the same family that later opened the legendary restaurant Commander's Palace.) Commander

COMMANDER'S

AROMATIC COCKTAIL BITTERS

These Bitters are the most palatable and flavorous ever yet prepared from aromatic and bitter ingredients it stimulates the appetite and invigorates the functions of the Stomach, thereby preventing dyspepsia

A teaspoonfull can be taken with either Sherry or Madeira, or if preferred with a little Anisette and Brandy with or without water which then makes a very light and pleasant tonic.

PREPARED BY

A. COMMANDER,

SOLE PROPRIETOR

Office 36 Magazine St. 85 Arcade Alley. NEW ORLEANS,

Label for Commander's Bitters.

worked for Handy at the Sazerac House in the late 1880s, and he was rather blatant in imitating his former employer's product. The label on Commander's bottle was absolutely identical to Handy's, down to decorative details, the font, and the text. The only difference was the substitution of the name Commander's for Handy's at the top of the label and of Commander's name and address at the bottom. Commander hired a popular and energetic salesman who promoted his bitters aggressively, claiming they were just as good as Peychaud's but cheaper. He apparently put a considerable dent in the Handy Company's market, for their local sales fell from eighty-one cases a month to a mere twelve. In August 1894, Thomas H. Handy and Co. took Commander to court.

Commander's defense was simple and audacious. Handy, his attorneys claimed, had no right to trademark his bitters because he was simply selling what had been sold as Peychaud's bitters for much longer. Commander couldn't have been trespassing on Handy because, his argument went, Handy was already trespassing on Peychaud! The court ruled in favor of Handy, noting that the Handy Company's branding was very different from Peychaud's bitters, while Commander was clearly copying Handy's branding outright. Handy and Co. was awarded the princely sum of $450.

So now that this bitter legal battle is behind us, let's see if we can find a Sazerac cocktail somewhere in all of this. So far, we have a Sazerac House that dates back to the late 1850s, though its ownership had changed hands and its building had been razed and rebuilt. Brandy cocktails had been served both in New Orleans (and just about everywhere else) since the antebellum era, and some were even flavored with a splash of absinthe. Sazerac de Forge et Fils had long been the most prized brandy in the city, though by the time of the bitters dispute, it had become rare and prohibitively expensive, thanks to the phylloxera epidemic that had all but decimated French brandy production in the 1870s. The signature drink served at the Sazerac House took on the actual name Sazerac cocktail sometime in the 1890s, and by this point it was being made with rye, not brandy. In 1902, the *New Orleans Item* declared that Thomas H. Handy and Company's Sazerac cocktail was "one of the institutions that has made New Orleans famous among visitors." Thomas H. Handy and Company trademarked the brand name Sazerac and began selling a premixed bottled version of the cocktail. The firm established agencies in large cities across the country as well as in London and

Hamburg, and it advertised its products in newspapers across the country. (And it still does today, since the Sazerac Company, as the firm is now known, includes Buffalo Trace, Glenmore, Barton, and Medley along with Sazerac rye in its stable of brands.)

As of 1915, the Sazerac House, still at the same Royal Street location, was selling the "world renowned Sazerac cocktails" for twenty cents each. A New Orleans classic had arrived.

Southern Punch:
"The Killer of Time,
the Destroyer of Bitter Memory,
the Mortal Enemy of Despair"

In most of the country, punch had fallen out of favor long before the Civil War. As the tavern gave way to the saloon, the libations of the colonial era—toddies, slings, flip, and punch—were eclipsed by single-serving formulations like cocktails, juleps, crustas, and fizzes. The new mixologists of the hotel bar put their ornate bowls and ladles into storage and replaced them with shakers and bar tumblers. In the South, though, punch lived on, but not as a libation for tipplers whiling away an evening at the punch house. It became instead the traditional lubricant for large ritual gatherings, with secret recipes concocted by members of militia units and social clubs and handed down from one generation of members to the next.

But let's set the proper expectations here. If you grew up in the South, you may be thinking of booze-free pink fruity drinks or that big glass bowl with a ring of lime sherbet floating in it at the wedding receptions in the church fellowship hall—the kind that some joker was always trying to spike with vodka. That's not the sort of punch we are talking about here. There would have been no need to spike the punch at a gathering in the late nineteenth-century South for it was foundationally an alcoholic thing.

Chatham Artillery Punch

In the 1850s, the Republican Blues, an elite Savannah militia unit, traveled to drill with the companies in Macon. Upon their return home to Savannah, they were welcomed by the city's other elite militia unit, the Chatham Artillery, and Sergeant A. B. Luce of the artillery concocted a new punch for the occasion. He took a horse-watering bucket, filled it with ice, then poured in a quart each of brandy, whiskey, and rum along with sugar and lemon juice. Then he filled the bucket to the brim with Champagne and stirred it together.

The punch was a hit—literally. Looking back on the occasion in 1885, the *Augusta Chronicle* recalled that "every single man of the Blues was put under the table by this deceiving, diabolical and most delightful compound." That concoction became the signature beverage of the Chatham Artillery, broken out at any and all important occasions in the city of Savannah. "As a vanquisher of men," the *Chronicle* concluded, "its equal has never been found. It is as mild as a syllabub, seemingly, but it conquers like a cyclone."

The Chatham Artillery had been organized in 1786, and like all militia units, their original purpose had been to serve as military reserves in case of war. The line militia units, which most men joined, met for drilling infrequently—as seldom as twice per year. The elite units like the Chatham Artillery functioned more like semi-independent social organizations, complete with corporate charters, bylaws, and dues. During the Civil War, most militia units had been absorbed into the Confederate army (the Chatham Artillery had served as Wheaton's Company of the Georgia Artillery). But afterward, the units returned to their more usual role as reservists and, in the case of the elite units, at least, prestigious, self-selected social clubs. They played a ceremonial role in civic celebrations and parades, and they escorted prominent politicians who came to visit a community. A committee of stewards elected from the unit's members was responsible for planning parades, securing meeting spaces, and, perhaps most important, providing the refreshments for company gatherings.

The Chatham Artillery's favorite form of refreshment soon gained national notoriety. In 1886, the artillery celebrated the centenary of the unit's founding, and they prepared a large quantity of punch for the occasion. "When the affair is fired off," the *Macon Telegraph* predicted, "three States will feel the shock, and an epidemic of headache sweep the whole coast country." The *Western Druggist*, a journal published far away in Chicago, described it as "the killer of time, the destroyer of bitter memory, the mortal enemy of despair." The oldest member of the Chatham Artillery was always the custodian of the precious secret formula for the punch, and when he died, the recipe was passed on the next oldest member.

If you get a chance to sample Chatham Artillery Punch and end up getting laid low by it, don't feel bad. In its day, that potent brew took out many a strong imbiber, including famous war heroes like Admiral George

Dewey, who had led the US victory over the Spanish fleet at the Battle of Manila Bay in 1898. Dewey's exploits made him a national hero, and he was honored by parades and gala balls all across the country, including a big Dewey Day in Savannah in 1900, which at least thirty militia companies and five bands traveled to attend.

Admiral Dewey and his wife arrived on a special train from Washington the morning of March 19. Despite a gusty rain, the streets from the station to their hotel were lined with cheering crowds. The weather had lifted by the following morning, and Dewey took a river excursion on the revenue cutter *Hamilton*. A public reception was arranged that evening at 9:00 p.m., and five thousand people gathered at the DeSoto Hotel to salute the admiral. Shortly before the event was to begin, they were informed that Dewey had taken ill during the river cruise and was still too indisposed to appear. Most newspapers accounts were discreet, reporting the admiral's malady as merely "indigestion" that had occurred during the cruise. Some, like the *Boston Herald* added a few more relevant details, noting that "as a result of a combination of 'artillery punch,' of which the admiral drank only a glass, and salad, he had a severe attack of indigestion, and was compelled to leave the table."

The admiral rallied the next day, and fifty thousand people thronged the streets of Savannah to watch some four thousand troops parade in his honor. The Chatham Artillery, having given the admiral one sort of explosive salute the day before, saluted him during the festivities with a volley from the brass ordnance that had been presented to them by George Washington more than a century before. One can only imagine what that cannon fire did for the good admiral's head.

By the time Admiral Dewey encountered Chatham Artillery punch, it had been somewhat modified from its original antebellum form. The Savannah *Morning News* tracked down the gentleman responsible for the concoction served to Dewey on his trip down the river. The punch maker, who requested anonymity, insisted that his creation wasn't strong at all. "The admiral simply could not stand acids," he declared, "and there is much of it from the fruit that is used." The punch served to the admiral had been made from two gallons of Catawba wine, one gallon of Santa Cruz rum, and a case of Champagne augmented by half a gallon of tea, the juice of three dozen lemons, three cans of sliced pineapple, a jar of maraschino cherries, and six sliced oranges. "'Chatham Artillery Punch,' its maker explained, "is not what it was formerly. Why it is weak as water in comparison to that which was once mixed for the mystification of all who indulged in it."

Here, then, is a recipe for Chatham Artillery Punch, and it's my best approximation of the "weak as water" version that laid out Admiral Dewey.

Admiral Dewey's Artillery Punch

SERVES 1 THIRSTY
ARTILLERY UNIT AND
GUESTS (AROUND 160)

2 gallons Catawba wine

1 gallon Santa Cruz rum

½ gallon tea

Juice of 3 dozen lemons

3 cans sliced pineapple

1 jar maraschino cherries

6 sliced oranges

6 bottles Champagne

Prepare the base punch stock in advance. Combine the Catawba wine, rum, tea, and lemon juice in a large container and stir well. Cover and let stand for up to a week, stirring every now and then. At serving time, pour into a large punch bowl filled with ice. Add the fruit and the Champagne and stir well to blend. And, no, this punch is not as weak as water.

A Note on the Spirits: Most artillery punch recipes call specifically for Santa Cruz rum, which once meant rum produced on what is now called Saint Croix in the US Virgin Islands. (The Spanish called it Santa Cruz.) Today Saint Croix is home to Cruzan Rum Distillery, one of the world's largest rum producers, but its main product is a clean, lighter-bodied rum more in the style of the Cuban rum that became popular after Prohibition. Most cocktail enthusiasts seem to agree that Appletons X/V, which hails from nearby Jamaica, is probably more similar to the heavy, dark rum that would have been used back in the glory days of Chatham Artillery punch.

Good luck finding Catawba wine these days. In *Imbibe!* David Wondrich recommends substituting for Catawba "any sweetish white—yea, even unto a white Zinfandel." I'm not so sure about that. As we saw in chapter 9, most Americans in the nineteenth century found the Catawba wine to be too dry for their tastes, and it wasn't until Nicholas Longworth made a sparkling wine from the Catawba grapes that he found a ready market. I would recommend subbing in either Champagne or a drier white wine in recipes that call for Catawba wine and not (shudder!) a white Zinfandel.

Charleston Light Dragoon Punch

Just up the coast from Savannah, the Charleston Light Dragoons had
a punch of their own, and its potent formula achieved its own measure
of infamy. Founded in 1791, the Light Dragoons were an elite cavalry
unit composed of some of the city's wealthiest residents. The unit had
served in the Civil War as Company K of the Fourth Regiment South
Carolina Cavalry and saw considerable action. It was right after the Civil
War that they first concocted the punch that became the signature of
their gatherings.

Many different recipes for Charleston Light Dragoon Punch have been
published over the years. The ingredients they all share are whiskey, rum,
sugar, lemons, sparkling water, cherries, and ice. Brandy appears in some
recipes but not others, as does tea, raspberry cordial, pineapple, oranges,
and ginger ale. The earliest version I've been able to find appeared in an
odd volume called *Favorite Food of Famous Folk* (1900), which was compiled
by, of all people, the Ladies of the Guild of St. James Parish Church in
Pewee Valley, Kentucky. Sarah Barnwell Elliott, a Savannah-born novelist
and women's rights advocate, contributed the recipe for Charleston Light
Dragoon Punch. Her note accompanying the recipe says simply, "I send
you the best punch recipe that I know . . . it comes from Charleston, S.C.,
where they know a good deal about such delightful things."

A few years later, another version was published in a volume called
*Famous Old Receipts Used for a Hundred Years or More in the Kitchens of
the North and South* (1908). The author notes that he secured the recipe
"through the kindness of Mr. Louis F. Sloan, who now concocts it for all
the functions the Dragoons have." Sloan, a cotton broker and commercial
merchant, was the unit's designated punch maker in the early 1900s. A
good four decades later, John Laurens contributed his version of Charleston
Light Dragoon punch to the Junior League's volume *Charleston Receipts*
(1950), and since it's a classic Charleston cookbook that has never been out
of print, that recipe has received the widest circulation in recent years.

The ingredients in Sarah Barnwell Elliott's version are similar to those
in the Chatham Artillery Punch, starting with a quart each of whiskey,
rum, and French brandy along with lemon juice and sugar. To this, though,
Elliott adds black tea, maraschino cherries, and, instead of Champagne, it
gets its fizziness from Apollinaris water and ginger ale. The Sloan version
is a little simpler, with no brandy, tea, or ginger ale. It calls for a whole lot
of whiskey (1½ gallons) and a touch of Jamaican rum (just ½ pint) cut

with sugar and lemon juice, plus maraschino cherries, sliced pineapple, and a small tumbler of raspberry cordial for flavoring. Instead of sugar, the 1950 version from John Laurens gets its sweetness from a combination of grenadine, curaçao, and raspberry syrups, and he adds a dose of green tea and orange juice to the mix.

Of the three, the version published in *Famous Old Receipts*, being attributed directly to Louis Sloan, seems closest to the source, but each version has interesting ingredients that aspiring punch makers could try. The recipe below is based on Sloan's, with a few mixing details borrowed from John Laurens's version in *Charleston Receipts*.

Pre-Prohibition Charleston Light Dragoon Punch

SERVES 28

5 lemons

½ pound Demerara or turbinado sugar

1 cup water

1½ liters rye whiskey (Rittenhouse bottled in bond would do nicely)

250 milliliters (⅓ bottle) Jamaican rum (such as Appleton V/X)

1 small (10 ounces) jar maraschino cherries

1 can (14 ounces) sliced pineapple

4 ounces raspberry cordial

1½ liters Apollinaris or other sparkling water

Juice the lemons and strain to remove the pulp. Combine the lemon juice, sugar, and water in a saucepan over medium-high heat. Stir until the sugar is dissolved, remove pan from heat, and allow to cool. Pour lemon and syrup mixture into a large jug or similar container, then add the whiskey, rum, cherries, pineapple, and raspberry cordial, stirring constantly as you add each ingredient to ensure they blend properly. Allow to rest refrigerated at least four days before use, stirring it periodically.

At serving time, place a large block of ice (which you can make by filling a large pan like a loaf pan with water and freezing) in a punch bowl, pour over the punch stock, and add the sparking water. Stir to blend and, if you like, garnish by floating a few very thin slices of lemon on the surface.

The Charleston Light Dragoons continued on as a military and social organization for the sons of the some of the city's most prominent families until the early twentieth century. The unit served in France in World War I as the Headquarters Company of the Thirtieth Division, and after the armistice was disbanded. The veterans met occasionally for several more years, but as an official organization the elite unit was no more.

Their famous punch lived on, though. The noted Charleston gardener Emily Whaley had an encounter with Light Dragoon Punch on her wedding day in 1934, which she recalled in her memoir *Mrs. Whaley Entertains*. Instead of rye whiskey, this version was made with moonshine. It steeped for several days, and when the guests arrived at the reception at her father's house, they found the punch waiting in large ice-cold basins. It didn't take long for the potent brew to have its effect. One guest, Whaley recalls, wound up trapped in the kitchen, unable to get his bearings and find his way out. He ended up disposing of his portion of the punch in the woodbox. One groomsman managed to lure a bridesmaid off to a comfortable bench in the garden where, Mrs. Whaley recalled, "in the middle of his tender, loving speech he threw up." The reception and the marriage it celebrated continued unimpeded, but young Mrs. Whaley learned an important lesson about entertaining. "To this day," she declares in her memoir, "I won't serve a punch. You just can't gauge how strong they are."

Other Famous Southern Punches

The Chatham Artillery and Charleston Light Dragoon are the most famous of the Southern militia punches, but other companies made their own punches, too, though their recipes have been lost to the hangovers of history. Punch was more than a militia tradition. In nineteenth-century Charleston, it was served at the most formal of occasions, like the Saint Cecilia Society ball. Established in 1766 as a musical society to stage subscription concerts, it had evolved into a purely social organization by the time of the Civil War, holding balls each January and February for the city's elite. The names of the society's members were secret, as were the dates of their balls. Invitations were delivered directly to members' homes by servants wearing white gloves. Early in the twentieth century, as more and more ambitious men sought to join, the society limited its membership to male descendants of previous members—a pretty sure way to keep out carpetbagging financiers and local insurance salesmen. During the Depression, the society started limiting itself to a single annual ball, and that tradition continues today. The gentlemen still dress in tails, the ladies still carry cards to schedule dance partners, and the socially ambitious in Charleston still fall all over themselves to try to get in the door.

Saint Cecilia Punch

5 lemons

750 milliliters brandy

1 pineapple

1¼ pounds sugar

3 cups green tea

375 milliliters (½ bottle) Jamaican rum (such as Appleton V/X)

750 milliliters peach brandy (see note below)

3 liters Champagne

1½ liters carbonated water

Slice the lemons thinly and put them in a jar with the brandy. Allow to steep for 24 hours. Several hours before serving time, brew 3 cups of green tea and, while still hot, add in the sugar and stir until dissolved. Slice the pineapple and put it into your punch bowl along with the lemon slices and the brandy they steeped in. Add the sweetened tea, rum, and peach brandy. Stir well and allow to rest refrigerated until serving time.

When ready to serve, add the Champagne and carbonated water and stir to blend.

A Note on Peach Brandy: Good luck getting your hands on that (see chapter 3 for details). Depending upon where you live, you might be able to use something like Peach Street Distillers peach brandy. If you can't, though, please do not use a bottle of the flavored neutral spirits sold as peach brandy today. Old-school peach brandy does not have much, if any, of a peach flavor to it. Use a good apple brandy instead, such as Laird's bottled in bond.

Otranto Club Punch

The Otranto Club was a hunting organization that owned a large parcel of land about ten miles outside of Charleston. The land used to be part of a plantation named Otranto, and the organization used the old plantation dwelling as their clubhouse. They also came up with their own signature punch for club gatherings, the recipe for which was included in *200 Years of Charleston Cooking.*

Otranto Club Punch is notable for not being notable—that is, for its deceptively bland flavor. When mixed together, the green tea, sugar, and lemon somehow manage to almost completely neutralize the harsh bite of the brandy and rum (and the rye, too, if you're using it). It tastes for all the world like a drink that's been heavily watered down, and yet the alcoholic ingredients outnumber the nonalcoholic by a whopping 3-to-1 ratio (plus whatever sparkling water suits your taste). In other words, it will knock you on your keister before you even realize it.

Otranto Club Punch

SERVES 20 TO 30

12 ounces Demerara or
turbinado sugar

3 cups strong green tea

Juice of 10 lemons,
strained

750 milliliters peach
brandy (see note on
peach brandy in Saint
Cecilia Punch recipe,
page 197)

750 milliliters Jamaican
rum (such as Appleton
V/X)

1½ liters California
brandy or good rye
whiskey (I'm partial to
a rye like Rittenhouse)

Appolinaris or sparkling
water

Dissolve the sugar in the warm green tea. Add the lemon juice, peach brandy, rum, and the brandy or rye and allow to steep (several days greatly improves it). At serving time, fill a bowl with ice, pour over the punch stock, and top with as much Appollinaris or sparkling water as suits your taste. Or to serve individual portions, fill rocks glasses with ice, pour a few ounces of the stock into each, and top with sparkling water.

The Decline of Punch

During the twentieth century, old-fashioned punch recipes gradually gave way to debased imitations. Punch blenders started adding a lot of cut-up fruit to the bowl, and increasingly it was canned fruit instead of fresh. Bottled or frozen juices replaced freshly squeezed, and soda water or ginger ale supplanted Champagne. The original punch recipes were essentially bowls of booze cut with just enough sugar, citrus, and tea to fool imbibers' tongues into thinking they weren't drinking pure liquor. Prohibition pretty much put an end to that practice, and punch emerged on the other side a pale, sickly-sweet shadow of its former self. By the time the Junior League of Charleston published its famous cookbook *Charleston Receipts* in 1950, the ingredients list for the Charleston Light Dragoon punch had expanded to include both red and white canned cherries along with a quart of grenadine syrup, a bottle of curaçao syrup, a quart of raspberry syrup, and the juice of six dozen oranges. Punch continued its long decline from there. Alcohol was eliminated altogether, and soon the giant blocks or rings of ice that were floated in the bowls were replaced by floating blobs of lime sherbet and other indignities.

These days, though, classic Southern-style punch is starting to be rediscovered for the beauty that it is. It's turning up on the cocktail menus at the South's more ambitious bars, where bartenders are not only re-creating the old traditional recipes of the militia companies and social clubs but also are starting to create their own varieties, many of which— as they were as far back as the colonial days—are allowed to steep and mellow in jugs and barrels for weeks or even months. Far from a tame refreshment for teetotalers, we are learning, this old-school concoction can really pack a punch.

16

Southern Suds:
The South Masters Brewing

Beer—especially pale lagers in their modified, industrial American incarnation—is an inseparable part of present-day Southern culture, be it Miller High Life tallboys drunk in the infield of stock car races or cans of Bud passed around at Lowcountry South Carolina oyster roasts. Over the past decade or two, the products of the big breweries have been joined by the output of a flourishing new microbrewing and craft brewing industry. In 2013, the Brewers Association tabulated more than 450 craft breweries in operation in the South. Southern beer drinking has never ridden higher than it is today.

Or has it? Southern food historians have tended to give beer a quick, dismissive treatment and move on to other subjects, making a passing reference to a few notable Southern brands like Dixie and Lone Star or novelties like Billy Beer, that short-lived marketing scheme from Jimmy Carter's somewhat disreputable brother. Far more attention has been given to the South's notable contributions to the world of soft drinks— Coca-Cola, Pepsi Cola, Barq's Root Beer, RC Cola, Dr. Pepper. Beer was certainly rare in the antebellum South, since the climate and lack of ingredients made it difficult to produce locally, but matters were very different during the New South era. The forty-year period between 1870 and 1910, in fact, marked the golden era of Southern beer, and the South developed a flourishing brewing industry that made a wealth of regionally brewed brands available to its residents.

Here's my advice for enjoying a nice beverage with this chapter: go down to your local good beer store and buy yourself a growler. Two decades ago this would have been virtually impossible for most Southerners, but today, if you live in a city of any decent size, you can pull it off. For your selection, look for something produced within one hundred miles of your home, and don't buy some dark ale or hopped-up IPA. For classic Southern beer, you'll want a crisp, clear lager, like the Charleston Lager from

Palmetto Brewery in Charleston or the American Common Lager from Fullsteam Brewery in Durham, North Carolina.

Take it home, keep it cool, and enjoy a tall glass on your back porch on a warm summer afternoon. That's precisely what Southerners were doing back at the turn of the twentieth century.

The Germans to the Rescue

The first few generations of British immigrants to the South had to abandon their native beer, but a later wave of immigrants—those arriving primarily from Germany—refused to let go so easily. They found inventive ways to brew beer despite the obstacles of climate and geography, and their efforts not only allowed their fellow German-Americans to enjoy good beer but, after two centuries of scarcity, finally brought to reality the long-running Southern dream of an abundant beer supply.

New Orleans had the highest proportion of foreign-born immigrants of any Southern city. From 1820 to 1870, it was one of the country's busiest points of entry, second only to New York City in the number of newcomers who arrived through its port. At the start of the Civil War, Louisiana boasted some twenty-five thousand German-born residents, most of whom lived in New Orleans. After the war, Germans continued moving to the city in large numbers, both directly from Germany as well as from Northern cities, turning their eyes southward and seeking agricultural opportunity. By 1870, the state of Louisiana boasted more than fifty German-language newspapers and magazines, and an estimated one-fifth of the state's population spoke German.

Back in Germany, the beverage of choice for these immigrants had been lager beer, but that was hard to get their hands on in New Orleans. The heat of the South had always impeded brewing, and for lager, it made things doubly difficult. A fragile yeast is used to make lager, and the wort—the sweet, grain-infused base—is fermented at a much lower temperature than English-style ale. The cool temperature slows the chemical reactions that convert sugar to alcohol, resulting in a clearer, crisper brew. In Bavaria, German brewers did their work in the late fall and stored their beer all winter covered with ice harvested from nearby lakes—hence the name lager, which means "storage" or "warehouse" in German.

In the antebellum American South, there was no place for brewers to lagern their beer on ice, so German immigrants in New Orleans had to make do the best they could. They tried at first to import true lager from Northern brewers. Saloonkeeper Christian Kolst imported the first recorded shipment of lager from Pittsburgh's Schenk Brewery. By 1854, beer was arriving regularly from Philadelphia's Engel and Wolf and trade with other brewing cities, including Saint Louis and Milwaukee, soon followed. Such trade was expensive and unpredictable, though. Without climate-controlled shipping and storage, barrels of beer often froze in the winter and exploded in the heat of summer, so imported lager remained an expensive luxury.

Most families had to make do with a home-brewed version called city beer, a low-grade product that tasted, as one drinker put it, like "a molasses brew and wormwood." By 1845, two men named Wirth and Fischer had opened the Stadtsbreuerei (City Brewery). At least five other breweries produced city beer during the 1850s, all for local consumption, since the product did not keep well enough to ship. Germans in New Orleans did what they could to preserve their beer drinking culture, including opening several beer gardens in the Bayou Saint John neighborhood. The largest of these, the Tivoli Garden, was described in the newspapers as "thickly planted with choice trees and shrubbery beneath which were benches and tables, and amid which were latticed bowers and arbors." Within these gardens, men and women enjoyed both imported lager and local city beer along with food and conversation, and they danced in a large, open ballroom to waltzes played by German musicians. The *Picayune* noted that "German beer, quite bitter and strongly flavored with hops, was the favorite beverage, accompanied by a curious German doughnut and ginger cakes." Another writer described the "beer men with large baskets filled with beer jugs, which pop like champagne bottles and emit a frothy, yellow fluid that will make you sleep before it makes you tipsy."

A few German immigrants made efforts at establishing breweries in other Southern cities too. Egidius Fechter, who was born in Baden-Württemberg, Germany, arrived in Atlanta in the early 1850s and started a brewery near Howell Park in the West End. Fechter most likely was making schenk or "steam beer," which could be produced in three days without refrigeration but had limited shelf life. In 1858, Fechter's brother Dionis opened his own operation, called the City Brewery. Both breweries appear to have suspended operations during the Civil War, bringing a halt to Atlanta's supply of locally brewed beer.

After the Civil War, the industrious German brewers of New Orleans decided it was time to figure out how to make proper lager in the South. Georg Merz had begun brewing city beer at Old Canal Steam Brewery in the 1850s, and on December 1, 1864, he introduced the first locally brewed lager to the city. Merz used ice shipped in from Maine to cool the beer, but this source proved unreliable and prohibitively expensive. So he started experimenting with mechanical refrigeration. Around 1870, he imported a small ammonia absorption machine made by Charles Tellier of France and soon had it operational in his brewery. A reporter visited the factory in 1872 and reported that the machine "supplied the large storeroom, holding five thousand barrels of ale and lager beer, with dry cold air at a temperature of fifty degrees, the temperature outside being eighty five degrees."

While Merz's lager found a ready market with New Orleans residents, he does not appear to have sold any outside of the city. Brewers initially faced numerous challenges to selling beer at any appreciable distance from the place where it was brewed. Their product was highly perishable, going flat and stale very quickly. Ceramic containers were expensive, and glass bottles were fragile and prone to breakage. But a series of new inventions made things a lot better. Cold filtration systems allowed brewers to rack pure beer directly into bottles and kegs, and with pasteurization—heating the finished beer to 145 degrees and cooling it in the bottles—they could kill the microbes and wild yeasts that lead to spoilage. New manufacturing techniques developed after the Civil War made glass bottles cheaper and more durable, and new types of stoppers and closures replaced unreliable corks and kept the beer fresher. The Hutchinson stopper, patented in 1879, used a wire loop to seal a rubber gasket in the top of the bottle. More popular for beer bottling was the so-called lightning stopper, which used a porcelain or rubber plug held fast by a thick wire over the top. In 1892, William Painter invented the crown cap—a metal cap with a cork gasket that was crimped onto the top of the bottle, forming a tight seal. The crown cap proved the most durable and long-lasting form of sealing bottles. By 1915, all major bottlers had switched to the cap, which is still the predominant closure for bottled beer today.

Most important for bringing beer to Southern drinkers in bulk, though, was the postwar railroad boom, for the new rail systems allowed brewers to ship their beer long distances and develop broad distribution networks developed through a system of agents. At first, much of this beer was being made outside of the South. Cincinnati, with its large population of German immigrants, had eighteen active breweries producing 550,000 barrels per year, and much of that beer was shipped southward. In the early 1880s, W. O. Muller of Asheville, North Carolina, was an agent for "the celebrated" Foss and Schneider Cincinnati lager beer. Hermann Schubert, the proprietor of Schubert's Hotel in Knoxville, advertised himself as the sole agent for Kauffman's lager beer, a major Cincinnati brand that sold more than fifty thousand barrels a year in its flourishing Southern trade. The city of Cincinnati did not have the Southern market all to itself. In addition to the Cincinnati beer from brewer C. Mortimer, Theodore Joseph of Raleigh advertised that his saloon carried a full line of bottled beer that included Jacob Seeger's Baltimore lager, Frederick Lauer's Reading, Pennsylvania, lager, E. Anheuser's Saint Louis Bavarian Beer, and the Celebrated Star Lager from Saint Louis.

The prominence of Northern and Midwestern beer in the Southern trade began to ebb in the mid-1880s, when the South's own brewing industry began to flourish. The seeds had been planted just before the Civil War in the border state of Kentucky, where cold winters and milder summers allowed access to natural ice and cool underground storage facilities, making brewing feasible for a substantial portion of the year. Those conditions coupled with Louisville's large immigrant population helped that city develop a number of breweries by the eve of the Civil War. Farther to the east, the Robert Portner Brewing Company of Alexandria, Virginia, developed one of the first major Southern beer distribution networks. Portner, a native of Prussia, founded his brewery during the Civil War and established a flourishing trade among occupying Union soldiers. He branched out after the war and started selling beer to saloonkeepers across the Potomac River in Washington, DC, and soon the nation's capital was his largest market. But he was competing against sixteen other brewers for the DC business and needed new markets. To the north and west, established German-American breweries already had Pennsylvania locked up. The state of Virginia, however, offered virtually a wide-open field.

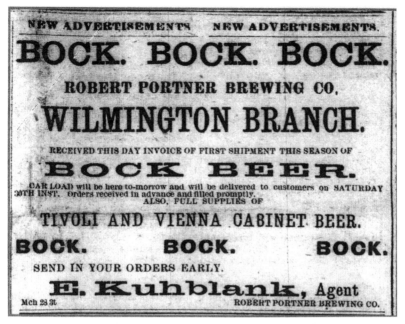

Advertisement for Robert Portner's Bock, 1889.

Portner established a branch location and bottling plant, which he called his Southern depot, in Norfolk in 1876. A growing railroad hub, the city gave him access to towns throughout the James and York River valleys. The Norfolk branch showed brisk sales, so in 1880, Portner added more branches in Lynchburg, Virginia, and Charlotte and Wilmington, North Carolina. In 1881, he pushed even farther south to Augusta. Portner's Export Tivoli brand beer was advertised in Augusta as "Always on Hand . . . in kegs and bottles for family use and shipping." The beer typically sold for $2.50 for a dozen quart bottles, which included a deposit on the containers.

After the Civil War, Dionis Fechter reopened his Atlanta City Brewery at its original location on Marietta Street, and in 1868, he and several partners opened a new, larger brewery at corner of Harris and Collins (now Courtland) Streets, where they employed ten workers and produced both lager and porter. One of his partners, Michael Kries, set out on his own and founded the Fulton Brewery in 1866. The firm sold its lager and ale by the keg, gallon, or in whatever pitchers or pails their customers brought to the brewery. Other competing breweries soon opened their doors, including the short-lived Atlanta Steam Brewery and the Georgia

Spring Brewery in the West End, which was both a brewery and a destination resort complete with dancing platforms, a saloon, shooting gallery, and a small lake with boats.

Dionis Fechter died in 1874, and his brother Egidius inherited his interest in the Atlanta City Brewery. By 1875, Egidius had added an ice machine built by the Columbus Iron Works, and within three years the company had $60,000 in capital investment and was producing ten thousand barrels of beer each year, which it was starting to distribute across the South in competition with big brewers like Portner. The brewery made its own kegs and barrels on the spot—as many as 550 per day—using Georgia oak staves bound with strong iron hoops, and it malted its own barley too. Those grains were boiled for twelve to fifteen hours in a giant copper kettle with a one hundred–barrel capability, creating a wort that was cooled by flowing over a series of ice water–filled copper cylinders into a fermenting tub in the cellar. After fermenting for twenty days, it was moved into a 1,600-gallon resting tank in one of the brewery's nine underground vaults, where it was stored surrounded by blocks of ice for thirty days then moved into another reservoir filled with beechwood shavings, which filtered and purified the beer, for another thirty days. The operation consumed the entire output of the Atlanta Ice Factory, some two thousand tons per year, and employed twenty-five people. "The employees of the brewery," a reporter from the *Macon Telegraph* noted, "drink beer all the time, and yet they are never drunk. Their bibulous capacity is simply extraordinary."

The success of the Atlanta City Brewery and its peers caused other brewers to turn their eyes southward, and most of them were German-born immigrants who got their start in the breweries farther north. Philip Schillinger, for instance, who ran the Phoenix Brewing Company in Louisville, visited the rapidly growing city of Birmingham, Alabama, in 1884, and as a local business directory later explained it, "was quick to perceive the many advantages offered, chief among them central location and clear field." Along with three of his sons, Schillinger moved south and opened the Birmingham Brewery, complete with two Arctic refrigerators to cool the cellars and storage vaults. By 1886, they were selling ten thousand barrels a year, primarily within the city.

Around the same time, two German-American brothers-in-law, Edward W. Herman of Louisville, Kentucky, and August J. Schweers of Cincinnati, moved to Augusta, Georgia, where they broke ground on a

TRY

"Belle

OF

Carolina,"

PURE EXPORT
BEER,

AND BE CON-
VINCED.

Brewed and bot-
tled by

Augusta

Brewing

Company.

A. BINDEWALD, Mgr.,
Charlotte, N. C.

Advertisement for Augusta Brewing Company's Belle
of the Carolinas beer, 1897.

brewery in July 1888. Adjoining the brewery were the company's offices
and bottling plant along with a cooper's shop for making barrels and
kegs and a wagon shed and blacksmith's shop that supported the teams
of horses and delivery wagons. Emblazoned on the side of the brewery
building in bold, ten-foot-high white letters were the words Belle of
Georgia, the company's flagship brand. Herman and Schweers also
launched a Belle of Carolina brand, which was sold across the Savannah
River in neighboring South Carolina, along with Dixie, Palmetto State,
and Bohemian.

These new Southern breweries used networks of agents to take
their beer to markets outside the city in which it was brewed. An agent
generally contracted to receive beer in barrels or kegs, and he would, in
turn, bottle it and sell it locally. Bottled beer was particularly popular
in saloons, but it was beginning to be drunk in private homes as well,
and beer agents regularly made home deliveries. In June 1898, the
Augusta Brewing Company advertised in the Columbia, South Carolina,
newspapers that they sold their Export Beer, Belle of Carolina, and

Palmetto State beers "exclusively by beer dispensaries." They listed nine agents in the state, ranging from Greenville in the western part of the state to Darlington in the east. Other agents took the brewery's products throughout Georgia and into North Carolina.

The town of Salisbury, North Carolina, offers a representative example of how expansive the beer distribution network had become by the early twentieth century. In 1907, the seventeen thousand residents of Salisbury had a choice of three different lager beers, all of which were produced in the South. Charles H. Russler was an agent of the East Tennessee Brewing Company, which shipped its beers 250 miles from Knoxville, Tennessee. Jonathan F. Ludwick represented the Augusta Brewing Company from some 200 miles south in Georgia. And Daniel L. Springs bottled and sold beer that was shipped in 350 miles from the Robert Portner Brewing Company in Alexandria.

Within cities, breweries developed a network of saloons to get their product into the hands of patrons. These became known as tied houses because of their exclusive ties to a single brewery. The Birmingham Brewery, for instance, bought or leased buildings that they, in turn, rented to saloonkeepers, who were obligated to sell only their product. The firm also extended loans to their tenants to help them pay for expensive beer and liquor licenses. Their local rival, the Schillinger Brewing Company, not only bought an extensive amount of real estate in Birmingham but also owned and operated some local saloons outright, many of them serving the city's large African-American population.

The King of Beers Emerges

Just as it had in the whiskey industry, the industrialization of beer production drove scale and consolidation in the beer trade. Through larger production, brewers were able to decrease their marginal costs. With refrigeration and mechanization, they could produce beer more cheaply and year-round. And with improved bottling techniques and the efficient distribution system provided by railroads, they could ship their product greater and greater distances. These changes favored the larger manufacturers. In the North and the Midwest, it meant the large industrial breweries were able to squeeze out the smaller regional ones, many of which failed in the 1870s and 1880s. The situation intensified in the 1890s when English investor syndicates consolidated and vertically integrated many of the major American breweries, increasing production and slicing prices to gain a national market share. Soon those giant brewers began looking southward too.

No one man more fully embodied the new realities of industrial brewing than Adolphus Busch of Saint Louis, Missouri. The youngest of twenty-one children, Busch immigrated to America in 1857 and settled in Saint Louis, where he became a partner in the brewery founded by his father-in-law, Eberhard Anheuser. Adolphus Busch was less a brewer—he hired men to do that for him—than a master marketer. He conquered the Saint Louis market by hiring so-called collectors who visited each saloon that carried Busch's beer, spending generously to treat patrons to the company's brand and regaling them with tales and orations. The collectors visited the weddings and funerals of prominent personages like saloonkeepers and wholesalers and lavished them with gifts during the holidays. Busch issued a series of commemorative paintings illustrating historical events like Custer's last fight as well a portrait of Busch himself with the Prussian statesman Otto von Bismarck. Eventually, Busch found an even better way to ensure a loyal network of saloons as his customers: he helped aspiring saloonkeepers obtain their city license, glassware and fixtures, and a lease on a storefront. In exchange, he charged the new customer nine dollars per keg instead of six dollars, to offset the expenses sunk in establishing the joint.

Beyond just conquering Saint Louis, Busch soon figured out how to take his product nationwide. In the 1870s, he and his partners developed a method of pasteurizing beer, which allowed it to stand up to temperature fluctuations and, consequently, be transported long distances. He also teamed up with a local merchant named Conrad to create an American version of the clear, light beer being brewed in the city of Budweis in Bohemia—a beer Busch named Budweiser. Then he set out across the country to promote the brand and to establish a network of agents in every city he could visit. Adolphus Busch was producing thirty-five thousand barrels of beer per year in 1875. By 1901, he sold more than one million, and most of that was his Budweiser brand.

Busch made particularly deep inroads in the South. In 1890, liquor, beer, and tobacco dealer W. O. Muller of Asheville, North Carolina, who just a few years earlier carried Foss and Schneider Cincinnati lager beer from Cincinnati, announced that he was an "Agent and authorized Bottler of the Celebrated Anheuser-Busch St. Louis Pale Lager Beer

Anheuser-Busch advertisement, 1899.

and Original Budweiser Export Beer." Muller was the first to introduce Anheuser-Busch's beers to the city, which he "received in car load lots in a refrigerator" and delivered to "the trade of a wide contiguous territory." By 1908, muckraker Will Irwin of *Collier's* was decrying "the Grip of Anheuser-Busch on the South," noting that the firm maintained an agency in every large city and even owned several breweries in the region, like Caddo Brewery in Shreveport, which was controlled directly from Saint Louis.

Busch's broad footprint squeezed most of the Cincinnati breweries out of the Southern market, but amid the onslaught of Budweiser, plenty of smaller local breweries flourished. In 1877, G. H. Herbers founded the Memphis Brewing Company, and by 1890 the firm was selling pilsner, export, Tennessee pale, Bavarian, and its own version of Budweiser. At one point, more than 1,500 workers worked at the brewery, and by 1903, production was up to 250,000 barrels per year, making it the largest brewery in the South. Down in New Orleans, Valentine Merz, the nephew of local beer pioneer Georg Merz, founded Dixie Brewing Company in 1907. A German-born brewer named William Ostner moved from

Saint Louis to Jacksonville, Florida, in 1913 and opened the Jax Brewing Company. Charleston was supplied by the Palmetto Brewery, which by the 1890s was producing one thousand gallons of beer per day.

Statistics from the United States Brewers' Association reported that the combined production of Southern breweries in 1911 exceeded 2.5 million barrels. Thanks to ice and modern distribution networks, the three-century-old Southern dream of a tasty, reliable supply of beer was finally a reality.

Workers at the Palmetto Brewery, Charleston, South Carolina, 1880.

17

The South and Temperance

We're about to talk temperance and Prohibition, so why not do what many Southerners did when reformers tried to cut off their cocktails and mix up a whiskey and Coke? That combination of hard and soft drinks, as we will see, has quite a long history in the South.

Now, those of more refined tastes may balk at the notion of mixing good whiskey with a sweet soft drink, but the flavors actually pair quite nicely together. To help draw them out even further, Stephen Dennison, the chef-mixologist for BourbonBlog.com came up with the idea of making a simple syrup from Coca-Cola and using it in a whiskey cocktail—an ingenious touch that inspires the recipe below.

Bourbon and Coke Rebooted

SERVES 1

2 ounces bourbon

¼ ounce Coca-Cola simple-syrup (see recipe below)

2 dashes Angostura bitters

Twist of lemon, for garnish

Place the bourbon, syrup, and bitters in a cocktail shaker filled with ice. Shake until frost forms on the outside of the shaker, then shake 10 seconds more. Serve up, in a cocktail glass with a lemon twist for garnish.

Coca-Cola Simple Syrup

MAKES 1½ CUPS

1 (175 ml) bottle of Mexican Coca-Cola (the kind made with real cane sugar)

6 ounces granulated white sugar

Combine the Coca-Cola and sugar in a small pot over high heat and stir until sugar is dissolved. Allow syrup to come to room temperature, then put in a jar and refrigerate for up to several weeks.

Early Temperance Movements in the South

Most accounts of Prohibition begin with its roots in the temperance movement, and they tend to focus on the Ohio-based Woman's Christian Temperance Union and the larger-than-life religious kook Carrie Nation and her Kansas-based antisaloon crusade. Antebellum Southerners, admittedly, had been slow to join the early temperance movement, but after the Civil War, the drive to rid society of alcohol found a much more welcome reception down South. In the march toward national Prohibition, in fact, Southern states were at the front of the procession.

The movement in the South had a very different character than in the North and Midwest. It was much more locally focused and employed different tactics. Much of the Northern antisaloon rhetoric focused on the immigrant classes, particularly those from southern and eastern Europe. In the Southern temperance movement, the rhetoric was inseparably tied to "the Negro problem" as Jim Crow descended and racial animosity increased. Outright eradication of alcohol through legal prohibition was now the objective, and there were several competing approaches for how to achieve it. The first, commonly called Leonardism, after the prominent prohibitionist Reverend A. B. Leonard, tried to ban alcohol from the top down by passing statewide legislation. The so-called "local option" tactic tried to change things from the bottom up, allowing citizens to vote to ban alcohol in their particular county or city. The "high license" was a more expedient approach that attempted to limit alcohol consumption by putting high-dollar license fees, ranging from $100 to $2,000, on saloons and liquor dealers. All were attempted with varying degrees of success in the South during the last decades of the nineteenth century.

The state of Georgia, the *Cincinnati Commercial Tribune* declared in 1885, "is unquestionably more thoroughly saturated with prohibition sentiment than any other State in the Union." The Peach State had been founded as a temperance colony a century and a half earlier, and it led the way on local option. Evangelicals played a key role in Georgia, and none was more influential than Sam Jones. As a young man in Cartersville, he had been unable to attend college due to illness, but he still managed to read enough law to pass the bar and take up a career as a lawyer. He didn't pass too many other bars after that. By the young age of twenty-one, he managed to achieve such a notorious reputation as a drunkard that his bride's own father refused to attend their wedding. Within a few years, Sam Jones had boozed himself out of a law career and was driving wagons for a living. In 1872, his dying father called him to his bedside and pled with him to stop drinking. Sam Jones promised that he would. A week later, he confessed his sins, was born again as a Christian, and took up a new career as a Methodist preacher.

Evangelist Sam Jones.

Jones quickly showed a natural talent for preaching, and he started traveling the state sermonizing and raising money for the North Georgia Orphans Home. In the cities, his revivals drew crowds of thousands. A master storyteller with a wry wit, Jones emphasized living the good life through simple messages like "quit your meanness." He was a foe of sin in all its forms—baseball, card games, dancing, and dime novels—but he held out special contempt for his own weakness: alcohol. "I'm for everything that's against whiskey," he declared in one of his more eloquent sermons, "and against everything that's for whiskey. . . . I'm a concentrated, consolidated, eternal, uncompromising, every-day-in-the-year, stand-up-to-be-knocked-down-and-dragged-out prohibitionist." The liquor trade was the handmaiden of the devil, Jones insisted, and, "I have entered the fight against the devil. I will kick him as long as I have a foot. I will hit him as long as I have a fist. I will bite him as long as I have a tooth; and then gum him till I die!"

Jones's wit and charisma made him the most popular Southern preacher of his era. His folksy style inspired many imitators, including the young Will Rogers, and he could be profoundly persuasive. In 1885, Jones traveled to Nashville to preach at a three-week revival series, and one night a notorious riverboat captain named Tom Ryman showed up hopping mad. Ryman had made his fortune operating a fleet of thirty-five river boats, and he had had enough of Sam Jones's preaching against the evils of gambling and alcohol, the foundation of Ryman's business. He planned on heckling the preacher, but instead he ended up getting converted. Ryman ordered all the barrooms on his boats to be closed, and he had placards with Scriptures installed on the walls of the staterooms. Captain Ryman later used his wealth to build the Union Gospel Tabernacle for Jones and other evangelists to preach in. After the captain's death, the hall was renamed the Ryman Auditorium, and it eventually became the famed home of the Grand Ole Opry.

In the mind of Sam Jones and the preachers who followed in his footsteps, it was not just drunkenness but drinking itself that was the sin. Jones made frequent visits to Atlanta to condemn its sinful ways, railing against its residents as "beer kegs and whiskey soaks." He was particularly troubled by the exponential rise in beer drinking that had occurred since the Civil War, and Jones sneered at efforts to portray beer as a temperance drink. "Why, I got stinking drunk years ago on beer," he said. "And of the nastiest, suck-eggiest, doggiest drunks a man ever got on, a beer drunk is the worst."

The rhetoric of Sam Jones—folksy, energetic, blissfully free of dogma and doctrine—appealed mostly to a rural audience, and it was in the countryside that Southern prohibition sentiment gained its initial force. The governor signed the local option into law in 1885, and within a year, 108 counties had voted themselves bone dry, and 12 more had adopted partial prohibition, leaving just 11 "whiskey counties" in Georgia. The Kansas City Times commented, "The prohibitionists of Georgia are smarter than their Kansas brethren, in that they have made less noise and accomplished more."

Before long, though, critics were calling Georgia's prohibition experiments "a grim burlesque." Fifteen illegal saloons were said to be in operation in Athens, the home of the University of Georgia. The federal government kept right on accepting the twenty-five-dollar tax from liquor dealers regardless of where they lived, and Pulaski County, despite having voted itself dry, had twenty-three federally licensed liquor dealers living in it. It was the cities—Macon, Augusta, Savannah, and, more than any other, Atlanta—that kept all of Georgia, if not soaking wet, at least thoroughly damp. Atlanta's population of 50,000 was served by 118 saloons, or almost one for every 400 residents. Wholesalers brought in whiskey by the carload, and the Atlanta City Brewery churned out keg after keg of crisp lager. County lines were quite porous when it came to stopping the flow of alcohol, and the state's pottery works were doing a booming business, turning out tens of thousands of little brown jugs, which would be loaded on wagons to ferry corn whiskey from the wet districts to the dry. One wholesale house in Savannah was reported to have delivered ten thousand jugs in a single month to thirsty Georgians in dry counties. If the drys were going to fully stamp out alcohol in the rural parts of the state, they were going to have to make the cities go dry too.

The Atlanta Campaign

In 1885, temperance advocates in Fulton County, in which Atlanta is located, succeeded in gathering enough petition signatures to force a local option referendum. The so-called Atlanta Campaign was the first serious effort in the country to vote a large city dry, and residents were deeply divided on the subject. Nearly every pastor in the city advocated prohibition, but 80 percent of the doctors opposed it because they needed alcohol to practice medicine (for the patient, one assumes, not the doctor, but you can never be too sure). Some of the most ardent antiprohibitionists in Atlanta were prominent businessmen who feared a ban might hurt the economy. After all, the city's saloons did $2 million a year in business, and Atlanta's eleven wholesale liquor dealers pulled in another $4.5 million, contributing more than $32,000 a year in license fees to the city's coffers.

The prohibition campaign created a curious dilemma for Atlanta's African-American community, which held the swing votes on the prohibition measure. Black leaders had long been accused by white prohibitionists of siding with the liquor interests, so ministers went out of their way to voice their objections to liquor sales and implore from the pulpit that their congregations vote dry. At the same time, a large number of African-Americans worked in the hotel and restaurant industry, and banning alcohol sales would threaten their livelihoods. The owners of the Kimball House, in fact, loudly declared that they would be forced to close the hotel if they could not operate their barroom. The Atlanta Campaign gave African-Americans their greatest political visibility and political influence during the New South era. They gathered with white temperance groups for joint rallies, speaking together from the same platform. Influential members of the African-American community found themselves courted—in some cases, even offered bribes—by both drys and wets seeking to secure the votes they could command.

At daybreak on November 25, 1885, the day of the dry vote, processions took control of city streets as voters, both black and white, gathered to march to the polls. The wets wore red badges printed with the word liberty. The drys wore blue. One of the dry processions was 1,200 strong and led by a brass band. Along the streets, ministers beseeched voters in the wet caravans to change their minds, making dramatic harangues against the liquor traffic. Temperance organizations provided free lunches near the polls, with women serving lunch to black and white voters alike. Just after 11:00 a.m., nearly one hundred African-American employees, gaily dressed, left the Kimball House and marched together to the polls, where they unanimously cast their votes in favor of liquor sales.

Their votes weren't quite enough to tip the balance. The following morning, the pro-dry *Atlanta Journal* trumpeted, "HAIL YE FREEMAN! THE SHACKLES OF WHISKEY SHAKEN OFF BY ATLANTA!" The *Atlanta Constitution* was more subdued, running a conciliatory editorial stating that the city was "entering upon the most tremendous experiment tried by any city of more than fifty thousand people" and that the citizens had volunteered to "blaze the way for cities, whether it leads to disaster or prosperity." With more than seven thousand ballots cast, it was the largest electoral turnout in the county had yet seen, and the drys had prevailed by a slim 226-vote majority.

The law didn't take effect until July 1, 1886, so Atlantans had plenty of time to prepare. Saloonkeepers, hoteliers, and liquor retailers were obviously going to be hard hit, but so were the operators of the city's pharmacies and soda fountains, since in addition to an array of flavorings, customers could also get a shot of hard liquor in their drinks. One druggist in particular took a hard look at his future. Like many pharmacists, John Pemberton had long sold tonics and medicinal wines under names like Southern Cordial, Gingerine, and Lemon and Orange Elixir. His big hit was a product he called Pemberton's French Wine Cola. It was a blatant rip-off of Vin Mariani, a best-selling tonic made from Bordeaux wine infused with coca leaves. Pemberton's knock-off added cola nut and damiana to the mix, and he advertised it throughout the city as a cure for nervous disorders and impotence.

In the wake of the prohibition vote, Pemberton could read the writing on the wall for his French Wine Cola. He began working in his home laboratory on a temperance drink, experimenting with essential oils from fruits and other ingredients that could replace the wine in his cola concoction. He added sugar to mask the bitterness of the oils and citric acid to cut the sweetness, then sent the syrup down to Veneable's soda fountain to see how it tasted when mixed with carbonated water. On May 29, 1886, a month prior to the advent of citywide prohibition, Pemberton and his partners declared in an *Atlanta Journal* ad: "Coca-Cola. Delicious! Refreshing! Exhilarating! Invigorating!" The vote against hard liquor in Atlanta had birthed what would become America's most popular soft drink.

Prohibition arrived with little fanfare on July 1. Many saloons closed, some draping their fronts in black banners of mourning. A few joints on Marietta Street remained open, selling only lunch and nonalcoholic summer drinks, but most owners were emptying their shelves and having their furniture hauled off to auction. A dejected John McMahon, proprietor of the Big Bonanza saloon on Decatur Street, told the *Macon Telegraph* that his business, which now consisted of selling buttermilk, ginger pop, soda water, and lemonade, had fallen from $100 a day to $5, and his rent alone was $100 a month.

It didn't take long for Atlanta's wets to find a loophole, though: in a concession to local vineyards, "domestic wines" had been exempted from prohibition. They petitioned the US District Court to block enforcement of the law as unconstitutional, since it discriminated against wines produced in other states in restraint of interstate commerce. The judge refused to take immediate action, but he ruled that if in enforcing the law the authorities interpreted "domestic wines" to mean only wine produced in the state of Georgia, then the law would indeed be discriminatory and could, therefore, be deemed unconstitutional. Enterprising wets threw open wine rooms throughout the city, stocking their shelves with wines from Ohio and California, and the cops left them alone. A single bust for selling nondomestic wine could put the constitutionality of the entire prohibition law in jeopardy. John McMahon was finally able to pay his rent, for he quickly jettisoned the buttermilk and ginger pop and converted the Big Bonanza into a wine room.

Atlanta's wets weren't content to just sip a little vino. As 1887 opened, dozens of wine room owners were arrested for selling hard liquor alongside their domestic wines. In February 1887, detectives followed a wagon from the Atlanta City Brewery, which was still making beer but supposedly not selling it inside the county, as it delivered two barrels to the local icehouse. Later in the day, those were taken to Kenny and Werner's wine room on Alabama Street, where the detectives seized them. Because the dry law banned just the sale, not the possession, of alcohol, residents could place an order with a whiskey agent outside the county and have a bottle shipped to them. A number of remarkably efficient whiskey agents set up shop in Atlanta. A man could go to one of them and order a quart of whiskey to be shipped to him from Griffin, a wet town some forty miles away. Within two minutes, the delivery would arrive.

As Atlanta approached the first anniversary of its pioneering prohibition law, both wets and drys took stock of its performance. The *Atlanta Avalanche* and the *Macon Telegraph* called the experiment an economic disaster, claiming that rents were down 30 percent and houses stood vacant throughout the city. The city's new mayor, John Tyler Cooper, an avowed antiprohibitionist, repeatedly told the press that the law was a farce that stripped the city of liquor tax revenue without putting a dent in consumption. The drys told a different story. Henry Grady claimed in the *Atlanta Constitution* that drinking had been cut 80 percent, 130 barrooms had closed, and crime had plummeted. Instead of squandering their wages on getting drunk, workingmen instead bought food, clothing, and furniture for their families, and storefronts formerly occupied by saloons had been taken over by prospering tradesmen.

The real test came at the ballot box, since Georgia's law allowed counties to vote on the local option every two years. A new referendum was slated for November 26, 1887, and Atlanta was again divided into two warring camps. This time around, an unexpected voice emerged as the most influential in the whole debate. He was a black man who went by the name of Yellowstone Kit, and he traveled the South selling patent medicine. He had set up shop in a large vacant lot, where he staged concerts and sold his unique line of wares. Kit's shows, complete with a dozen-piece brass band, tightrope walkers, jugglers, and comedians, drew crowds as large as two thousand people. Each week, he would distribute bread among the poor, and a highlight of each evening was when he selected an infirm person out of the audience and gave the person a big wad of cash.

As November approached, Yellowstone Kit found himself besieged by both wets and drys, who believed he could sway critical African-American swing voters. Ex-governors, senators, and judges all came to visit the medicine salesman, and one prominent prohibitionist allegedly offered him $5,000 to go dry. The *Augusta Chronicle* declared Kit "the most skillful humbug of the age" and noted that "he has wonderful influence with the negroes, and besides cajoling them out of their scanty earnings, it is claimed that he can vote them." Four days before the referendum, Yellowstone Kit finally declared his allegiance. He was opposed to drinking liquor, he announced from the stage, but he favored repeal because he preferred well-policed and regulated saloons over bootleg liquor. Two days later, the city shut down Yellowstone Kit's medicine show, ostensibly because neighbors were complaining of the large disorderly crowds, but his voice had been heard.

On November 25, the night before the election, fifteen thousand people thronged the streets. Bonfires blazed, a half dozen brass bands played, and thousands of tin horns tooted. Two thousand people packed the Opera House to hear speakers deliver passionate antiprohibition oratories. When Yellowstone Kit arrived on the scene, driving his carriage through cheering throngs, he was seized by the crowd and passed over their heads to the speaking platform.

The next day's headlines blared, "Atlanta Goes Wet!" It did so by more than 1,100 votes, a stunning defeat for the prohibitionists. The drys cried foul, claiming the liquor interests had bought the vote and decrying the influence of Yellowstone Kit. The movement's biggest failure, grumped W. T. Turnbull, the chairman of the Young Men's Prohibition League, was they lost "the low class of negroes [who] were thirsty." Instead of prohibition, Atlanta put in place a high license system, imposing a $1,000 fee for saloons selling liquor. By February 1888, sixty-eight bars were in operation in the city.

For African-Americans, the Atlanta campaign marked the last time for almost a century that their votes would determine the outcome of an election. White evangelicals in Georgia and beyond drew a troubling conclusion from the Atlanta experience: that African-American voters were not the reliable antiprohibition voting bloc they had hoped for. Prohibitionists increasingly began to portray black men as unfit for holding the vote, and their efforts took on an increasingly fearful and inflammatory edge, contributing to a more general deterioration of race relations as Georgia and the rest of the South descended into the Jim Crow era.

The Dispensary Movement

Atlanta was an important test of the local option as a prohibition tactic. South Carolina was the proving ground for a very different approach: the state control of liquor sales through what became known as the dispensary model. Liquor sales had been illegal in rural areas of South Carolina since 1880, and under an 1882 local option law, seventy-eight towns had voted themselves booze-free in the space of a decade. Prohibition sentiment was riding high, and the temperance forces, sensing a chance for total victory, stepped up the fight and in 1892 secured a referendum on statewide prohibition. Voters overwhelmingly approved the measure, which instructed the legislature to enact a complete ban. The House duly passed a prohibition bill and sent it to the Senate.

That's when Governor Benjamin "Pitchfork Ben" Tillman stepped in. Tillman had risen to power as a populist champion of small cotton farmers, in opposition to the conservative elite. A farmer himself, Tillman capitalized on a surge of resentment against bankers, merchants, and politicians, advancing the notion that city folks—especially those in Charleston—had a stranglehold on the countryside. Though a teetotaler himself, Ben Tillman had little interest in prohibition. For him, the game was all about power, and Tillman resented the fact that liquor was prohibited in rural areas but could be sold in towns and cities, which generated lots of tax revenue for the municipalities.

So Tillman decided not to get rid of the liquor system but to turn it to the advantage of rural residents and his own political ambitions. The prohibition measure passed by the House exempted medicinal alcohol, designating a state commissioner who would dispense wholesale liquor to permit holders in each county, who in turn would sell it to druggists for use in medicine. Late in the legislative session, Tillman took a pencil to the text and made a few strategic edits, striking all references to medicine and druggists. That transformed the measure from a prohibition bill into a state dispensary bill, and he rammed it through the Senate on a seventeen to eight vote. The House, being told they could take the dispensary bill or nothing, opted for the dispensary, and thus, in a move that satisfied neither wet nor dry, South Carolina began a remarkable experiment that gave the state a full monopoly on the sale of liquor.

Starting July 1, 1893, a dispenser would be established in the seat of each county that had not voted itself dry through the local option, and each county dispenser got its liquor from the central dispensary in

Columbia. Tillman appointed D. H. Traxler, a devout churchman and husband of one of the state's Woman's Christian Temperance Union leaders, as his first state dispensary commissioner. The two teetotalers must have made quite a pair when they traveled to Cincinnati to study the liquor business and secure an initial supply of booze. When they returned home, they set up what would soon become the largest bottling plant and wholesale liquor operation in the world.

By the second day of the dispensary regime, Tillman was already receiving reports that blind tigers were in open operation in many towns and cities. The term *blind tiger*, which was used widely in the South to refer to what elsewhere might be called a speakeasy, dated back to at least the 1850s. In 1857, the *Spirit of the Times* told the story of its origins. Its narrator stopped off at a small town along the banks of the Mississippi and found a house with a hole cut in the side and, over the hole, a sign reading, Blind tiger, ten cents a sight. He put down his dime but found that "instead of showin' me a wild varmint without eyes, I'll be dod busted if he didn't shove out a glass of whiskey. You see, that 'blind tiger' was an arrangement to evade the law, which won't let them sell licker there." The nickname was soon applied to any establishment that sold liquor illegally.

Charleston was the home of the blind tigers in South Carolina. In the eyes of the fundamentalists in the upper part of the state, the city had always been a den of license and wickedness. If Charleston did not accept dispensary liquor, Tillman thundered, he would make it "dry enough to burn" and would send enough special constables to "cover every city block with a man." On July 15, Tillman's detectives made their first arrest in the city. The violator was Vincent Chicco, a saloonkeeper who was charged with selling beer to a detective at his Market Street establishment. Almost immediately, a local judge ordered Chicco released on $500 bail and promptly issued a warrant for the officer's arrest on charges of assault.

Thus began three decades of infamy for Vincent Chicco, the King of the Blind Tigers and archnemesis of Pitchfork Ben Tillman. Born in Italy in 1851, Vincent Chicco had left home as a teen to become a sailor, and on one of his voyages, his ship stopped in Charleston and he decided to stay. Chicco became a naturalized citizen in 1874 and entered the grocery trade. As was common in that era, his store also included a saloon where men could enjoy a beer or dose of whiskey. After 1894, Chicco's business was listed in various city directories as a grocery, a delicatessen, a cigar shop, a café, and a restaurant. But customers knew what they could find there. For years, Chicco handed out aluminum tokens the size of a quarter. On one side were the words "Good for 5¢ in Trade at Chicco's Cafe"; on the other, just in case some of his more dense patrons might not get it, an image of a tiger's head, his eyes covered by a blindfold.

To stomp out scofflaws like Chicco, Tillman dispatched special constables to all corners of the state, and they effectively became the governor's own private police force. State law authorized them to search the vehicles of common carriers without a warrant, to seize vehicles used to transport liquor at night, and to enter homes and businesses suspected of holding illegal whiskey. In December 1893, the first violent clash involving Tillman's constables occurred when an African-American man was shot and killed during a bootlegging arrest, and three months later, a constable killed one man and wounded another in the town of Willington. These deaths and stories of the constables' raiding private residences—plus a steady drumbeat of abuse from the state's anti-Tillman newspapers—fanned the flames of resentment among many of the state's citizens.

The conflict erupted into a full-on battle in March in what has variously been called the Darlington Massacre and the Darlington Rebellion. It began when four of Tillman's constables began raiding suspected liquor dealers in Darlington, and local crowds confronted them with jeers and insults. Tillman sent eighteen additional constables from Charleston as backup, but the abuse continued as they raided barrooms and illegal liquor dealers. On March 31, things came to a head. The constables had finished their last raid and made their way to the railroad station to await their train back to Charleston. A large crowd of men and boys gathered to give them a jeering send-off. At some point, a fight broke out in the crowd, and as the police chief was breaking it up, a young man named Frank Norment cursed Officer J. D. McClendon with "a vile epithet." It was disputed later whether McClendon fired in anger or self-defense, but he shot Norment dead and a general eruption of gunfire followed. One constable was killed and several others were severely wounded. The remaining constables fled down the railroad tracks and took refuge in the wooded swamps while an angry mob scoured the countryside, searching for the hiding constables.

Upon learning of the shootings, Governor Tillman ordered all of the militia companies in Columbia to assemble and proceed by special train to Darlington. Under state law, members of militia units could refuse to serve as long as they had not yet donned their uniforms. To a man, the members of the three companies declined Tillman's orders, and their ranks were dismissed. Adjutant General Hugh L. Farley departed the city by train and, following Tillman's orders, proceeded first to Sumter and then to Manning, only to have the local militia units in both towns refuse to join him too. General Farley proceeded to Darlington alone.

The fury of the mob in Darlington only increased after the fallen men were buried the following morning. Tillman responded by declaring martial law, seizing control of the railroads and the telegraph lines. Militia companies from the western part of the state, where Tillman had his greatest political support, heeded his orders to assemble, and they were rushed to Columbia via special trains. By Sunday afternoon, twenty-seven companies had assembled in Columbia along with hundreds of so-called wool-hat boys who responded to Tillman's call for volunteers, and that won the day for Ben Tillman. The fugitive constables returned to Darlington under military escort, where an inquest quickly exonerated them from wrongdoing. By April 5, the situation had settled enough for Tillman to send the militia home.

Tillman's victory not only bolstered the dispensary regime but also earned him broad praise from national newspapers for his firm stand against public disorder. In the years that followed, the governor and his allies undertook all manner of legal and legislative wrangling to protect what the newspapers labeled Tillman's Baby. In 1893, the state Supreme Court declared the dispensary law unconstitutional, but after a justice retired, Tillman filled the spot with his own appointee and the court reversed its decision. The dispensary continued to be plagued by legal wrangling and the constant competition from the blind tigers, but once the system was up and running it sent a steady stream of revenue flooding into state coffers—$414,000 in 1899, almost half the state's total tax receipts.

The blind tigers in Charleston—and, especially, Vincent Chicco— remained a thorn in Tillman's side for years. Chicco took to calling his Market Street establishment the second Fort Sumter because it had resisted so many sieges. Even after Tillman was elected to the US Senate in 1895, he remained a passionate defender of the dispensary system, and his battle with Vincent Chicco, whom he labeled "a kind of Dago devil," heightened into a personal crusade. Chicco dished it right back, selling a line of cigars he called the Two Determined, which came in boxes with a picture of himself and Tillman on the lid. The idea, Chicco explained to the press, was that Tillman was determined that Chicco should stop selling liquor, and Chicco was determined to keep right on selling it.

THE TWO DETERMINED

"The Two Determined": Ben Tillman and Vincent Chicco.

Ultimately, the dispensary experiment in South Carolina was undone not by blind tigers and the illegal liquor trade but by the human frailty of those selected to run the enterprise. Starting in 1905, a legislative committee began investigating the dispensary operations, and their report revealed a morass of corruption. County dispensers routinely cooked their books, "misplaced" liquor, and failed to remit payments to the state dispensary. They readily accepted—and often demanded—bribes from whiskey houses, including free trips, free liquor shipments, and outright cash payments. The testimony from the hearings sent shock waves of scandal reverberating across the state, and the following year, antidispensary majorities were elected to both houses of the state legislature. They promptly abolished the central state dispensary, leaving it to each county to decide for itself whether to continue its local dispensary or go dry. By 1915, public sentiment had so turned against the dispensary that outright prohibition once again gained favor. In August, voters approved a referendum mandating statewide prohibition, and the entire state went dry on January 1, 1916.

"The Negro Problem" and the Drive Toward Prohibition

As the nineteenth century gave way to the twentieth, the push toward complete prohibition gained momentum in the South, and it was tightly linked to racial politics and the deepening fear and oppression of the Jim Crow era. Back when New South sentiment was at its peak in the 1880s, many white evangelical leaders had espoused an optimistic message of harmony and reconciliation, portraying slavery as a dark episode best left in the past and welcoming universal male suffrage. Along with free public education, temperance was portrayed as a key reform needed for moral uplift and future prosperity in the South for whites and blacks alike. They were joined in this sentiment by New South economic boosters like Henry Grady of Atlanta, who championed the economic benefit of uplifting African-Americans in the South, and by black leaders like Booker T. Washington, who saw alcohol as a barrier to individual success.

White evangelicals started changing their tune after the Atlanta Campaign and similar efforts, like the failed 1887 attempt in Tennessee to pass a constitutional amendment prohibiting liquor, which African-American votes were instrumental in defeating. Events on the national scene made white Southerners even more leery of the black vote. In 1888, the year following the wet victory in Atlanta, Benjamin Harrison won the White House and the Republicans took over both houses of Congress. In 1890, Senator Henry Cabot Lodge introduced the so-called Force Bill, which meant to end election fraud in the South and ensure African-Americans' right to vote, to be enforced by military force if required. White Southerners were enraged, fearing a return of neo-Reconstructionist governments and African-American political power.

Fear of the black vote and black drinking became tightly entwined in the harsher stereotypes of African-Americans that were promulgated during this era. Where previous white myths had tended to infantilize African-Americans—portraying them as loyal, childlike creatures who needed to be patronized and protected by the white community—Jim Crow imagery increasingly demonized them. Alcohol played a central role in the popular image of the "black beast," with cheap whiskey the trigger that could unleash primitive urges. If you believed the worst of the propagandists, every black man in the South was only a few shots of cheap whiskey away from being transformed into a mad beast that would steal, murder, and rape white women. Newspaper editors routinely lamented urban conditions that left male African-American workers unsupervised and uncontrolled, fearing, as the *Birmingham News* put it, "the menace of the liquor filled negro," and their worries focused in particular on "the negro saloon."

In cities across the South, reformers locked horns with wets over the sale of alcohol to African-Americans. In Birmingham, the board of aldermen was dominated by prosaloon Democratic party insiders. They had strong ties to saloonkeepers and liquor dealers and, especially, to Philip Schillinger of the Schillinger Brewing Company, which owned many Birmingham saloons and had exclusive tied house arrangements with many others. Starting in 1889, a succession of reform mayors failed to impose a $1,000 high license on saloons and isolate such establishments in a single saloon district, forbidding them to operate elsewhere. In 1904, George Ward, a "good government" candidate, was elected on a saloon-reform platform, and after much wrangling, he cut a deal with Philip Schillinger and the saloon men that effectively created a red-light district in the middle of a lower-class African-American neighborhood.

The simmering racial tensions underlying the Southern prohibition movement came to a full boil in Atlanta in 1906. Like all Southern cities, Atlanta had its entertainment district, which was centered on Decatur Street. Though many of the saloons on Decatur served both whites and blacks, the drys made much of the fact that unemployed black men frequented them and that many were rumored to be decorated with pictures of nude women. John E. White, a prominent Baptist minister, labeled "Decatur Street dives" as "breeding places of lust and animal insanity." At weeklong revivals, Sam Jones railed against "the liquor traffic" and enumerated the many evils caused by black men drinking alcohol. More and more, fearful white leaders concluded that statewide prohibition was their only course, arguing, as one white supremacist put it, that a stronger race must "forgo personal liberty" to protect an inferior one from "weakness and folly." And increasingly, they came to believe that total disenfranchisement of African-Americans was a necessary prerequisite to being able to close the saloons.

The 1906 Georgia governor's race pitted two newspapermen, Hoke Smith, the former editor of the *Atlanta Journal*, against Clark Howell, the active editor of the *Atlanta Constitution*, and the contest devolved into what one historian has termed "a bitter Negrophobe campaign." Smith staked out a plan to reform the electoral process in such a way as to strip the vote from African-Americans "without disenfranchising a single white man." Amid this heated political rhetoric, white paranoia over black sexuality—specifically, of black men raping white women—reached the level of outright hysteria. In early August, the editors of the *Atlanta Georgian* and the *Atlanta News*, which had been playing up for months any and all rumors of attacks on white women by black men, declared that the city was experiencing an "epidemic of Negro assaults," and they blared each alleged crime in banner headlines. Many of the incidents hardly amounted to actual assault (in one complaint, a woman simply drew her window shades and spied a strange black man on the sidewalk), but that didn't keep Charles Daniel, the *Atlanta News*'s crusading young editor, from fanning the flames, declaring that for a black man who attacked a white women, "lynching is too good . . . and hanging is a mercy."

On Saturday, September 22, the evening edition of the *News* announced that a black man had attempted to assault a white woman near the Sugar Creek Bridge. That was followed quickly by an extra edition with the headline "TWO ASSAULTS" in massive type across the entire top half of the page. Just hours later, a second extra declared "THREE ASSAULTS," followed quickly by another declaring four. By early evening, a mob of white men had gathered, their rage rising with each new extra edition that hit the streets. Finally, they smashed the windows of a black barbershop on Peachtree Street, chased two barbers into the street, and beat them to death with clubs and fists. Mayor James Woodward tried to calm the mob, imploring them that "the honor of Atlanta before the world is in your hands tonight!" but he was shouted down with cries of "nigger lover!" White mobs roamed the darkened streets with torches, unleashing their rage upon whatever black residents they could find. Several passengers were dragged from streetcars and clubbed, and at least three died from their wounds. The mob shattered the plate glass windows of black restaurants and stores. The arrival of the state militia along with a heavy rain finally dispersed the rioters around 2:00 a.m.

For the next three nights, the militia patrolled the streets, but there was still sporadic violence. Finally white leaders, fearing continued disorder and under the scrutiny of national press coverage, sought dialogue with leaders in the black community, and an uneasy truce fell over the beleaguered city. All told, somewhere between two dozen to forty blacks as well as two whites were killed in the violence. In its aftermath, one thousand black residents left the city permanently. Many African-American business owners moved their shops from the central business district to Auburn Avenue, further segregating the city. Within a few years, most white Atlantans had managed to put the incident out of mind, but for many African-American leaders, it discredited forever the accommodationist strategy advocated by Booker T. Washington.

White leaders in Georgia took away a very different message. "You may say the bloodshed in Atlanta was inevitable," said Hoke Smith, who argued that the black vote was controlled by the liquor interest. Smith swept to victory in the governor's race. As he promised, among his first acts in office was a measure instituting a strict grandfather clause. With the black vote suppressed, one wet county after another went dry through local option elections. The following year, Georgia passed a statewide prohibition measure. None of the four alleged assaults on white women in Atlanta reported in the newspapers was ever substantiated.

Whiskey Paranoia

The antisaloon forces were soon joined in their efforts by muckraking reporters like William Henry "Will" Irwin, who wrote a series of articles on the American saloon for *Collier's* magazine. Irwin traveled around the South to expose the tactics of saloonkeepers and liquor dealers, with a particular emphasis on those catering to African-American customers. Most inflammatory was Irwin's assertion that booze was responsible for the interracial violence in the South, and he held up as an example the case of Charles Coleman and Margaret Lear in Shreveport, Louisiana. In 1906, Coleman, an African-American man, was charged with the rape and murder of Lear, a fourteen-year-old white girl. Witnesses testified that Coleman had been drinking, and he accosted Lear as she walked home from school and attempted to drag her off the road, presumably to rape her. When she resisted, he shot her with a pistol and killed her. Coleman was quickly captured, and the governor had to send multiple companies of the state militia to the city to prevent him from being lynched. After a four-hour trial, the all-white jury took just three minutes to return a guilty verdict, and Coleman was hanged a week later.

When Irwin incorporated the case into his antisaloon series for *Collier's* two years later, he declared that the real murderer was not "the poor black beast" but the white men who manufactured the gin that got him drunk. In "every low negro dive in the South," Irwin charged, liquor firms sold cheap brands of gin with obscene brand names and lurid images on the label meant to advertise "by suggestion, by double meanings, that these compounds contain a drug to stimulate the passions which have made the race problem such a dreadful thing in the South." Irwin called out specifically Lee Levy and Company of Saint Louis, claiming they made "a popular and widely sold brand" that was so offensive that "if I should give its name here, or attempt to describe its label, this publication could not go through the mails." Irwin named Blumenthal, Bickart and Company of Atlanta and Dreyfus, Weil and Company of Paducah, Kentucky, makers of Devil's Island Endurance Gin, as similarly egregious panderers.

The real villains in Southern lynchings, Irwin charged, were not the white men who did the actual killing—Irwin wrote off their crimes as the acts of "temporary brutes in their mob anger." No, the true criminals were the greedy liquor promoters who sold the gin. African-American laborers, in Irwin's formulation, were little more than primitive brutes, "a web of strong, sudden impulses, good and bad." They would come into town on a Saturday afternoon, plunk down fifty cents for a pint of Levy's gin, and their animal lust would be enflamed by the label on the bottle with its obscene pictures of white women and suggestions of aphrodisiacs and potency enhancement. Though Irwin never came right out and said it, all the liquor producers he targeted had Jewish names, offering a little two-for-the-price-of-one bigotry.

In June 1908, Lee Levy & Co. was indicted in the state of Tennessee and charged with circulating obscene literature. The literature, in this case, was the labels on their gin bottles, for the government contended that "by holding the labels in a certain position the picture presented is one that tends to arouse depraved passions in a negro." In November 1908, *Collier's* gushed that "Lee Levy, manufacturer of the worst brand of 'nigger gin,' indirect accomplice in heaven knows how many Southern outrages," had been indicted by a federal grand jury on multiple counts of sending obscene matter through the mails. In the face of the investigations, Levy and other liquor producers had yanked the offending brands of gin from the market and they were now hard to find "even in the lowest negro groggeries."

In retrospect, Irwin's sensational charges don't hold water. He portrayed the murder of Margaret Lear as having occurred when the schoolgirl walked past "a negro saloon" and "out of that saloon staggered Charles Coleman—'drunken,' ran the testimony at the trial, 'on cheap gin.'" Newspaper accounts of the crime and trial, though, show that Margaret Lear actually passed by Lee Gullatt and Co., a retail grocery. They state only that Coleman had been drinking and do not specifically mention "cheap gin." The linkage to liquor brands like Levy's was made only by Irwin and only two years after the fact.

All told, Lee Levy was a relatively small player in the industry, and if his brand was "popular and widely sold," as Irwin claimed, not a lot of people seemed to know it. The Memphis *Commercial Appeal* at the time noted "their sales are insignificant." The other liquor dealers called out by Irwin were slightly larger fish. Bluthenthal, Bickart and Company, an Atlanta-based wholesaler, included among its twenty or more brands Mobile Buck Gin, whose labels promised one could "regain your lost courage, vim, vigor, energy." Devil's Island Endurance Gin was one of a dozen brands trademarked by Dreyfus, Weil and Company of Paducah, Kentucky, and they definitely aimed toward the racy in the advertising cards for their product. One shows a young, fancily dressed man (a white man, it should be noted) peeping in the slightly ajar door of a beach dressing room, behind which can be seen a woman in a partial stage of undress. "They will peep," the card declares, adding, "those fellows who drink that Devil's Island Endurance Gin Seem to have the very 'devil' in 'em."

The name of Lee Levy's gin was too scandalous for Irwin to print, but Prohibition historian Daniel Okrent uncovered it in the records of Levy's obscenity trial: Black Cock Vigor Gin. Okrent was unable to track down any bottles, but he notes that the trial records indicate that the label had a picture of a naked white woman on it. Advertising cards for Levy's gin, however, are more suggestive. One shows a cabin with an African-American woman (of the old mammy stereotype) standing in the door, the words Drink Black Cock Vigor Gin emblazoned next to her. In front of the cabin, a black rooster is chasing a white chicken, and along the bottom of the card is the motto "Hustling for Business." Another is more explicit in promising potency enhancements, claiming in verse that it will "make your limbs grow" and "keep muscles hard from head to toe."

Laden with innuendo? Certainly. So indecent that it will "arouse depraved passions" within drunken men? Not terribly likely. A federal judge seemed to agree. Lee Levy and his partner Adolph Asher were found guilty of sending obscene material through the mail, but the judge only fined them a total of $500 and noted that he would have dismissed the charges altogether if they had pled guilty.

Irwin's muckraking conflated the paranoid fears of white Southerners about black sexuality with the long-standing (and still ongoing) tradition of using sexuality to sell booze. Images of scantily clad women had been used to promote liquor for decades, and men's concern over their potency (or lack thereof) has long been a gold mine for marketers. The wholesalers' ads actually seem aimed more at insecure middle-aged white men than at black laborers. One newspaper ad for Mobile Buck Gin, for instance, shows a white man staring into a mirror with the slogan "Are you satisfied with yourself?" An advertising card for Devil's Island Endurance Gin promises, "It Makes My Home Happy and Brings My 'Happy' Home." Even the imagery on Black Cock Vigor Gin—old mammies in turbans, grossly caricatured black men urinating on a fence to illustrate that the gin is "good for the kidneys"—seems aimed to amuse racist white consumers and not to appeal to African-American customers.

The muckraking rhetoric, though, helped lock in the white conviction that African-Americans and alcohol were a dangerous combination, and that fear helped pave the way to the passage of broader dry laws and outright prohibition. One by one, Southern states followed Georgia's lead and instituted statewide prohibition—Mississippi and North Carolina in 1908, Tennessee in 1909, Virginia in 1914, and Arkansas and South Carolina in 1915. The *State* newspaper in Columbia reported that the support for statewide prohibition came from two groups. The first was the expected contingent that believed that the liquor traffic itself was morally wrong. The other might not have problems with whites drinking liquor but believed it was "economic insanity" to allow intoxicants to be sold "in a commonwealth 55 per cent of whose people are negroes, for the most part ignorant laborers, and where illiteracy abounds."

By this point, Southern drinking culture remained intact only in the states of Texas and Louisiana. As the rest of the South grew drier, New Orleans, which *Travel* magazine dubbed "that mighty oasis," began flourishing as a winter tourist city complete with grand hotels, famous saloons, and a distinctive local style of jazz. The Saint Charles Hotel was joined by several new grand establishments as the city's tourist trade boomed, including the 330-room Hotel Monteleone and the six-story Hotel Grunewald (which is today known as the Roosevelt). Instead of the traditional hotel bar with its brass footrail, the Grunewald had the Cave, a lavish room with grottolike decor that included plaster rock formations, waterfalls, and statues of nymphs and gnomes among the stalactites and stalagmites. Some consider it the first nightclub in America. The Sazerac Saloon, with its sanded floor and seventy-five-foot-long bar, was still

Advertising card for Lee Levy & Co.'s Black Cock Vigor Gin.

Advertising card for Lee Levy & Co.'s Black Cock Vigor Gin.

serving its famous Sazerac cocktails, and Henry Ramos's line of shaker boys were still frapping out foamy gin fizzes at the Stag.

If New Orleans was the great oasis in the almost-dry South, Texas was hanging on as a bastion of dampness. By 1895, about one-quarter of Texas's 239 counties, most of them in the rural northern part of the state, had voted themselves dry under the local option. Central Texas, which had a large German-American population, remained resolutely wet, but the drys were starting to make inroads there too. Fearing that the wave of prohibition that had already swept across most of the South was on course to roll over the entire nation, the German-American-led beer industry decided that they were going to go all out to save Texas. The Lone Star State was one of Anheuser-Busch's largest markets, and Adolphus Busch used his influence in industry councils to persuade eight other breweries to pool their efforts and fund a committee to promote antiprohibition measures in Texas. The committee sent checks to penurious editors at country papers, who were happy to write scathing antiprohibition editorials in return. Busch's field force included four agents dedicated to drumming up the African-American vote, and their kit included not just wet propaganda tracts but a poster of Abraham Lincoln and cash to pay the poll tax for black voters. In 1910, agents of the beer industry were mysteriously able to overturn a prohibition measure that had passed in east Texas; Busch explained in a letter that the victory had been accomplished through "means that are best not written about."

Texas was still wet when Adolphus Busch died in 1913 from cirrhosis of the liver. The brewers' hard-nosed tactics may have won them the battle, but they contributed to their losing the war. When the Anti-Saloon League uncovered details about the brewers' Texas campaign, it cranked up its propaganda machine and blared the lurid stories nationwide. Testimony about the skulduggery of the beer industry played prominently in the congressional hearings in the run-up to national prohibition, but it was the outbreak of World War I that sealed the fate of the beer and liquor industries. Dry activists linked the names of Busch, Pabst, and Schlitz to the German-American Alliance, and the die was effectively cast. Outright national prohibition loomed ahead.

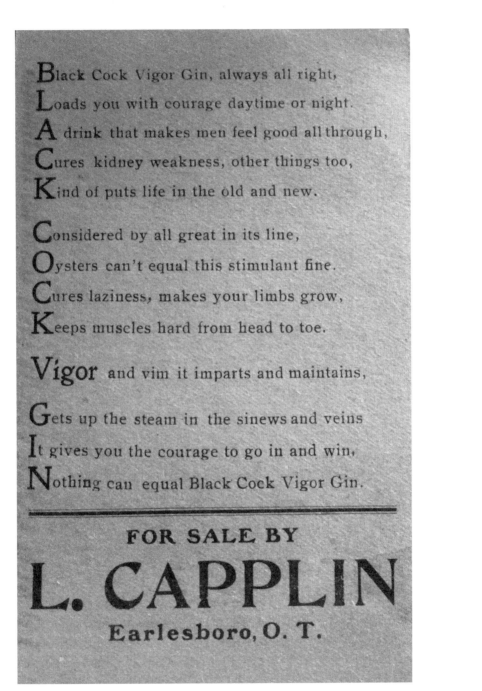

Black Cock Vigor Gin, always all right,

Loads you with courage daytime or night.

A drink that makes men feel good all through,

Cures kidney weakness, other things too,

Kind of puts life in the old and new.

Considered by all great in its line,

Oysters can't equal this stimulant fine.

Cures laziness, makes your limbs grow,

Keeps muscles hard from head to toe.

Vigor and vim it imparts and maintains,

Gets up the steam in the sinews and veins

It gives you the courage to go in and win,

Nothing can equal Black Cock Vigor Gin.

FOR SALE BY

L. CAPPLIN

Earlesboro, O. T.

Advertising card for Lee Levy & Co.'s Black Cock Vigor Gin.

18

National Prohibition

On January 16, 1919, Nebraska became the thirty-sixth state to ratify the Eighteenth Amendment, giving it approval from three-fourths of the states and making it law. As was specified in the amendment, one year after ratification—that is, at the stroke of midnight on Saturday, January 17, 1920—the manufacture, sale, and transportation of intoxicating liquor was prohibited in all of the United States.

Most of the South had been living under state-imposed prohibition for years, and the only ones whooping it up on Friday, January 16, were the drys. In Atlanta, a crowd of thousands craned their necks to watch an aerial funeral procession consisting of a trio of airplanes, led by a giant Curtiss biplane, that buzzed over the city, scattering the supposed ashes of John Barleycorn. A parade was led by a man dressed in a striped top hat with white whiskers and riding in a wagon, its sides emblazoned with signs that read Uncle Sam is on the water wagon. The festivities concluded at dusk with a giant bonfire in the center of the city, and a barrel of moonshine whiskey and a large copper still were tossed into the flames. Similar gatherings, many of them also involving the torching of confiscated moonshine, were conducted throughout Georgia.

The drys hoped that the national ban would finally stanch the flow of whiskey and beer that had kept Southern states wringing wet despite local prohibition laws, but that quickly proved not to be the case. National Prohibition did have a transformative effect on what and how people in the South drank, though, one that lasted long after repeal. Every single aspect of the drinking culture—the distillers, the type of drinks made, the role alcohol played in society, even the nature of illegal moonshine whiskey—was stripped down, shuffled around, and transformed during the years that alcohol was illegal. Drinking in the South emerged on the other side of Prohibition looking very different than it had going in.

The Fate of the Distilling Industry

Nationwide, the whiskey that was left in distillers' warehouses on January 20 was placed under lock and key by the Feds, and John F. Kramer, the Treasury Department's general prohibition commissioner, ordered 2,500 watchmen be hired to guard the stocks. It was estimated that this supply, which totaled some twenty-nine million gallons and would be sold only as prescription medicine, would last until 1925. Medicinal permit holders could distribute only 100-proof, bottled in bond spirits, and pharmacists could sell them only to customers with prescriptions from their doctor. A doctor could prescribe a patient up to one pint of 100-proof spirits every ten days, and doctors and dentists could buy twelve pints per year for office use. Within six months, fifteen thousand physicians had permits to prescribe whiskey, which, it turns out, was good for treating everything from asthma to old age. ("Take three ounces every hour for stimulant until stimulated," one doctor's instructions read.) Those distillers or wholesalers who weren't fortunate enough to get their hands on such a permit were out of luck. Almost all the rural distilleries closed their doors, and most were dismantled and their equipment sold. The great consolidation of the whiskey trade was under way.

A few distillers moved outside the US border to continue operations. Joseph L. Beam and his son Harry moved down to Juárez, Mexico, where they operated the Waterfill and Frazier Distillery. Others threw in the towel altogether. Edmund H. Taylor Jr., the passionate champion of good whiskey and the Bottled-in-Bond Act, opted for a genteel retirement, turning his energies to breeding Hereford cattle during the final years before his death in 1923. Jim Beam sold his Clear Springs Distillery and tried his hand at other enterprises, including the Sunlight Mining Company, the Sunbeam Quarry Company, and a failed attempt at citrus farming in Florida, which left Jim Beam and his family broke. Once-thriving whiskey towns like Tyrone, Kentucky, became virtual ghost towns, and historians estimate that 5 percent of the total jobs in the Bluegrass State were lost.

The South's thriving network of beer breweries suffered a similar fate. In Alexandria, the Portner Brewing Company stopped brewing operations in 1916 as, one by one, the states that were its best markets voted themselves dry. In 1916, the Augusta Brewing Company changed its name to the Augusta Ice and Beverage Company, and it invested $10,000 in retooling its plant to manufacture soft drinks and near beer. The latter product, one local historian recalled, "looked and frothed like real beer, but that was the only resemblance." The firm limped along for a few years before finally declaring bankruptcy in 1921.

Some breweries did manage to keep their doors open by selling nonalcoholic drinks, ice cream, and ice. The Tennessee Brewing Company in Memphis, for instance, survived as the Tennessee Beverage Company, making soft drinks and malt syrup. Down in New Orleans, Dixie Brewing Company became the Dixie Beverage Company, producing Dixo nonalcoholic beer along with ice cream and soda pop. The Falls City Brewing Company in Louisville, Kentucky, reorganized as the Falls City Ice and Beverage Company, and sold ice, soft drinks, and near beer. These were the rare exceptions, though. Over the course of a half century, the South had pioneered the use of artificial refrigeration and industrial techniques to create a thriving regional brewing industry. It took less than half a decade of Prohibition to wipe that industry almost completely off the map.

Bootlegging and Illegal Whiskey Distilling

At the outset of Prohibition, an active underground distilling industry was already up and running in the South, mostly in the hills and hollows of the Appalachians. The arrival of Prohibition changed the nature of the moonshining trade, degrading the overall quality of the spirits and making the enterprise much more violent and dangerous. The goal of moonshiners had always been to make whiskey that they could sell to consumers and not pay taxes on. In the Prohibition environment, when there was no legal high-quality stuff to compete against, the bar for what was salable dropped quite low, and moonshiners shifted their focus to turning out product as quickly and cheaply as possible. The big profits to be made lured many younger men into the trade, many of whom would never have been interested in whiskey distilling when there wasn't so much fast money in it.

During this period, the so-called thumper keg was widely adopted to eliminate the time-intensive second distillation run. This was a fifty-gallon keg placed between the cooking pot and the condenser, and the first run of spirits were poured into the thumper as they emerged from their first run through the still. The hot vapors from the pot produced a second distillation in the keg, along with the rhythmic thumping sound that gave the device its name. Even more deleterious was the substitution of raw sugar for most of the corn in the mash. Cheap corn sugar could be imported by the ton from the Midwest, and five dollars' worth of it could be converted to ten gallons of high-proof moonshine that would sell for forty dollars a gallon. If crafty distillers cut that booze further with water and adulterants, they could clear as much as $500 profit on a ten-gallon batch.

Moonshiners used tricks to speed fermentation, like plopping carbide chunks in the fermenter boxes to heat the mash, and they added things like sulfuric acid or lye to simulate a bead—the bubbles that form when high-proof whiskey is shaken. They colored the clear spirits with charcoal, fruit juices, caramel, and burned peaches. Deputy Sheriff Frank Hampe of Harris County, Texas, reported that during moonshine raids he frequently found that the barrels used for fermenting mash were left uncovered. "This allows the rodents and insects to fall in and die," he told the United Press. "Moonshiners make no effort to take the dead animals and bugs out." On one of his raids, he even found a dead pig in one of the barrels of mash they destroyed.

The profits to be made even from the lowest-quality rotgut drove moonshining to become a more organized operation. By 1922, newspapers were reporting that moneymen were setting up illegal stills and paying a regular wage to moonshiners to operate them on their behalf. Criminal gangs set up elaborate moonshining and bootlegging networks across the South. Prohibition also changed the geography of the moonshine trade. In the old days, it was a primarily local trade. Moonshiners would conceal barrels in a wagon and deliver them to nearby storekeepers. Many customers often came directly to the supply, bringing a jug to be filled at a drop point somewhere along a mountain road. The Prohibition years saw the rise of the moonshine trippers, who transported illegal liquor longer distances via automobile. Many of the South's cities—Knoxville, Asheville, Greenville, Columbus—suddenly became thirsty moonshine markets, and the trippers started making fast nighttime runs from the mountains down to the cities to supply them. The small five- or ten-gallon wooden kegs and ceramic demijohns that were popular in the early part of the century gave way to half-gallon glass jars—the type used by housewives for canning vegetables—packed twelve at a time into corrugated paper boxes. Even more popular were one-gallon rectangular tin cans with cork tops. Known as jackets, they could be stacked five a time in burlap sacks and tied securely together. Packed properly, ninety cans of whiskey could be carried in a Model T.

Long a mountain phenomenon, illegal distilling became more prevalent in the coastal South too. In Dare County, North Carolina, thirty steam distilleries were said to be producing fifty thousand gallons per week. In a direct reversal of the pre-Prohibition trade, most of this North Carolina liquor made its way to Baltimore, where it was artificially colored and sold as bonded whiskey. In Florida, where lots of sugarcane and sorghum was grown, distillers could buy cane syrup for $1.20 a quart and turn it into moonshine that sold for $6 a quart. In August 1922, officers in Marion County, South Carolina, turned up a copper still with 640-gallon capacity in the Pee Dee swamp. Operated by George Best, a prominent farmer, it was the largest still seized up to that time in the state.

Best's operation was an outlier for the early days of Prohibition-era moonshine, for most busts were of much smaller stills. But there were an awful lot of them. News of raids and arrests filled Southern newspapers in the early 1920s. Almost half of the 2,200 prisoners in the Atlanta federal penitentiary were serving liquor charges. In 1921, Deputy Sheriff Arnold in Duval County, Florida, offered a twenty-five-dollar reward for the return of Spine, a pig whose fondness for corn mash had helped his men uncover moonshine stills. The pig was believed to have been swiped by so-called blockaders.

All the arrests and investigative pigs had little effect on the supply of moonshine on the market. In November 1921, whiskey from the north Georgia mountains was selling in Athens for $1.75 per gallon, the lowest price in decades. "It is said that bootleggers peddle their drinkable wares in practically every skyscraper in the business section of Atlanta," one newspaper reported in 1921. "Businessmen know it and talk about it but they simply wink at it." Nat McWorter, an African-American bootlegger, operated a supposed soft-drink stand under the Washington-Courtland street viaduct. He owned two six-cylinder cars and claimed to have city detectives on his payroll. The superintendent of the nearby Atlanta Ice and Coal company complained to newspapers that "drunken negroes were so thick under there at times that 'they had to wheelbarrow them away,'" but the police did nothing to break up the parties. In cities like Lexington, Kentucky, the soft-drink stands were well known to have enamel coffee pots filled with moonshine behind their counters.

Rum-Running

Moonshiners' stills were only one source of illegal liquor in the Prohibition South. With close to three thousand miles of coastline stretching from

Texas around to Virginia, the region had plenty of secluded spots where small boats could land cargoes of liquor. The popular image of Prohibition bootleggers is based upon Chicago and Detroit—guys in fedoras with tommy guns and names like Bugs and Waxy. Some of the first large-scale bootleggers to gain public notoriety, though, operated in the South. Many were immigrants from Germany and Italy, and they tended to make their living in the grocery trade before Prohibition gave them an opportunity for much larger profits,

One such immigrant was Frederick "Fred" Haar, who was born in Germany in 1865 and by 1885 had arrived in Savannah, where he opened a grocery store and saloon. He and his son, William, were arrested several times between 1909 and 1916 for violations of state prohibition laws, and they stepped up their activities once Prohibition became nationwide. In July 1922, federal agents raided Fred Haar's grocery and seized $75,000 in cash, accusing Haar and several other men of evading federal income taxes. The income they had failed to pay those taxes on had not come from the sale of flour and potatoes, as the Feds were able to prove by examining Haar's bank accounts and property records. A year later, on August 16, 1923, a *New York Times* headline declared, "Biggest Liquor Ring Broken in Savannah." Eighty-four men, including a prominent Savannah banker, were rounded up by Secret Service and Treasury officers in a single one-day sweep and charged with conspiracy to violate the Volstead Act, the Federal legislation that defined how the Eighteenth Amendment was to be enforced.

William Haar, Fred's son, was accused of being the ring's leader. In the wake of the national Prohibition, he had gained control of a fleet of ships that took on loads of booze from Scotland, France, Cuba, and the Bahamas. They would sail to just outside the three-mile limit off the Georgia coast where US governmental jurisdiction ended. There they offloaded their cargo of Scotch whiskey, French brandy, and Caribbean rum onto fast motorboats that raced it to land in the swampy inlets around Savannah as well other points along the coast, from Wilmington, North Carolina, all the way down to Florida. From there, the liquor was broken up into lots of around five hundred cases, disguised as various types of merchandise, and distributed across the South by train, automobile, and coastwise craft. Some made its way as far north as New York and Philadelphia. All told, 126 people were indicted across the country for their involvement in the ring led by the so-called Savannah Four. William Haar and his two brothers, Carl and Fred Jr., were sentenced to a $10,000 fine and two years in the federal penitentiary, and their father, Fred, was sentenced to one year. William Haar was also assessed a tax of more than $1.9 million for unreported income between the years 1917 and 1921, though the Internal Revenue commissioner reduced that to a paltry $238,105 upon appeal.

Destroyed illegal whiskey, Girard, Alabama.

Savannah was just one point of entry; any city on the coast was poised to become a hub for illegal liquor. Just south of New Orleans, the Barataria Bay, once the home base of early nineteenth-century pirates like Jean Lafitte, emerged as the hotbed of twentieth-century outlaws too. The bay was screened from the Gulf of Mexico and crisscrossed by a network of navigable streams that reached almost to New Orleans, providing plenty of cover for rumrunner boats as they made their way to shore, where trucks waited to take the cargo inland. They got no interference from Sheriff L. A. Mereaux in Saint Bernard Parish, just to the east of New Orleans, who collected a toll on each shipment made through his jurisdiction and used the proceeds to maintain a mansion built in 1808 and his own private racetrack.

Plenty of ships were also landing illegal liquor in Mobile Bay. In 1922, Aubrey Boyles, the US district attorney for southern Alabama, began sending coded telegrams to Mabel Walker Willebrandt, the US assistant attorney general in charge of federal Prohibition, warning that a massive protection racket was going on in Mobile. Willebrandt called in M. T. "Lone Wolf" Gonzaullas, a former Texas Ranger who had become famous for rooting out moonshiners in the Southwest, and he began to infiltrate and document the inner workings of what soon became known as the Mobile Rum Ring. Early in the morning on November 13, 1923, federal agents swept through the city and confiscated eight trucks full of imported liquor worth more than $100,000. There was no place to store that much booze in the federal building, so agents stacked it in the alley outside and surrounded it with electrified barbed wire and guards armed with sawed-off shotguns.

By December, Boyles had indicted 117 people for conspiracy to violate Prohibition laws, including some of Mobile's leading citizens and Democratic public officials. They included the chief of police, the county sheriff and four of his deputies, the president of the People's Bank, and William H. Holcombe Jr., the former sheriff of Mobile County and a member of the Alabama state legislature. But the Mobile political machine wasn't going down without a fight. On December 18, the newspapers announced that a warrant had been issued for the arrest of US District Attorney Aubrey Boyles on charges of soliciting bribes. The allegations came from none other than the freshly indicted state legislator William H. Holcombe Jr., who claimed that Boyles had offered to let him escape prosecution in exchange for a fat payout. Boyles turned himself in and was released on a $4,000 bond, and he asked the US attorney general to relieve him of his duties until the charges were resolved.

To replace Boyles, Mabel Walker Willebrandt tapped a young lawyer named Hugo Black, who as the chief prosecutor of Jefferson County had been the nemesis of Birmingham's blind tiger operators. The Mobile Rum Ring trial began in April 1924, and it was the biggest case ever heard in the Mobile federal court. Lone Wolf Gonzaullas thrilled the press with his descriptions of the inner workings of the Mobile Rum Ring. The sale of booze was controlled by the so-called Big Six wholesalers, who operated front businesses like the Inkstand. Nominally an ink company, the store's back room held a bar "where all the vintages of yore were served to the thirsty." The bootleggers bought protection from the sheriff and the police department, and Percy Kearns, a prominent local attorney, served as the go-between, gathering the money from the rum ring and delivering it where it needed to go to keep the wheels well greased.

Treasury men study the "war zone" map of rum runners' positions in the office of General Lincoln C. Andrews (left), assistant secretary of the treasury in charge of Prohibition law enforcement.

The jury returned eleven guilty and thirty-three not guilty verdicts. Five of the Big Six ended up being convicted, as was Mobile Police Chief P. J. O'Shaughnessy, lawyer Kearns, and William Holcombe Jr. The cases earned Hugo Black a reputation as a resolute defender of the law and enforcer of dryness, and he banked off that in his successful run for the US Senate in 1926, which ultimately led to his appointment to the United States Supreme Court in 1937. Most of the defendants, though, weren't particularly damaged by the outcome, and the Holcombe-led political machine remained in power in Mobile.

The federal government took its fight against rumrunners not just into the cities but onto the high seas as well. By 1923, a rum row had developed off the coast in the Gulf of Mexico, where rusty old freighters and tramp steamers lay at anchor, their holds full and decks piled high with liquor. Safely outside the three-mile limit, the crews cheerily greeted Coast Guard cutters that came within hailing distance, and they held legitimate clearance papers showing they were en route to Mexican ports with their cargoes of liquor. The *Biloxi Daily Herald* noted that two such ships, one registered under the Honduran flag and the other under the British, appeared on rum row in October 1923 and five months later were still

Southern Spirits

"bound to Tampico," though they were certainly making very slow progress. In 1924, the United States signed a treaty with Great Britain extending the definition of a nation's coastal waters to twelve miles offshore, which quadrupled the distance that rumrunner boats would have to travel. Even before it was ratified, the ships in the Gulf's rum row, most of which were flying under British flags, mysteriously disappeared—finally arriving, perhaps, at their destination in Tampico.

Industrial Alcohol

Beyond medicinal whiskey, smuggled imported liquor, and moonshine, there was one other common way that Southerners got their hands on booze. Plenty of companies were still legally making industrial alcohol, which was used for manufacturing everything from perfumes to hats. "A very well known antiseptic solution," the *Macon Telegraph* reported in 1920, "manufactured in a very near-by Southern State, which carries a large percentage of alcohol, has come into enormous demand in this, as well as other Georgia cities." That firm was said to be making more than one hundred barrels per week. Between 1920 and 1925, though the sale of hats remained relatively constant, the production of industrial alcohol in America tripled.

The government mandated that denaturants like sulfuric acid or iodine be added to industrial alcohol to make it undrinkable, but that didn't stop people from trying. By 1925, so-called cleaning plants dotted the countryside, where industrial alcohol was passed through a still to remove the denaturants and then colored and flavored to pass for aged whiskey. In 1926, the federal Prohibition administrator for Kentucky and Tennessee reported that "so-called moonshine" made from redistilled industrial alcohol was selling for less than the real stuff that mountaineers made from raw ingredients and was forcing the real moonshiners to seek other means of income. "Our agents have seized real moonshine but three times in six months," he reported, "and these seizures were but a few gallons each." Less sophisticated bootleggers undertook to rectify various forms alcohol—paints, shoe polish, perfumes—using cruder methods, like filtering it through newspapers or felt hats, with, at best, spotty levels of success. Repeated cases of blindness and paralysis were attributed to victims' drinking spirits containing wood alcohol and other poisonous substances.

In March 1930, a full decade into Prohibition, a new sort of paralysis suddenly appeared. The typical victim was an alcoholic male, usually unemployed or holding a low-paying job in an urban area, and living alone in a cheap rented room in a seedy part of town. First his legs would begin to get limp below the knee, and within days they would be so floppy that the person couldn't walk. The source of the affliction was quickly identified as Jamaica ginger extract—commonly known as jake—a patent medicine that had been around for decades and whose popularity had soared during Prohibition. A two-ounce glass bottle could be bought for thirty-five cents in drugstores and groceries, and it contents were up to 85 percent alcohol. At some drugstores, a back room served as a sort of impromptu saloon, where customers could take their bottle of jake and a Coca-Cola and concoct their own libations. By April, the partial paralysis was already being called jake leg, and health departments across the South and Midwest started banning the sale of Jamaica ginger extract. Johnson City, Tennessee, was struck particularly hard. "You can go on the streets of Johnson City now," one victim wrote to the surgeon general's office, "and in the run of a day, you can count three or four hundred people in the same condition I am in."

The cause of the poisoning remained a mystery until a sample of Jamaica ginger extract was tested in the Bureau of Prohibition lab and found to contain triorthocresyl phosphate (TOCP), a plasticizer used to keep synthetic materials from becoming brittle. How it got into the patent medicine was the next question. At the outset of Prohibition, the federal government had ordered that the amount of solids in fluid extracts be doubled, an attempt to make patent medicines so unpalatable that people would be discouraged from drinking them. They tested compliance by boiling away the alcohol and weighing what was left behind. Boosting the regular solids in Jamaican ginger, it turned out, transformed it from a pale orange liqueur to a nasty, bitter black syrup. So patent medicine manufacturers had started adding castor oil, which had a higher boiling point than alcohol and was left behind with the ginger during boiling tests. It was all well and good until a Boston firm named Hub Products, in an effort to find something cheaper and less prone to separation than castor oil, doctored up 640,000 bottles of Jamaica ginger extract with TOCP, which was thought to be nontoxic to humans but had never been tested as a food additive.

Victims formed groups and petitioned the government for relief or aid, but their pleas fell on deaf ears, in large part because they tended to be lower-class men and chronic alcoholics. William "Alfalfa Bill" Murray, the governor of Oklahoma, lumped "the man with 'jakeitis'" in with stock exchange investors as "people I haven't much use for." One minister in Johnson City declared from the pulpit, "God is hanging out a red flag as a danger sign to those who violate his law." The two owners of Hub Products, Harry Gross and Max Reisman, were convicted in federal court, but they were sentenced only to probation despite having paralyzed tens of thousands of victims.

The Demise of the Southern Cocktail

At the onset of national Prohibition, it wasn't clear what would happen to the great oasis of New Orleans and its famous cocktails. In February 1920, the *New Orleans States* reported the fates of some of the Crescent City's most noted bartenders. Henry C. Ramos had taken his gin fizzes to Cuba, where he was doing a land office business, but many of his mixologist peers exited the liquor trade. Those who chose to stay in the hospitality business ended up converting their bars to nonalcoholic enterprises. Oscar Dubar of the Crescent Hall Bar, for instance, retooled as an oyster bar and cigar stand, while Aristide Martin of the Sazerac Bar switched to making sandwiches in his old location. A great many of these so-called conversions, though, turned out to be little more than a veneer, and within a year, the path New Orleans was going to take through Prohibition was clear. After surveying ninety-two cities, sociologist Martha Brensley Bruere declared scientifically that New Orleans was the wettest place in the country. "There is general disregard of the law and scorn for it," she wrote in *Does Prohibition Work?* "Most of the men drink something every day."

New Orleans was the most wide-open, but plenty of other Southern cities had their own illicit restaurants and bars. Galveston, Texas, became a notorious gambling and drinking resort town during Prohibition, featuring Sam and Rose Maceo's high-end Balinese Room at the end of a seventy-five-foot pier extending out into the Gulf. John Newman Harris had moved to Savannah and established a successful grocery business during World War I, but after Prohibition arrived, he moved into a different line of work. In 1923, he was among the dozens of men swept up alongside William Haar in the Savannah Four raids and was sentenced to eight months in the federal pen. After his release in 1924, Harris built a roadside diner, Johnny Harris Tavern and Bar-B-Cue, on a dirt road that ran from downtown Savannah out to the riverfront village of Thunderbolt. It sold food and beer to motorists heading out to the yacht club and casino at Thunderbolt and the beach islands beyond. Harris did so well at it that in the 1930s he upgraded to a new restaurant and nightclub that featured a twelve-sided grand ballroom with a thirty-foot domed ceiling painted to resemble the night sky so patrons could dance "beneath the stars." The Johny Harris Restaurant is still in business today.

Up the coast in Charleston, Vincent Chicco, the King of the Blind Tigers, kept right on going at his so-called grocery store on Market Street. Other Charleston grocers were dealing in illicit booze too. Henry Otto Hasselmeyer had arrived from Germany around the turn of the century at the age of twenty. He got married, bought a three-story building, and opened a grocery. When Prohibition arrived, Hasselmeyer worked out a nice side business to complement his grocery sales. His mother-in-law would sit in the back of the store wearing a big apron and shelling beans and peas for Henry to sell. Interested patrons soon discovered that beneath that apron was hidden a bottle of booze, and for a small charge, she would gladly dispense them a dose.

In 1929, Dr. James M. Doran, the US prohibition commissioner, delineated for a reporter what people were drinking and where they were getting it. In Northern cities, much of the liquor was brought in by sea or smuggled over the border from Canada. "Through the south and into the southwest," he said, "it's a proposition of pure moonshine and corn liquor. In Florida and through the Gulf area there's a little imported liquor mixed up with the local moonshine. You'll find almost entirely moonshine up the Atlantic coast to north of Baltimore."

Even when they could get their hands on the good stuff, the flavors were different than before. The US Custom Service posted legal advertisements for all the alcohol they nabbed, and the ones from Florida showed seizures consisting mostly of rum, Canadian rye whiskey, Scotch whisky, and gin. Thanks to bootleggers' boats, Southerners were being reintroduced to an old favorite spirit that had long fallen out of favor—rum—but it was nothing like the harsh, dark rums of the nineteenth century. Bacardi had been founded in 1862 in Santiago, Cuba, and it brought new innovations to the Cuban rum industry, including the use of column stills, a filtering system to remove impurities, and blending distillates to create a light, crisp rum. During Prohibition, Bacardi tripled the size of its shipments to the Bahamas and the French Island Saint-Pierre off the coast of Newfoundland—both of which were notorious ports for smugglers. The hogo bite of old Jamaican rum was eclipsed by the smooth, cleaner Bacardi style, removing one of the key notes in the palette of Southern spirit flavors.

The Great Mint Julep Controversy of 1933

Perhaps no one wanted to see the end of Prohibition more than Irvin Shrewsbury Cobb. A portly, cigar-chomping man with a receding hairline and thin-lipped grin, he was America's highest paid journalist and a star of radio, movies, and the lecture circuit. Kentucky-born and unashamedly fond of good bourbon, Cobb signed on as the chair of the Authors and Artists Committee of the Association Against the Prohibition Amendment and became one of the most ardent campaigners for repealing Prohibition. In 1929, he published *Red Likker*, a rabidly antiprohibition novel about the American whiskey industry that traces the rise and fall of a fictional distillery named Bird and Son. Over the course of his five-decade career as a writer and humorist, Cobb was awarded the French Legion of Honor and even had a brand of cigars, a hotel, and a bridge over the Ohio River named after him.

It is also my contention that, more than any other single person, Irvin S. Cobb was responsible for fabricating the image of bourbon whiskey as the quintessential spirit of the South, in direct contradiction to more than a century of brandy and rye drinking. He started doing so even while it was still illegal to make bourbon whiskey in America.

In July 1933, Cobb challenged Eddie of the Astor, a well-known bartender from New York's Hotel Astor, to a mint julep showdown. Cobb had overheard Eddie state (correctly) that a proper julep should be made with brandy. "Brandy?" Cobb reportedly declared. "Putting brandy in a mint julep is like putting ketchup in iced tea." The very contest shows that there was still was rich diversity in the julep world at the time. Cobb's challenge, columnist H. Allen Smith noted, originated out of "a controversy over the potability of the Kentucky mint julep as compared with all other forms of julep." H. L. Mencken, the famed Baltimore journalist and critic, upon hearing of the challenge, harrumphed that both parties were wrong. "In Maryland we use rye whiskey. Bourbon puts too much meat on the consumer."

The contest took place in Cobb's Park Avenue apartment, and Heywood Broun, the popular columnist for the *New York World-Telegram*, was enlisted to judge. For his Kentucky julep, Cobb used a bottle of Belmont bourbon distilled in 1901, which he obtained from Louisville's Pendennis Club. Cobb provided a bottle of brandy to Eddie of the Astor, and when the bartender requested a bit of old Jamaican rum for his cosmopolitan julep, he was given the closest thing Cobb had on hand: Bacardi. Judge Broun downed three of Cobb's bourbon juleps and three of Eddie's brandy versions in alternating succession, then promptly retired to a bedroom for a nap. He awoke a half hour later, fortified himself with three cups of coffee, then banged out a decision on Cobb's typewriter. "Judgment is rendered in favor of Mr. Cobb and the mint julep compounded out of Kentucky Bourbon," he declared. "Eddie of the Astor is guilty of a heresy in using brandy as a base." He took the opportunity to take a poke at rye, too, declaring it "Communistic, Atheistic, and against the dignity of man" to commit "such gross violations of the code as using rye whiskey, or that great abomination, the gin julep."

Eddie of the Astor took the defeat graciously, though he noted that he was a little out of practice, thanks to the whole Prohibition thing. He added, "I wish the press to know that it was not really Mr. Cobb that won, but really his liquor." There he had a valid point: it's sort of hard to compete with 32-year-old bourbon when all you've got is a bottle of Prohibition-era brandy and Bacardi rum. But Cobb had won the battle. It was just the first of the many in his propaganda campaign that ended up elevating bourbon in the popular imagination as the quintessential spirit of the American South. But first, it had to be legal to make the stuff again.

One by one, fed-up states began voting to denounce or modify the Volstead Act, and a handful even voted to repeal their local enforcement acts—New York in 1923, Montana in 1926, and Wisconsin in 1929— leaving enforcement of Prohibition up to the Feds. The Hoover administration stuck to its dry guns, arguing that all that was needed was even more aggressive law enforcement, and Congress doubled down, passing strict new laws making violating the Volstead act a felony and subjecting offenders to much harsher sentences. These measures, which many viewed as legislative overreaching, only increased popular support for repealing Prohibition. The public was outraged by cases like that of Mrs. Etta Mae Miller of Lansing, Michigan. A mother of ten whose husband was already serving time for a liquor law violation, Miller was sentenced in 1929 to a mandatory life sentence for her fourth Volstead Act conviction under Michigan's new "habitual criminal" law.

In the 1932 presidential campaign, the platform for both the Republicans and the Democrats included a plank promising to repeal the Eighteenth Amendment. On November 9, Americans voted Franklin Delano Roosevelt into the White House in a landslide election, giving FDR 57 percent of the popular vote and the electoral votes for all but six states. The writing on the wall was easy to read: the end of Prohibition was near.

19

Four Roses and Rebel Yell: Rebounding from Prohibition

In July 1935, the Kingfish—aka Senator Huey P. Long of Louisiana—was staying at the New Yorker Hotel in Manhattan, and he spied a sign in the bar promising a Ramos gin fizz. Wondering if he could get the real thing in New York, Long ordered one. He took one sip and proceeded directly to his room, where he telephoned Seymour Weiss, the manager of the Hotel Roosevelt in New Orleans, and instructed him to send his best gin fizzer by the first plane to New York City. Sam Guarino, the bar manager of the Roosevelt, arrived the next morning, and Long assembled a group of reporters at the New Yorker.

Sam Guarino took his place behind the hotel's Horseshoe Bar and proceeded to mix up a big batch of fizzes, with Long assisting with the shaking and providing a torrent of invective about deceitful congressmen and the Bolshevist tendencies of President Roosevelt. As they passed the glasses around, the Kingfish stentoriously related how his own grandpappy, John D. Long, was responsible for the invention of the Ramos gin fizz. In 1852, the Kingfish said, his grandfather stopped into the Roosevelt Hotel in New Orleans and found the young bartender about to be fired because he didn't know how to mix drinks. Taking pity on the young man, Grandpappy Long jumped behind the bar and, despite not being a drinking man, spent the entire day teaching him how to mix drinks, culminating with instructions on how to concoct the Ramos gin fizz, a proper version of which the New York scribblers now had their chance to try.

Long's story, of course, was complete hogwash, starting with the fact that the Roosevelt Hotel did not exist until 1923, but it helped get Long and his Ramos gin fizz demonstration reported in papers all across the country. What got the Kingfish into hot water, though, was not his fast and loose treatment of facts but rather his taste buds. Right after Sam Guarino had combined the ingredients, Long instructed him to add a dash of vanilla. Old-school cocktail lovers went nuts. The *Omaha World Herald* reported that "bartenders below the Mason-Dixon line are throwing up their hands in horror at the mere thought of vanilla in the gin fizz." Curly O'Connor, head bartender at the Waldorf Astoria scoffed at Long's fizz as "a soda fountain concoction." He recalled being in New Orleans back in 1888, when the cocktails were shaken for a full ten minutes before serving and didn't contain any vanilla. A few days later, Long backpedaled, explaining that vanilla does not properly belong in a Ramos gin fizz but that "some connoisseurs liked a dash of it," himself included.

It was just one of many small stumbles as Southerners tried to reclaim a drinking culture that had been all but obliterated. Prohibition's fourteen-and-a-half year interregnum hadn't stopped Southerners from obtaining and consuming alcohol, but it did permanently change what and how they drank. The process of rebooting not just a distilling and brewing industry but also an entire drinking tradition was not a simple one, and the way it unfolded wound up shaping and, in many cases, distorting the we way we think today about Southern drinks—what they are, where they come from, and how they should be consumed. More than any other period, the decades after repeal formulated the fuzzy haze of myth and legend that defines Southern drinking today. It's not just a matter of historical forgetfulness, either, for there was plenty of storytelling and deliberate myth-making by those trying to sell liquor to the public in a challenging marketplace.

When it entered the dark dry days of Prohibition, the South enjoyed a vibrant if somewhat turbulent drinking culture. What emerged on the other side was something very different. You could make a Ramos gin fizz to accompany this chapter if you like (see the recipe on page 180), but it wouldn't really be appropriate. A more suitable drink would be a mint julep, and one made with bourbon in "the old Kentucky way," preferably as dictated by the marketing department of a postrepeal whiskey company. The recipe on the following page is a good candidate. It's taken from *How to Make Old Kentucky Famed Drinks*, a small two-by-4-inch promotional booklet published by the Brown, Forman Distillery Co., Inc., in 1934. Its opening recipe is the Pendennis Club mint julep, as made by Martin Cuneo, the head bartender at the elite Louisville social club.

Martin Cuneo's Pendennis Club Mint Julep

SERVES 1

1 tablespoon granulated sugar

Spring water

1 large bunch fresh mint, about 5 inches long

Cracked ice

3 ounces bourbon

To make properly, you should use a 16-ounce silver julep cup. If you aren't fortunate enough to have one, a large glass tumbler will do. Put sugar in glass, add a small amount of springwater (just enough to wet it thoroughly), and stir till sugar is well dissolved. Remove three sprigs of mint from the bunch and add to cup. Fill cup with cracked ice. Add bourbon and stir gently. Add additional ice if needed to refill cup to the top. Let stand a few minutes until sides of the cup or glass are well frosted. Take the remainder of the mint, trim ends, and place on top of ice, and forcing the sprigs down into the ice. Cut a straw to the proper length so that when placed in the cup, it will just protrude about the lip of the cup. As Cuneo's instructions note, "The nostrils of the drinker should be practically buried in the mint leaves during the act of drinking."

Repeal

On April 10, 1933, Michigan became the first of the thirty-six states needed to ratify the Twenty-First Amendment and repeal Prohibition. By the end of November, the number was up to thirty-three and the country began preparing itself for legal booze. President Roosevelt was on call to race back to Washington from his part-time residence in Warm Springs, Georgia, to declare repeal just as soon as the thirty-sixth state ratified the amendment. Domestic distilleries were working overtime, churning out new spirits at top speed, and importers were loading liquor onto fast boats in foreign ports in anticipation of the event. Three states—Ohio, Pennsylvania, and Utah—all ratified the amendment on the same day, December 5, 1933. The failed experiment of national Prohibition was over.

The post-Prohibition experience in the South was quite different than it was in other parts of the country, for Southerners didn't suddenly pop the caps for newly legal celebratory parties. The Twenty-First Amendment allowed each state to determine its own alcohol laws, and of the twenty-three states that allowed liquor sales immediately upon repeal, only one was in the South—and it was Louisiana, of course. Legal drinking returned to the rest of the South in fits and starts, as state by state and county by county, residents determined whether to allow alcohol sales. For decades, the South was a patchwork of wet, dry, and damp areas.

Georgia ended its statewide alcohol ban in 1938 and reverted to local option. Within weeks, twenty-five counties had voted themselves wet. The measure passed in Fulton County by a margin of three to one, and on April 25, a dozen liquor stores opened their doors in Atlanta. "With their tongues hanging out," the *Atlanta Constitution* reported, "hundreds of Atlantans flocked to the legal liquor stores to make purchases of state-stamped legal whiskey, many of them buying legal liquor for the first time in their lives." Tennessee followed suit with local option the following year. Mississippi was the last state in the Union to end statewide prohibition, remaining dry until 1966.

An Industry Rebuilds

A handful of Southern brewers had managed to limp through the dry years selling ice and soft drinks, and once their states went wet, they switched right back to fermenting malt and hops. In Memphis, the Tennessee Beverage Company reverted to the Tennessee Brewing Company, and it brought to the market a string of poorly selling brands before finally striking gold with their catchily named Goldcrest 51 and its memorable red circle logo with the number 51 inside, commemorating the number of years the company had been in business. In Galveston, the Galveston-Houston Breweries renovated their plant and resumed sales of Southern Select beer, while Howard Hughes spun up the Gulf Brewing Company on the grounds of the Hughes Tool Company, where he introduced Grand Prize, which soon became the best-selling beer in Texas.

In Jacksonville, Florida, the Jax Brewing Company, which had ridden out Prohibition as Jax Ice and Cold Storage, reclaimed its old name and started pumping out Jax beer again. Branded "the Drink of Friendship," Jax's crisp pilsner sold in local bars for ten cents a glass. Down in New Orleans, the Jackson Brewing Company was selling a beer named Jax too—named in honor of nearby Jackson Square. The two breweries ended up agreeing to split the South, with the Jacksonville Jax selling east of Mobile and the New Orleans Jax to the west. Two other pre-Prohibition breweries, Dixie and National Brewing, resumed operations in New Orleans too.

The South was once again awash in beer, and while the big national brewers like Anheuser-Busch and Schlitz had a large foothold in the market, there was a great diversity of smaller regional beers that were available. These local brands took on particular identification in the cities in which they were brewed, becoming a key element of a night on a town in a particular part of the South. "Between the repeal of Prohibition and the year I got out of high school," Jacksonville newspaperman Bill Foley recalled, "Jax Beer was as much a part of the Southern saloon as punchboards and pig's feet. . . . Jax was a kind of beer you didn't mind spilling, which if you play enough Nine-Ball and listen to enough hillbilly music in the course of an evening, you are bound to do."

There were plenty of options for those who wanted a shot of hard liquor alongside their beer, but not the same regional diversity. In the nineteenth century, small distilleries had once dotted the hills of North Carolina and Georgia, many of them operating a few months out of the year and others only when there was a bumper crop of apples or peaches. In the postrepeal world, fruit brandy distilling—with the exception of moonshiners still dodging taxes up in the hills—was a thing of the past. Many of the smaller old firms in the major distilling centers of Kentucky, Pennsylvania, and Maryland were gone, too, having shut down their plants and sold off their equipment and brands. Many of those brands did return to the market, but often in name only.

As Prohibition had ground on, a series of mergers and consolidation had shuffled the ownership of old brands and stocks of liquor from one company to another, eventually concentrating control in the hands of a small number of firms. One of the biggest players was Lewis Solon Rosenstiel, who had started off selling bulk medicinal whiskey before teaming up with D. K. Weiskopf, who owned the old Schenley Distillery in Schenley, Pennsylvania. Together they formed the Schenley Products Company, which proceeded to acquire the makers of Golden Wedding, Echo Springs, Old Overholt, and Ancient Age. The old Whiskey Trust, which had once dominated alcohol production in the Midwest, reorganized into the National Distillers Products Corporation and began buying up precious supplies of whiskey as well as the brands of many of the old distilleries. Their merger with the American Medicinal Spirits Company in 1929 made National Distillers the largest player in the market.

On the eve of repeal, these firms had twenty million gallons of whiskey aging in their warehouses, and fully half of it was in the hands of National Distillers, who by then owned the Old Taylor, Mount Vernon, Old Crow, Old Overholt, and Old Grand-Dad brands. (That's a lot of olds, but as we'll see, old was a big thing in whiskey marketing.) Another five million gallons were in the hands of Schenley, and the remaining 25 percent was scattered among a few smaller players, including Frankfort Distilleries, Inc., which held the Four Roses brand, and Glenmore, which owned Kentucky Tavern. That twenty million gallons was a mere fraction of the demand of a nation that during Prohibition was consuming 200 million gallons of spirits every year, but inventory was not the only issue. "The major part of the problem before the whiskey companies is one of merchandising," *Fortune* magazine commented in December 1933. "For only through expert merchandising can the whiskey business be kept in relatively few hands—few enough for the government to see they are kept clean."

The men who now controlled the liquor industry were determined to prevent the return of the many ills that plagued their trade before Prohibition. Back then, it had been a sprawling, disorganized business, with thousands of companies of all sizes—distillers, blenders, rectifiers, brokers, and wholesalers—selling in an unruly market. Distillers sold their barrels as soon as they entered the warehouses, and they didn't worry too much about what happened to their contents after that. Those spirits could be modified and blended in any number of ways, then put in bottles that were labeled with just about anything.

The state and federal governments wanted to ensure a large, centralized alcohol industry too. President Roosevelt issued an executive order creating the Federal Alcohol Control Administration (FACA) to administer a code of fair conduct for the liquor industry, which restricted entry to the distilling business and required permits for any person wishing to import, sell, or produce distilled spirits, wine, or beer. When former bootleggers, moonshiners, and smugglers started applying for those liquor permits, the FACA quickly put in a place a requirement that applicants could not have a felony liquor law violation on their records. The permits and code of conduct helped cement the emerging oligopoly in the reviving American spirits industry.

One big barrier for distillers trying to reenter the business was lack of capital. Many of the old distilleries had been torn down during Prohibition, and most of the ones that remained were in disrepair and needed a thorough overhaul before being ready to resume production. Then there was the problem of aging. Whiskey from Scotland and Canada, which had been manufactured years before and already was properly aged, was flooding the country, making it difficult for American distillers to compete with their immature products. A four-year bottled in bond whiskey could not be introduced until at least 1938, so investors had to fund operations for almost five years before they could see a return.

In Kentucky, many old pre-Prohibition distillers started getting back into the whiskey game. Joseph L. Beam returned from Mexico and helped organize the Heaven Hill Distillery in 1935. John P. Dant, the son of J. W. Dant, built a distillery at Meadowlawn in Jefferson County, where he and his successors produced Old Boone, Distiller's Choice, and Old 1889. Jim Beam had sold his Clear Springs Distillery at the onset of Prohibition, but the family had bought the property occupied by the Old Murphy Barber Distillery in Clermont, intending to quarry on the site, and they had the equipment of the old F. G. Walker Distillery in storage. So at the age of 69, Jim Beam went back into the bourbon business with his thirty-three-year old son, T. Jeremiah, as well as his brother Park and nephews Earl and Carl. The Beams needed capital to rebuild, and they turned to a trio of Chicago investors, who contributed $15,000 apiece. The James B. Beam Distilling Company incorporated on Aug 14, 1934, finished construction on the distillery in just four months, and in March 1935 made their first batch of mash since 1919. Beam had lost the rights to Old Tub bourbon when he sold the Clear Springs Distillery, so he switched to Colonel James B. Beam Bourbon, which later became Jim Beam Kentucky Straight Bourbon Whiskey.

Not all of the firms that got back into the market were as successful as Heaven Hill and Beam. The mergers and consolidations continued during the post-Prohibition period as the bigger players kept snapping up old brands from struggling small distilleries. At the time of repeal, Brown-Forman was still a relatively minor player, though it had enjoyed the benefits of having a medicinal distilling permit during Prohibition. Under the leadership of Owsley Brown, the son of founder George Garvin Brown, the firm grew rapidly, and within a decade had expanded to become the largest independent distilling company in the United States. Old Forester had long been their flagship brand, and through a series of postrepeal acquisitions, Brown added three distillery plants as well as brands like Early Times and Kentucky Dew. Two Canadian firms, Seagram and Hiram Walker, grabbed a large share of the postrepeal market too. Both had prospered during American Prohibition, when they sold a tremendous volume of their spirits in Canada and had no idea how bottles bearing their labels kept being found across the border in the United States.

A Patchwork Quilt of Laws

As Southern states went wet again, each put in place its own layers of regulations on top of the federal provisions to try to keep the alcohol industry in check. These measures differed greatly from state to state, creating a patchwork system of rules and regulations that to a large extent persists today. The so-called control states, in an echo of South Carolina's dispensary experiment from half a century before, gave the state a monopoly on alcohol sales. North Carolina, Virginia, Alabama, and Mississippi all fell into the control model, and they remain so today, though many of their rules have been tweaked over the years. Virginia, for instance, allowed licensed retailers to sell wine, but they had to buy it from the state as a wholesaler. North Carolina initially imposed a state monopoly on all alcohol sales, though they later relented on wine and beer. The government remains the state's liquor retailer today.

The government had no intention of allowing the saloon—which *Fortune* magazine declared "the most glaring evil" of the pre-Prohibition liquor trade—to return to American life. At both the national and state level, stiff regulations were placed on establishments that served liquor by the drink, many of which focused simply on trying to keep those places from looking like old-time saloons. Screening devices were banned to remove the sense of privacy that might lead to debauchery. The number of entrances were regulated, with back entrances and private back rooms banned. Many states specified that only legitimate restaurants could serve spirits, and they required a minimum number of square feet of kitchen space and percentage of revenue to be derived from food. To prevent the return of the so-called tied house—saloons that had exclusive contracts with or were owned outright by a particular brewery—laws restricted a supplier from obtaining control over a retailer. Perhaps most significant, states implemented the so-called three-tiered distribution system, which separates producers from retailers by requiring brewers and distillers to sell to independent wholesalers who, in turn, sell to retailers.

The Southern states went wet slowly and in a piecemeal fashion, with most reverting to local option, which allowed politicians to cater to their dry constituencies. The local option still exists in many Southern states today, and though over time, more and more counties have voted alcohol in, there are still a substantial number of dry counties dotting the South. Eighteen out of Texas's forty-seven counties are still dry, as are twenty-six out of Tennessee's ninety-five. The local option created all sorts of bizarre alcohol rules, and visitors traveling from one part of the South to another over the past half century have found local regulations that seem unusual if not downright eccentric. Many resulted from legislatures trying to avoid the many pains and problems that had led to Prohibition in the first place. Others are like the camel, that famous horse designed by committee, for they resulted from the intense negotiations and compromises between wets and drys to get a measure on the ballot. In Georgia, many municipalities prohibited stores from advertising cold beer on signs outside their businesses—hence the sign at the local convenience store near my childhood home that proclaimed, "We can't say it, but we've got it!" Many states prohibit the sale of alcohol on Sundays altogether, while others, like Alabama and Kentucky, allow it only after noon. Stores can't sell alcohol on Christmas Day in Georgia and Mississippi, and until just recently, South Carolina mandated that liquor stores had to be closed on election day. In Tennessee, wine can be sold only in licensed liquor stores, not grocery or convenience stores, while in South Carolina, liquor stores are forbidden from selling beer. (In New Orleans, of course, there are drive-through daiquiri stands open twenty four hours a day.)

One common phenomenon in the South was the so-called damp county, where some forms of alcohol (say beer) were legal and others weren't (like wine and hard spirits). Until 1973, the town of Oxford, Mississippi, the home of the University of Mississippi, allowed the sale of beverages with more than 4 percent alcohol but, in a particularly perverse move for a college town, would not allow the sale of beer! It took a campaign of students picketing the mayor's home to get a local option vote on beer, and Oxford finally went fully wet by a slim margin. The ordinance implementing beer sales, though, had its own strange twist: beer could not be sold refrigerated unless the establishment had a license for on-premise consumption, which meant you could enjoy an icy Bud at the neighborhood bar but couldn't pick up a cold six-pack at a grocery or convenience store. That absurd law persisted until 2013.

The Decline of Rye and the Preeminence of Story

The swamp of laws and regulations were challenging enough, but the makers of aged rye and bourbon whiskey faced an even larger problem: shifting consumer tastes. For nearly fifteen years, almost all of the good whiskey that was available had been Scotch, and the tastes of whiskey lovers had shifted toward that smokier spirit. Even more drinkers had become accustomed to clear spirits. "Before prohibition gin went into Martinis and Negroes," *Fortune* magazine not so tastefully declared in 1933. "The younger drinking generation was weaned on it and an entirely new body of drinkers, women, preferred it to whiskey." Bacardi remained synonymous in many Americans' minds with rum, becoming almost a generic term, and they expected it to be light and crisp, not dark and funky.

For whiskey makers to get back into this market, branding and story were far more important than trivial details like who distilled a particular spirit and where. And that raises a thorny question about the fate of rye whiskey in the twentieth century. Though bourbon was much beloved before Prohibition, especially in Kentucky and the Deep South, rye had been by far the whiskey of choice for most Southerners. Both bourbon and rye distillers were decimated by the dry years, but for some reason, bourbon managed to stage a comeback after repeal while rye slid slowly and surely into obscurity.

Spirits historians have offered various explanations for rye's collapse. Some propose that a generation of drinkers weaned during the dry years on white spirits like gin and Bacardi had no palate for the pungent, full-bodied rye whiskey. But this explanation should apply equally to bourbon, since in a side-by-side tasting the difference between a good bourbon and a good rye is subtle at best. Others have noted that Pennsylvania and Maryland, the great rye-producing states, had other industries to fall back on when Prohibition descended, so distillers there moved on to other fields of endeavor. The more rural and agricultural Kentucky didn't offer nearly as many options, the explanation goes, so distillers clung to their trade and went right back to it as soon as it was legal.

This sounds reasonable on the surface, but in the immediate wake of repeal, whiskey was being distilled and sold by just a handful of firms, and those firms had both rye and bourbon brands in their stables. Many owned distilleries not just in Kentucky but in Maryland and Pennsylvania too. National Distillers, for example, controlled the Large Distillery in

Pennsylvania, the Mount Vernon Distillery in Baltimore, and the Sunny Brook and Wathen Distilleries in Louisville. In their advertisements and promotional materials, these distillers tended to push both styles with equal billing, often as two flavors of the same brand. The day after repeal went into effect, Goodman and Beer Co., a New Orleans liquor wholesaler, advertised itself as the exclusive distributor for James E. Pepper and Co.'s bourbon and rye whiskey. Frankfort Distilling was marketing Paul Jones Whiskey in both bourbon and rye varieties, touting that they were made from the pure limestone water of Kentucky and Maryland. Their print ads bore the emblem, Kentucky for Bourbon, Maryland for Rye.

With two plants in Maryland and two in Kentucky, Frankfort was ready for action on both the rye and bourbon fronts. It started advertising widely in November 1933, grooming the market before repeal had even gone into effect. Whiskey in general had been tainted by the tricks of bootleggers and moonshiners, and the public, distillers concluded, first needed to be educated and reassured. "How can I be sure of getting good whiskey?" one Frankfort advertisement asked. The answer, of course, was to choose one of the company's brands. To further allay adulteration concerns, the firm introduced its patented "bootleg-proof Frankfort Pack"—a carton with a tin top and bottom that had be destroyed before the bottle could be removed.

Another concern was that, after more than a decade of shaking up martinis with bathtub gin, consumers might no longer remember how to mix proper drinks. To assist with that problem, Frankfort Distilleries engaged the longtime bourbon champion and julep partisan Irvin S. Cobb. The firm published *Irvin S. Cobb's Own Recipe Book*, a slim paperbound volume that was sold for ten cents by mail and in liquor stores across the country. It contained authoritative directions for making seventy-one famous drinks, together with "a rollicking dissertation on the joys of King Bourbon and its Brother Rye" penned by Cobb himself.

To today's eyes, Cobb's booklet is searingly offensive. It pages brim with line drawings of wide-eyed, grinning black men plucking banjos and shaking up drinks for elderly white gentlemen bedecked in nineteenth-century finery—top hats, ribbon ties, flowing white mustaches and beards. "The best Rye, as most everyone knows," Cobb declared, "has always come from Maryland, just as the best Bourbon has always come from Kentucky." The reason, he explains, is the limestone-seeped springwater that can be found only in those states. The fact that, at that time, Frankfurt Distilling maintained dual headquarters in Louisville and Baltimore may also have

The cover of Irvin S. Cobb's portrayal of drinking in the Old South.

had something to do with Cobb's assertion. The booklet invokes the name of Jerry Thomas, "the most illustrious of American barkeepers," and it presents the full canon of the pre-Prohibition bar: cocktails, fizzes, smashes, and slings. In his essay, though, Cobb casts "the queen mother of all the infusions—the Mint Julep" in the starring role, and he devotes a full sixteen pages to singing her praises.

Cobb decried the "high crimes and misdemeanors" in julep making, including crushing the mint, using peppermint springs, or—most egregious of all—finishing the drink with a dash of nutmeg across the top. He advanced a theory that the Civil War was caused not by slavery nor states' rights but rather by "some Yankee coming down South and putting nutmeg in a julep. So our folks just up and left the Union flat." He wraps things up with a misty-eyed memory of his uncle's solemn julep-building ritual, invoking pretty girls on porches and men plucking banjos and colts cavorting in pastures, working himself up to the elegiac declaration, "Oh, vanished lady! Oh, darky music! Oh, my Old Kentucky Home!"

The prominence of the julep is noteworthy, since the frosty creation that once dominated the Southern bar had all but disappeared by the turn of the twentieth century. In 1886, the *Macon Telegraph* had noted, "The mint julep still lives, but it is by no means fashionable." The writer decried the more recent notion that in a julep the mint should be crushed and shaken with water and whiskey, claiming, "No man can fall in love with such a mixture. Poor juleps have ruined the reputation of the South's most famous drink." By the turn of the twentieth century, the mint julep was in full-on retreat, both in the South and in distant hinterlands like New York City. By 1905, the New York *Sun* was mourning the loss of the julep amid "the passion for whiskey and water or 'highballs.'"

The postrepeal whiskey marketers, though, thrust the mint julep right back onto the stage. The dominant theme in the advertising of Frankfort and many other whiskey makers was nostalgia, looking to a misty past where gentleman in formal outfits sipped a range of decorous concoctions. The mint julep got resurrected as a liquid embodiment of this romantic Southern past, and in the process was endowed with many of the moony characteristics that have stuck to it ever since—the preeminent drink of Kentucky, of horse racing and beautiful women, and of a sanitized South where slavery was little more than a humorous, benevolent institution.

Though Cobb's probourbon propaganda helped get the ball rolling, it was that famous horse race at Churchill Downs in Louisville that forever cemented the notion that mint juleps are inseparable from Kentucky and bourbon whiskey. The Derby dates back to 1875, and by the early twentieth century, the mint julep had become one of the favorite drinks of racegoers, but there does not appear to have been a strong linkage in the popular imagination between the beverage and the Derby. That linkage seems to have been forged primarily through postrepeal marketing during the late 1930s.

Irvin S. Cobb's portrayal of drinking in the Old South.

A 1937 *Life* photo spread on the sixty-third running of the Kentucky Derby makes no mention of mint juleps. It does, however, include a photograph of four bow tie–clad African-American waiters from Churchill Downs Bar, and notes "no Bourbon-and-soda orders whatever are filled when the Derby horses are coming down the stretch." Mint juleps were, however, part of the festivities surrounding the horse race. Life's photographer went to a mint julep party hosted by one Julian P. Van Winkle, the president of the Stitzel-Weller Distillery, that was attended by many of Louisville's most prominent citizens and out-of-town guests. "The Van Winkle mint julep formula," the article noted, "is to use only 17-year-old stock—either 'Old Fitzgerald' or 'Old Mammoth Cave.'" Van Winkle was in the mint-bruising camp, muddling sugar and mint at the bottom of a silver cup, packing in finely cracked ice, pouring two ounces of bourbon over it, and adorning the top with a generous bouquet of mint sprigs.

In 1938, the mint julep was named the official drink of Churchill Downs, and Harry Stevens, the King of Sports Concessions, started serving them in glasses instead of paper cups. The glasses were so popular they kept

"Yes, suh, Colonel, I'se comin'!"

"One mo' sprig o' mint, wavin' its green head otah the silv'ry frost o' the glass. A dash o' powduhed sugah on the leaves—and there, bless yo' thirst, is a julep!"

AND there, bless your thirst, *is* a julep— if Four Roses mingles its fragrance with the fresh young mint.

Four Roses was born for just such a sublime duty. It has the rich bouquet that old-fashioned distilling methods give. It has the full, lush flavor that comes from Kentucky and Maryland limestone water.

And so when Four Roses goes into your julep, when its genial soul blends with the heart of the mint and rime forms on the glass, the drink you raise to your fortunate

lips is no longer a drink . . . it is a lyric of fragrance and friendliness.

We exaggerate? This afternoon, make yourself a julep—or have one made at your favorite hotel or restaurant. Be sure the whiskey is Four Roses! Then you'll get a julep at its finest.

Frankfort makes a whiskey for every taste: PAUL JONES, Old Oscar Pepper—blends of straight whiskies—Antique, Mattingly & Moore—blended whiskies—Shipping Port —straight whiskey. Send 10¢ for "Irvin S. Cobb's Own Recipe Book."

Lovers of fine gin will appreciate the rare flavor of Paul Jones ★★★★ Gin

FOUR ROSES WHISKEY

*Made by Frankfort Distilleries of Louisville and Baltimore
America's largest independent distillers*

Advertisement for Four Roses Whiskey, 1935.

disappearing from the tables, so the following year Stevens allowed patrons to keep their vessel for an additional twenty-five cents. Those glasses had colorful designs, and for those who managed to keep their faculties enough not to smash them, they became prized souvenirs for Derby-goers, some of whom made a big deal out of assembling a collection of the glasses from each year.

By the 1940s, the drink was permanently bound up with the Kentucky Derby, but more than that, it had been transformed into a symbol of a mythic Old South that never was. In 1947, in a review of an illustrated travelogue of the South, Nash K. Burger of the *New York Times* noted, "There are many Souths, but mostly, of course, there are two, the Old South and the New. Or in terms of their beverages, the mint-julep South and the Coca-Cola South." The julep's reinvention coincided with a more general mania for Old South imagery. Margaret Mitchell's best-selling novel *Gone with the Wind* won the Pulitzer Prize in 1937, and in 1939 was released as a blockbuster film. Advertisers across the country slapped Old South imagery on everything from hams to lumber, and nowhere were the images more pervasive that in the marketing of liquor. An ad for Paul Jones whiskey showed two veterans, one Rebel, one Union, sitting beneath a tree with glasses, remarking, "It was back in '65 . . ." Four Roses Whiskey branded itself as "soft as Southern moonlight," and it ran full-color magazine ads showing a pair of black hands holding a silver tray of mint juleps with the caption, "Yes, suh, Colonel, I'se comin'!"

That mint julep party hosted by the Van Winkle family in 1937 became a legendary event, held each year on Derby weekend. And that brings us around to Julian P. Van Winkle, known to one and all as Pappy. Good whiskey on its own could sell, and story and myth making could make inferior whiskey sell too. When the two came together, it proved a potent combination.

Julian P. Van Winkle had gotten started in the liquor trade when he took a job as a drummer for W. L. Weller and Son, a Louisville-based whiskey wholesaler and rectifier. Pappy covered the Midwest territory, heading out by train and horse and buggy for two-month swings through the mountains and farmlands of Kentucky, West Virginia, Ohio, and Indiana, where he visited the taverns in each town, told jokes, and sold Weller whiskey. In 1907, Van Winkle and Alex Farnsley, the drummer covering the Southern territory, became partners in the firm, which had long since given up the rectifying business and focused instead on wholesaling. In 1912, they contracted with the A. Ph. Stitzel Distillery to have one thousand barrels of whiskey produced for them under the W. L. Weller and Son name. By 1915, Van Winkle and Farnsley had purchased the controlling interest in their firm, and by the time Prohibition was looming, they had purchased a major stake in the Stitzel Distillery too.

During Prohibition, Van Winkle and Farnsley kept their fingers in the whiskey game as much as they could, keeping the Stitzel bottling plant running to package medicinal whiskey for sale to druggists. In 1929, Stitzel had been one of the few firms granted a license to produce medicinal alcohol, so they came out of Prohibition with an inventory of whiskey aging in barrels and a head start on most of the competition. In 1933, the distillery and the wholesale company merged to create Stitzel-Weller, and the combined firm built a big new distillery on a fifty-three-acre tract just outside of Louisville. Arthur Stitzel was the engineer, Alex Farnsley the money man, and Pappy Van Winkle the salesman. Not long after, they bought the inventory and brands of the Old Judge Distillery, including their flagship Old Fitzgerald. Stitzel-Weller made their bourbon with a mash bill that used winter wheat instead of rye as its secondary grain, which imparted a softer, less spicy flavor that became the hallmark of the distillery's brands.

Alex Farnsley's nephew was a politician named Charlie Farnsley, a lawyer and the former mayor of Louisville. In 1936, Charlie Farnsley came up with two brands, Rebel Yell and Lost Cause. The first had a white label with a picture of a cannon firing, the other a plain label with a heavy black border of the sort used to indicate mourning. The whiskey was made at his uncle's distillery, and Farnsley initially bottled them for personal use, often giving them as holiday gifts and distributing them liberally when lobbying state legislators in Frankfort. Farnsley, the story goes, also applied to trademark a brand named Damn Yankee, but it was denied with the notation "in bad taste."

Moonlight-and-magnolia marketing fell out of favor after World War II, but it came back with a vengeance in the 1960s. The centennial of the Civil War spawned a lot of backward-looking Old South nostalgia and romanticized depictions of the war. At the same time, it was the height of the Civil Rights movement, and many white Southerners resistant to social change embraced old Confederate imagery like the Stars and Bars battle flag, which was hoisted above the domes of state capitols across the South, as a defiance to integration and federal attempts to impose Civil Rights laws. For whiskey marketers, it created an environment in which images of the Old South could once again sell.

It was during the early 1960s that Stitzel-Weller decided to start selling Charlie Farnsley's private Rebel Yell brand, a six-year-old, 90-proof bourbon, to the public. Pappy's son, Julian Van Winkle Jr., who by then had become executive vice president of the distillery, noted in promotional letters that the bourbon had "special appeal to men who regarded themselves as true Southerners, with pride in themselves and their heritage . . . It harks back to the grand old days when the South was famous for its gracious living, rich food and fine whiskey." In a stroke of marketing genius, Stitzel-Weller limited the territory where they sold Rebel Yell. As Van Winkle Jr. put it, they were "once more marketing only in the South after an absence of many, many years." Such language suggested this particular bourbon, which had been created just three decades before in 1936, was actually a much older product, and the firm played up that Sold Only in the South tag line in any number of advertisements. One that ran just before Christmas in 1965 declared, "Anyone can give whiskey. Only a Southerner can give Rebel Yell . . . and in full-dress gray!" The bottles were sold inside a velvet bag that was the same color gray as Confederate uniforms.

Stitzel-Weller weren't the only ones waving the Confederate flag. The Brown-Forman company promoted a story that its Old Forester brand of bourbon was named for Nathan Bedford Forrest, the famous Confederate general—and, incidentally, the first grand wizard of the Ku Klux Klan, though in the 1960s that was apparently not a marketing liability. As bourbon historian Mike Veach has uncovered, Brown-Forman's own records show that the brand was actually named for Dr. William Forrester, a Louisville physician who was also a Civil War veteran but not one that 1960s liquor buyers would have ever heard of.

On the one hand, such lost-cause marketing was a reflection of the turbulent, contradictory times, tapping into the nostalgic myths white Southerners were telling themselves about a past that was becoming increasingly difficult to justify. And those myths could move booze. The imagery, though, has had a lasting effect on our cultural memory of drinking in the antebellum South, cementing the hazy notion of old colonels sipping cold mint juleps on the veranda, made with bourbon and served by happy black retainers in a tranquil world that never was.

Moonshining

Long-aged bourbon and mint juleps weren't the only Southern drinks draped in a mantle of myth. Moonshiners had their share of misty legends, though they were increasingly difficult to square with the reality of bootlegging in a postrepeal world. The federal excise tax, which rose steadily from two dollars per gallon in 1933 to nine dollars in 1944, ensured a market for those who could make their liquor cheap. But even in dry counties, legally distilled booze could be slipped in from wet territory, so moonshiners couldn't make nearly the profits they enjoyed when whiskey making was illegal throughout the country. Hubert Howell, an old-timer from Cherokee County, Georgia, recalled that in the 1920s he sold whiskey for two dollars a gallon. After 1933, he could sell it for only a dollar and ten cents, and it cost him a dollar and a half to make. After repeal, a much harder edge set in, and moonshining became a serious and often deadly business and, increasingly, a form of organized crime.

Several areas emerged as leading moonshine centers in the postrepeal years. Each had a long history of whiskey making, an isolated terrain, and in the depths of the Depression and even afterward, little other economic activity going on. Perhaps most important, they were all relatively close to large cities that served as ready markets. By World War II, Dawson County, Georgia, which is about fifty miles north of Atlanta, was producing up to one million gallons of whiskey a year. Its county seat, Dawsonville, was so tiny that its only telephone was the pay phone at a service station. Ford coupes twisted their way down the narrow, winding roads to Atlanta, loaded with a half ton of shine in one-gallon tin cans or boxes of half-gallon Ball jars. Cocke County in northeastern Tennessee served cities in three states: Lexington, Kentucky; Asheville, North Carolina; and, Johnson City, Tennessee. The area along the Yadkin River in Wilkes County, North Carolina, which had a whiskey and brandy tradition stretching back to the 1750s, was a short drive from Charlotte and Winston-Salem, and the so-called Dark Corner of western South Carolina was convenient to Greenville and Spartanburg. Sugar rolled into these regions by the boxcar. One Tennessee storekeeper reported that he was selling two hundred bags of it per week. At one hundred pounds per bag, that totaled more than one million pounds of sugar in a year. Very little of it was being used to bake cakes or sweeten iced tea.

Twentieth-century moonshining was not just a mountain phenomenon, though. In southeastern North Carolina, the Lumbee Indians had small family stills hidden in the swamps near their tobacco farms, and they pooled their output to make up truckloads for shipping. Moonshiners in the Big Bend region along the Saint Marys River on the border of Georgia and Florida sold whiskey to trippers from Jacksonville and Miami. Their stills were secreted away in remote areas, accessible only by a still jigger—a sort of dune buggy that could navigate trails and rude roads to carry sugar in and bring out whiskey on the return trip.

The bootleggers' cars got faster with each passing year. The 1934, '37, and '38 Fords became favorites of the trippers, and they machined off the cylinder heads to increase compression and bored out the cylinders and put in oversized valves to increase stroke. They removed the bracing between the backseat and the trunk to add more cargo space and installed double shocks and override springs to handle the extra weight. The 1940 Ford became the all-time favorite moonshiners' car because of its folding seats and its speed and maneuverability; loaded down with 120 gallons of booze, it handled the curves of mountain roads even better full than when empty.

In the north Georgia, east Tennessee, and Carolina mountains, speed-hungry daredevils engaged in car-to-car combat with lawmen. They mastered the bootlegger's turn—throwing their cars sideways, skidding and spinning around in middle of road to head back the other way. They threw tacks and spikes in the paths of their pursuers. They rigged up smoke-bomb tanks, which burned oily cloths saturated in moonshine, creosote, and crankcase oil to lay down a thick screen of black smoke from the rear of the car. "You'd have to roll your door window down to see out," one revenuer recalled to moonshine historian Joseph Dabney. "And you couldn't turn on your windshield wipers—that just made it worse." Trippers even began loading up the oil with cayenne pepper so the smoke would burn their pursuers' eyes.

Some revenuers tried to beat the trippers at their own game. When their government-issued six-cylinder Fords proved no match, they seized a bootlegger's hot rod and used it to chase his comrades. "We were as crazy as the damned moonshiners," recalled Bill Griffin, a former Bureau of Alcohol Tobacco and Firearms (ATF) agent. "A bunch of kids having a good time." Burton Carroll, a Fulton County policeman, recalled that, even if they could catch up with a bootlegger, the hardest part was stopping them. "We either had to bump them off the road, wreck them, or puncture their tires," he recalled. His favorite trick was to wait until the car he was pursuing entered a curve and then bump it from behind to make it spin out of control.

The experience the trippers gained souping up their delivery cars soon carried over to the world of auto racing. In 1939, the first race held on the clay track at Atlanta's Lakewood Speedway was won by twenty-year-old Lloyd Seay, a notorious moonshine tripper who drove a 1938 two-door Ford with drilled manifolds. Seay went on to win several more races at Lakewood as well as in Greensboro, High Point, Daytona Beach, and Allentown, Pennsylvania. In North Wilkesboro, North Carolina, Junior Johnson started his driving career hauling the whiskey his daddy made to customers down to Statesville. In 1955, he drove in his first NASCAR race and finished the season with five wins.

These twentieth-century moonshiners have been imbued with just as much hazy romantic mythology as Lewis Redmond and his peers were back in the heyday of the Reconstruction-era moonshine wars. Books are filled with tales of camaraderie and respect between hunter and prey, what Joseph Dabney has called "the code of mutual respect . . . Though they were on opposite sides of the law, a strong bond of friendship held them together." Dabney cites as an illustration the incident when a revenue agent named Bill Webster was seriously injured when his car crashed while pursuing a Ford coupe. Webster's opponent, who turned out to be a tripper named Roy Hall, sent the lawman a big bouquet of flowers with a card signed only "the Coupe."

If you start to poke at such stories too much, though, the fun and rosiness starts to dissolve. Take the case of John Henry Hardin, the moonshine king of Georgia. Joseph Dabney called him "a man of great nobility and integrity and honor." Former ATF agent Duff Floyd remembered, "He would not lie to you. His word was his bond." Hardin was a successful corn and cotton farmer on the Etowah River, and he regularly had one team of workers farming and another making whiskey in the woods. He had as many as twenty big steamer stills at a time that supplied a steady stream of trippers who came in from Rome, Marietta, and Atlanta. He was finally brought up on federal charges when he was in his early seventies. Floyd recalled visiting Hardin in jail right before he got sent away on those federal charges and remembers shaking his hand and telling him, "John Henry, you are the best gambler I've even known . . . You've been very kind to us. Every man that worked down here against you appreciates your attitude." John Henry Hardin died in 1943, not long after being released from the federal pen, an invalid and a pauper. Six years later, the Army Corp of Engineers dammed the Etowah River, and

Hardin's farmland and old distilling patches were covered by the waters of Lake Allatoona.

There is a little bit more to the story of John Henry Hardin than usually gets told, though. His word may have been his bond, but he was happy to grease the palms of law enforcement. He served two years in the federal pen after being convicted of bribing a federal Prohibition officer in 1921. On June 19, 1932, Hardin's thirty-year-old son, Paul, shot and killed his wife and four small children in their home near Canton, Georgia, and then killed himself. Paul Hardin had been arrested back in January on liquor charges and was free on a $3,000 bond pending trial. John Henry Hardin discovered the bodies, and he told the police that he believed his son had become deranged brooding over his upcoming trial.

And then there's Lloyd Seay, the moonshine tripper who drove his 1938 two-door Ford to multiple victories at Lakewood Speedway and other Southern raceways. On September 1, 1941, he changed the number on his car from the lucky 7 to the more ominous 13, but he won the one hundred–mile Atlanta Labor Day race anyway. The following day, he was shot dead at his cousin's home in Dahlonega, Georgia, in a dispute over a load of sugar.

And that's the troubling pattern that keeps intruding into the romantic tales of noble, peaceful moonshiners, those good ole boys never meaning no harm who just want to distill a little corn and be left alone. An awful lot of violence and tragedy seems to surround them. The bootlegger's son kills his family and commits suicide. The moonshiner-turned-race car driver is murdered in a dispute over whiskey ingredients. That pattern stretches all the way back to the early days of moonshining just after the Civil War, when the notorious outlaw Lewis Redmond got arrested for attempted murder after supposedly going straight for decades.

When you look too closely, there isn't much beauty or romance to be found in the drinking of bootleg whiskey, either. Most of that moonshine wound up in poorer African-American neighborhoods in Southern cities. Much of the liquor produced in the remote Big Bend region was bought by a woman named Teresa Brown, Florida's moonshine queen. She sold it in her notorious Come and Go nightclub in Jacksonville—a den of prostitution—as well as at her home. In the latter, she had copper tanks rigged up in the attic with pipes running down the wall to a faucet, which was hidden behind furniture and from which she filled customers' orders. In Miami, bumper joints sold moonshine for fifty cents a shot. Atlanta was the undisputed moonshine-consuming capital of the South. In the 1940s, it was estimated that fifty thousand gallons of untaxed whiskey flowed down the so-called Toddy Trail of state highways from the mountains into the city each week.

Booze was back in the South, but amid the strains and machinations of an increasingly oligarchic spirits industry, the patchwork unevenness of governmental regulation, and the rough, raw nature of the illegal whiskey trade, the region had a long way to go to fully resurrect its long, rich drinking tradition.

20

King Pappy: The Decline and Rebirth of Southern Drinking

We opened this book with Pappy Van Winkle bourbon, and it's only appropriate that we end with it too. The trajectory of Pappy reflects the more general path of Southern drinking in the late twentieth century— a legacy that was slowly fading away and, just as it seemed done forever, came roaring back with a vengeance. And I can think of no better way to celebrate than to mix up a Julian.

Julian Van Winkle III says the only drink he can make other than a bourbon on the rocks is this variation on an old-fashioned. It's the way his grandfather, Pappy, liked to make a cocktail.

The Julian

SERVES 1

1 raw sugar cube

3 dashes Regan's orange bitters

3 dashes Angostura bitters

One ½-inch-thick orange slice

2½ ounces 107-proof 15-Year Pappy Van Winkle bourbon (or old Weller Antique 107, which is produced at the same distillery using the same wheated mash bill)

Cover a mixing glass with a paper bar napkin and put the sugar cube in the center of the napkin. Add the dashes of bitters onto the cube and let them soak in (the napkin will catch any excess). Drop the cube into the glass and discard the napkin. Add the orange slice and use a bar spoon or muddler to muddle the sugar into the flesh of the orange to create a thick syrup, taking your time and being careful not to squeeze into the bitter pith. Add 1 ounce of the bourbon and continue muddling for a minute or two. Add another ounce of bourbon and 3 or 4 ice cubes. Stir 30 seconds and pour into a rocks glass. Top with the remaining bourbon and stir briefly.

The Postwar Spirits Trade

The latter half of the twentieth century continued the consolidation process that had begun in the postrepeal days. The Big Four—United Distillers, Schenley, Brown-Forman, and Seagram—made out quite handsomely on military contracts during World War II, and they used those profits to keep buying up one small distillery after another. Seagrams snatched up H. McKenna, Cummins-Collins, Old Lewis Hunter, and Old Prentice, and amassed an inventory of bourbon that they would use in blended products after the war was over. Schenley produced more than two hundred million gallons of war alcohol and gobbled up a basket of distilleries that included Bardstown, John A. Wathen, and the Buffalo Springs Distillery. Schenley bought J. W. Dant Company in 1953. In 1956, Brown-Forman bought the Jack Daniel's distillery in Lynchburg from the Motlow family for $18 million, then snapped up Southern Comfort too. In 1966, American Brands bought Jim Beam and around the same time acquired all the old National Distillers plants, including Old Crow, Old Grand-Dad, and Old Taylor. The company later became Fortune Brands, and still later adopted the name of one of the old brands it had acquired, becoming James B. Beam Corp.

In the 1960s, foreign interests undertook their own buying sprees, rolling American whiskey brands into the portfolios of international conglomerates. France's Pernod Ricard bought Wild Turkey. Barton Brands was purchased by Argyle, the British subsidiary of Amalgamated, and later sold to Canandaigua Wine. The Four Roses Distillery remained in Kentucky, but it was owned and operated by Canadian-based Seagrams. After Lewis S. Rosenstiel died in 1976, his Schenley behemoth was bought first by Rapid American and then, in 1987, by United Distillers. United also snatched up Glenmore four years later, leaving Heaven Hill in Bardstown as the last fully independent, family-owned whiskey plant in Kentucky.

The same phenomenon was under way in the beer business. The big national brands like Busch, Pabst, and Schlitz ramped up their advertising, launching big-budget print campaigns and moving aggressively into the new medium of television advertising. In the 1950s, the industry started shifting from bottles to metal cans, which forced smaller breweries to invest in expensive canning lines if they wanted to stay competitive. Cone-topped steel cans had been introduced by Schlitz back in 1935, and Coors introduced the first aluminum can in 1959. By 1969, canned beer outsold bottled for the first time.

The Tennessee Beverage Company of Memphis, the makers of Goldcrest 51, closed its doors in 1955. That same year, the Spearman Brewing Company in Pensacola was purchased by a national beer conglomerate called the Hertzberg Foundation, which a decade later shut down the old brewery and stopped selling the Spearman brands. In 1956, Saint Louis's Falstaff Brewing, which had purchased the National Brewing Company of New Orleans back in 1937, added to its portfolio the Galveston-Houston Brewing Company of Galveston, Texas, in 1956, and the Mitchell Brewing Company of El Paso. The same year, faced with the reality that they had to sink a lot of capital into adding canning lines, the Jax Brewing Company of Jacksonville sold out to the similarly named Jackson Brewing Company in New Orleans, which now marketed Jax beer throughout the entire lower South. In the mid-1970s, Jax moved farther west when Jackson Brewing closed its doors and sold the brand to the Pearl Brewing Company of San Antonio, which continued to use the same formula and label design as the original Florida brewery.

The beer industry at this point was locked in a relentless race to the bottom, and breweries had to increase volume while reducing the cost of production. In the 1970s, many of the larger firms changed their recipes and brewing processes, reducing malted barley and adding corn syrup, increasing the heat of fermentation to speed brewing, and incorporating

A crossroads store, bar, and gas station near Melrose, Louisiana, 1940.

King Pappy

foam stabilizers and additives like silica gel to reduce cloudiness. Though still nominally making lagers in the style of the great nineteenth-century German-American brewers, brands such as Schlitz, Pabst, and Busch—the beers that had come to dominate the market not just in the South but across the country—were increasingly seen by consumers as lower-quality discount labels. The process was accelerated when Philip Morris acquired Miller Brewing in 1971, and the firm soon entered a fierce marketing battle with Anheuser-Busch, flooding magazines and the airwaves with a barrage of advertising that its competitors couldn't match.

In 1985, Dixie Brewing in New Orleans was purchased by Joe and Kendra Bruno. "It was this incredible old brewery," Kendra Bruno remembered. "But it practically cost us more money to put beer out from it than we made selling the stuff." Dixie Brewing filed for bankruptcy in 1989, through it was reorganized in 1992. Hurricane Katrina in 2005 damaged the old Dixie Brewing building, and looters carried off much of its metal equipment to sell for scrap. The company's products are now contract-brewed at Heiner Brau, a small brewery in Covington, Louisiana, and are available only in limited quantities. It's the last remaining brand from what was one of the South's greatest brewing cities. By 1983, the top six breweries—Anheuser-Busch, Miller, Heileman, Stroh, Coors, and Pabst—accounted for 92 percent of all beer produced in the United States. The era of the great regional Southern brews was over.

Moonshine's Last Hurrah

The 1960s also marked the last hurrah of the Appalachian moonshiner. Bootlegging had surged after World War II, when the excise tax on whiskey hit $10.50 per gallon. By 1960, it was estimated that one-fifth of the liquor consumed in the United States was distilled illegally, and the great majority of that was made and drunk in the South. But the forces of progress were aligning against illegal whiskey. "The moonshine industry in Virginia and the nation is suffering," the *Richmond Times Dispatch* observed in 1968, "from prosperity, shoddy workmanship, and intensive pressure from revenue agents." The entrenched poverty of the Appalachians that had helped keep moonshining part of the local economy was finally lifting. The Tennessee Valley Authority had brought electricity and factory jobs to eastern Tennessee, which induced a lot of men to turn away from their stills to seek more gainful employment. "When a factory moves into a rural area," the chief special investigator for the Alcohol and Tobacco Tax Division in Virginia reported, "there is almost an immediate marked decrease in moonshining in that area." As tourists and the developers of vacation homes began buying up land in the mountains north of Atlanta, former moonshining hotbeds like Dawson County started drying up too.

The quality of moonshine had gotten progressively worse, and it started to create a backlash with even the poorest drinkers. Since Prohibition, most of the South's moonshine had been made mostly from cane sugar with just a small amount of cornmeal to bind the mash. Things continued to go downhill in the 1950s and '60s. Most operations were quite filthy and disorderly, and the whiskey picked up wild yeasts from the air that created acetic acid (that is, vinegar) alongside the desired ethyl alcohol. Lead leached into the moonshine from the solder used to fasten pieces of homemade stills and from the automobile radiators that were widely used as makeshift condensers. The Internal Revenue Service (IRS) had 540 samples of moonshine tested at the army lab at Fort McPherson, Georgia, and discovered nearly one-third contained lead salts exceeding levels considered dangerous. Long-term drinkers were building up those lead salts in body, and so-called moonshine alcoholics started to be recognized by their bleeding lips and skin sores.

A lot of purple prose has been spilled to describe the kick of moonshine (Irvin S. Cobb, always good for a quip, likened it to "swallowing a lighted kerosene lamp"), but much of its sting probably came not from alcohol but from the other stuff lurking in the plastic jugs. Though it might come off the still at 125 or 130 proof, almost all bootleggers watered down their liquor to stretch out a few more bucks. Laboratory tests conducted by Virginia officials revealed that confiscated moonshine clocked in between 65 and 90 proof, compared to the 80 to 100 range for most legal whiskey. Many wholesalers used adulterants like bleach, paint thinner, and rubbing alcohol to give their watered spirits a diversionary kick.

As moonshine's quality tanked, the government stepped up its enforcement of revenue laws. After World War II, the Alcohol, Tobacco, and Firearms (ATF) division of the IRS started hiring college-educated men, including lawyers and accountants. While many were still tough, physical outdoorsmen of the old "still buster" mentality, they brought a higher level of technique to their investigations. Agents began using airplanes to spot stills from the air, and instead of just cutting up the stills they found, they started blowing them up with dynamite to ensure the parts could not be reassembled. Higher-ups put a stop to the hot-rodding and highway exploits of agents pursuing moonshiners. After losing too many new vehicles in crashes, they ordered their officers to stop blocking roads and bridges with their cars and to not engage in high-speed chases. Instead, they simply put investigators at the delivery spots to record the license number of the delivery car. After the car left, the investigators seized the liquor and then later went and found the car.

By this point, illegal whiskey making had been largely eradicated from the mountainous regions of the South. In 1970, Fred Goswick, who admitted to being an ex-moonshiner, opened the Dawsonville Moonshine Museum in the former moonshining capital of north Georgia. It included a display of four nonfunctional stills from various eras. The museum's tour guide, another ex-moonshiner named Carl Phillips, told visitors that he "couldn't commence to tell how much good stuff I've made. But you can't get away with it anymore." Moonshining in Dawson County, Phillips said, "is almost dead."

Illegal whiskey making had shifted into major metropolitan areas, including Atlanta, Augusta, Charlotte, and Birmingham, and the stills were set up not outside where they could be seen from the air but in houses and sheds where a search warrant was required for law enforcement to enter. In February 1971, a well-to-do neighborhood near Atlanta's Dunwoody Country Club was shaken by a huge blast when a whiskey still exploded in the basement of a two-story brick house. The larger operations were financed and controlled by organized crime syndicates. One Georgia bootlegger and his nephew were convicted in 1967 and charged with directing an operation moving twenty-one thousand gallons of untaxed whiskey in a six-month period, which was made in distilleries in fifteen different counties across Mississippi, Alabama, and Georgia. They hauled in sugar from New Orleans in tractor-trailers and distributed the output to illegal whiskey brokers in central Alabama. It was a multilevel of operation with captains, lieutenants, still hands, and drivers, and no one level knew the identities of the people in the other levels. The total operation was accused of defrauding Uncle Sam of $750,000 in excise taxes.

The poorest African-American neighborhoods in Atlanta remained the largest market for this new style of bootlegged liquor. In the early 1970s, an estimated five thousand to seven thousand gallons a day were flowing into the city. Cut with water, it was resold in shot houses, and there were said to be about two thousand of these joints in Atlanta, most of them tiny operations run by women in the kitchens of run-down residential homes. The operators would buy five or six gallons at a time and hide it around the house, selling it to customers for fifty cents a shot or by the pint or half pint to go. Shot house operators cleared around $200 a week, after paying off expenses like a $10 weekly protection payment to the neighborhood cops. In places like Richmond, moonshine was sold in the city's so-called nip joints for fifty cents a drink or two dollars a pint.

Stepped-up police and federal raids began to shut down some of the worst shot house operations. By 1974, inflation was taking its toll, too, as the price of a one hundred–pound sack of sugar jumped from twelve to forty dollars in the space of a year. At $2.50 a pint, the illegal whiskey was not much cheaper than the legal kind, and low-income drinkers increasingly switched to beer and wine.

Moonshining in the 1970s was far from a glamorous business—lead poisoning, criminal syndicates, poor alcoholics drowning their troubles and racking up debts at fifty cents per brutal shot. But moonshining had been one of the first subjects of the Southern myth-making machine, and the image of the outlaw bootlegger was just as appealing as mass media evolved from dime novels to movies and television. In 1958, Metro-Goldwyn-Mayer released *Thunder Road*, a Robert Mitchum drama about running moonshine in Kentucky and Tennessee. Mitchum played a Korean War vet who returns home and starts running shine for his father, delivering it in a souped-up hot rod while trying to fend off both revenuers and big-time gangsters trying to muscle in on their trade. The movie's dramatic car chase scenes helped make it a cult favorite, and it's still played occasionally in drive-in theaters.

In the late 1960s, Gy Waldron, a TV producer and commercial writer in Atlanta, started working on a film script he called *Moonrunners*, drawing on stories he'd heard as a child in Kentucky. It told the story of an old bootlegger named Uncle Jessie. As he worked on the story, Waldron got to know several ATF agents and learned how they tracked down bootleggers, and a producer friend introduced him to Jerry Rushing to add a little more color into the script. Rushing had been born and raised in a moonshining family in Monroe, North Carolina, and he hauled his first carload of bootleg whiskey at the age of twelve. Rushing and his brother did the driving, their Uncle Worley ran the still, and they even had a voluptuous cousin named Delane who was always hanging around. Rushing drove a 1958 Chrysler 300D, which he christened *Traveller* after General Lee's horse and had an oil-dump tank rigged up in the trunk. As organized crime got into the business and sentences got stiffer, Rushing had given up moonshining to work as a trapper and hunting guide, but his past exploits provided plenty of great material for Waldron's script.

Moonrunners was shot in Griffin, Georgia, and narrated by Waylon Jennings. It was released by United Artists in 1975 to mixed reviews, but it did well at the box office. Its real cultural impact came when Waldron elaborated on the movie's concept to create a pilot for a television show called *The Dukes of Hazzard* about a moonshining family in the rural South. It aired on CBS from 1978 to 1985 and was the second top-rated show in the country in 1980, doing immeasurable amounts of harm to America's image of Southern drinking—and of Southerners in general.

The Fate of Whiskey in a Vodka World

On May 4, 1964, a joint resolution of Congress proclaimed bourbon whiskey to be "a distinctive product of the United States" and refused to allow any whiskey created outside the United States to be labeled bourbon. Around the same time, whiskey began a long, slow decline in the American spirits market. The fondness for gin that had been established during Prohibition continued in the post-WWII era, and Bacardi's sales were strong too. But whiskey was hurt most by a new spirit on the American market: the clear, mild, almost flavorless Russian liquor known as vodka. G.F. Heublein and Bros. had purchased the rights to the Smirnoff vodka brand back in 1939, but they struggled with sales until after 1946, when the firm started promoting a new drink called the Moscow Mule that blended vodka with ginger beer and lime. Heublein poured money into marketing, promising, cleverly enough, that "Smirnoff Leaves You Breathless," and paying celebrities like Eva Gabor and Groucho Marx for endorsements. It was the perfect spirit for people who liked gin drinks but not the flavor of gin, and vodka martinis and vodka tonics abounded at the 1960s bar. By 1967, vodka had eclipsed gin as the country's most popular white liquor, and in 1976, its sales eclipsed whiskey for the first time.

By the 1980s, things were looking grim for the bourbon makers. International conglomerates were buying and selling bourbon brands like so many baseball cards, shuffling them from one balance sheet to another and squeezing out the few remaining family-run distilleries. For snooty consumers with a lingering taste for brown liquor, a single-malt Scotch was the new way to prove your connoisseurship. Out in the fern bars and nightclubs, the younger crowd was ordering ever more vodka and rum.

If bourbon was on the ropes, rye was in even worse shape. For decades, it was rare to find even a single lonely bottle on a liquor store shelf, and if you did, it was invariably Old Overholt or perhaps Jim Beam's yellow-label variety, draped in a fine layer of dust. Up in Baltimore, a shot of Pikesville rye remained a favorite of the old-timers in the working-class bars in Fell's Point, but with each passing year there were fewer and fewer of them left. Maryland rye, once prized for the sweet flavor imparted by the state's limestone-rich water, hit bottom in the 1970s. Majestic Distillers in Lansdowne distilled its last batch of Pikesville in 1972 and put it in barrels to age. It wasn't selling enough to distill anymore, and in 1982, Majestic sold the brand to Heaven Hill. The former Pikesville Maryland straight rye whiskey had to be renamed Pikesville Supreme straight rye whiskey, for though it was still sold only in the Baltimore market, it was distilled in Kentucky and shipped eastward on trucks.

There was still a flicker of life left in the bourbon market, though. One small operation that figured out a way to compete was Bill Samuels's Star Hill Distilling Company in Loretto, Kentucky, the producer of Maker's Mark, "the softest spoken of the bourbons." Samuels, who grew up in a whiskey-making family, had entered the business at a time when all the emphasis was on old: old brands, old spirits, old-timey imagery on the labels and ads. It mattered little that most of the companies selling the stuff were relatively new and had just bought old brand names from long defunct distilleries. Bill Samuels took a different route. He launched a totally new brand and didn't even try to pretend that it had an antebellum pedigree. Though they played up the company's use of old, slower distilling methods, Samuels's ads announced that he "did not simply resurrect the recipe of his father, grandfather, and great-grandfather (distillers all) but developed his own—one that was right for today's times and tastes." Their focus was instead on having a unique, soft flavor (thanks to the 14 percent wheat in its mash bill) and uncompromising quality control.

What was most significant about Maker's Mark was that it was unapologetically promoted as a luxury product. The top of each bottle was hand dipped in red sealing wax, giving it a distinctive, elegant look. The company's marketing played up the firm's small size and the amount of manual work involved in their process. Its ad copy read, "It tastes expensive . . . and is," and they asked its purchasers, "Do you think your preference for Maker's Mark is an extravagance?" That tactic kept them afloat during the lean 1970s, and in 1980, when the *Wall Street Journal* ran a front-page article on Maker's Mark, the firm's sales really took off.

Other distilleries picked up on the potential of selling luxury and soon introduced their own lines of premium bourbons. They were going directly after the Scotch sippers, introducing small-batch and special reserve lines— what's known in the trade as the high-end and super-premium categories. And it worked. By the late 1990s, affluent drinkers were passing up the Macallan and the Lagavulin in favor of a few fingers of Blanton's or Baker's over a single cube of ice. Today you can walk into your neighborhood liquor store and see row after row of bourbon bottles from dozens of different brands, some with the kinds of prices once commanded by only the rarest of single malts.

At first, bourbon's rise did little for its poor cousin rye. In 2005, Jim Beam, whose Old Overholt and Jim Beam Rye brands made it the country's largest rye producer, shipped 3.9 million cases of bourbon and only 32,000 cases of rye. At rye's lowest moment, though, the seeds of its rebirth were being sown. In 2006, Eric Asimov of the *New York Times* declared rye "the world's great forgotten spirit," and with considerable effort, cobbled together enough brands for a tasting. That and a few other articles created enough of a ripple of interest in rye that distillers to started socking a little more away in barrels to age.

Around the same time, bartenders were beginning to rediscover rye. Pre-Prohibition cocktails were suddenly cool again, and as bartenders dipped back into the old recipes of Jerry Thomas and other nineteenth-century mixologists, they suddenly realized that a great many of them called for rye. In 2008, Beam released (ri)1 (pronounced "rye one"), an ultrapremium whiskey with a sleek, modern bottle and a name like an algebraic formula. Between 2009 and 2011, the company's rye shipments increased 46 percent. Most of the major bourbon producers now maintain their own premium lines of rye whiskey, and they've been joined by an increasing number of smaller producers, like Whistle Pig from Vermont and New York's Tuthilltown Spirits, which makes Hudson Manhattan Rye.

The production of rye whiskey, once the pride of Pennsylvania and Maryland, has now shifted to Kentucky, where it's being made primarily by bourbon distillers. Of all the brands of rye on the market today, only Old Overholt has a direct lineage back to the pre-Prohibition days, though it passed through plenty of hands before being acquired by Beam.

But Southern whiskey lovers shouldn't care too much, since we've been importing rye whiskey from the Northern fringes for more than a century and a half. Now we can finally go back to putting it into mint juleps and old-fashioneds when we find ourselves fresh out of good brandy.

Rip Van Winkle Awakens

Perhaps no brand better reflects the dramatic rebirth that Southern whiskey has experienced over the past four decades than Pappy Van Winkle. Julian P. Van Winkle's old distilling company, Stitzel-Weller, produced 800,000 cases of bourbon per year in the 1950s and 1960s, including Old Fitzgerald, Cabin Still, and the sold-only-in-the-South Rebel Yell. Pappy himself kept an active hand in running the firm straight up until his death at age 91 in 1965, and afterward his son, Julian Jr., took the helm. Julian Jr. rebuffed several offers from larger distilleries to buy the firm, but the business's financials continued to worsen, and in 1972, he was forced by shareholders to sell to the Norton Simon conglomerate, whose Somerset Importers subsidiary owned Tanqueray gin, Johnnie Walker scotch, and Canada Dry ginger ale.

The Stitzel-Weller brands—Old Fitzgerald, W. L. Weller, Cabin Still, Rebel Yell—were tossed into the chaotic world of the liquor conglomerates, eventually ending up in the hands of United Distillers. They moved production of Old Fitzgerald to the new high-tech Bernheim plant and the bottling to a facility in Owensboro. In 1997, United merged with Grand Metropolitan to form Diageo, the world's largest producer of spirits. Along the way, the Old Fitzgerald label got sold to Heaven Hill, Rebel Yell to the David Sherman Corporation, and W. L. Weller to the Ancient Age Distillery, which would later become Buffalo Trace. The gates of the idled Stitzel-Weller distillery were chained shut.

Julian Van Winkle Jr. wasn't ready to quit the bourbon game, though. Teaming up with his son, Julian III, he launched a firm called J. P. Van Winkle and Son, and they started buying bourbon wholesale and selling it in hand-painted commemorative bottles made of porcelain. Many were in the shape of college football mascots, like the Kentucky Wildcat or Georgia Bulldog—the kind of thing you had to do to move bourbon in the 1970s. The Van Winkles had lost all the Stitzel-Weller brands, but they still owned rights to an old pre-Prohibition label called Old Rip Van Winkle, and they resurrected it, contracting back with Stitzel-Weller to have them produce a set amount of good bourbon for them each year.

Julian Jr. died of cancer in 1981, and his son, Julian Van Winkle III, took over the business. In 1983, he bought the old Hoffman Distillery on the banks of the Salt River in Lawrenceburg and set up a warehouse and bottling facility. At the time, bourbon was still in a free fall while vodka and rum were surging, and there was a huge supply of old bourbon gathering dust in Kentucky warehouses. Van Winkle started buying up inventory from struggling distilleries, focusing in particular on the ones that held his family's old brands and had made the bourbon using the old Stitzel-Weller wheated mash bill. In the mid-1990s, he launched a line of very old whiskeys—aged ten to twenty-three years—and named them Pappy Van Winkle after his grandfather.

In 1998, the twenty-year-old Pappy Van Winkle's Family Reserve received a 99 in the World's Spirits Championships in Chicago, the highest rating ever awarded a whiskey. To put his product in high-end restaurants and build cachet, Julian Van Winkle traveled around the country hosting whiskey-paired dinners. When his bourbon was embraced by celebrity chefs like Anthony Bourdain, Sean Brock, and David Chang, it rocketed into the firmament as the most prized and in-demand bourbon in the world.

"We apologize for the scarcity," Julian Van Winkle told me when I interviewed him back in 2012. "Most of the liquor stores are mad at us, and the consumers are mad at us too." But their hands were tied. They had upped the amount of bourbon they put away each year, but it takes at least a decade in the barrel to be ready for market. "We're just stuck with what we have," Van Winkle said. But considering the price they're commanding for each bottle, I suspect Mr. Van Winkle is doing just fine.

And speaking of treasures, what about that Pappy Van Winkle discussed on page 1 that was stolen from the Buffalo Trace Distillery? It turns out it was an inside job led by one of the senior employees on the Buffalo Trace Distillery's loading docks. The Pappy heist was part of a larger string of thefts committed by ring of conspirators that met while playing in a local softball league and ended up swiping and reselling cases and barrels of Eagle Rare, Wild Turkey, and Russell's Reserve worth more than $100,000.

The Return of Southern Spirits

It's not just whiskey that's enjoying a resurgence in the twenty-first-century South. With each passing year, it seems, more and more of the wine, beer, and spirits that had once seemed lost to the dustbin of history have started popping up again. A few decades ago, Madeira's winemaking families started reinvigorating their ancient industry, and now a remarkable wine that was almost extinct is making a dramatic comeback—and they're fine aged and blended Madeiras, too, not cheap cooking wine. Southern beer brewing, which was almost stamped out of existence by the market boot of international conglomerates, has roared back to life in just the past two decades too. Abita Brewing Company of Abita Springs, Louisiana, was founded in 1986, and in 1993, Ed Falkenstein and Louis Bruce opened the Palmetto Brewing Company in Charleston, the first brewery in South Carolina since Prohibition. In much of the South, there was a major barrier to craft beer production because state laws regulated the maximum alcohol that a beer could contain. In North and South Carolina, a grassroots movement called Pop the Cap convinced legislators to remove restrictions on high-gravity brewing. A wave of craft breweries started cropping up across the South, making locally brewed beer available for the first time in decades.

Though they lagged the brewers by a few years, Southern distillers have now launched a rebirth of what's often called artisanal distilling, a throwback to the late nineteenth century, when the South was dotted with small-scale distilleries turning out whiskey and brandy. As with beer, legislative changes were required to spur on this rebirth, including provisions to allow distillers to sell bottles directly to consumers at their distilleries—a key source of income—and amend licensing requirements geared toward limiting distilling to a few large firms. In 2009, for example, South Carolina created a new microdistillery category of liquor manufacturing for businesses producing fewer than 125,000 cases per year, and they reduced the biennial license fee from $50,000 to a far more affordable $5,000. By 2014, most states in the South had passed legislation that allowed distilleries to operate much more like wineries, and North Carolina, South Carolina, Tennessee, Texas, and Virginia each had a dozen or more distilleries in operation.

The modern liquor trade, ultimately, is all about story, and the long-standing romance of moonshining offered these modern-day distillers a splendid way to move their new products, which hadn't had time to age for years in charred barrels. With each passing month, more and more bottles of crystal-clear corn whiskey started appearing on the shelves of liquor stores throughout the South. They were produced by legitimate business folks who paid their taxes, but they packaged their spirits in Mason jars and paid homage to old-time mountain distillers in their marketing copy. Piedmont Distillers of Madison, North Carolina, teamed up with NASCAR legend and former-bootlegger Junior Johnson, using his mug shot in the marketing materials for their Midnight Moon line of corn spirits. In 2011, the Discovery TV network launched *Moonshiners*, a so-called reality show purporting to document the activities of moonshiners in Climax, Virginia. One of the stars, Tim Smith, soon brought out his own brand of Climax Moonshine. The big distillers weren't going to let this new category develop all on their own, and most of the big bourbon brands—Jack Daniel's, Jim Beam, Wild Turkey—quickly launched their own lines of white whiskey.

This isn't to say the stories aren't sincere. Many of the distillers, especially in the mountainous areas, have family connections to old moonshiners, and some even use old family recipes to make their products. In 2008, Kenny Greene, Keith Nordan, and Chris Hollifield launched the Carolina Distillery in Lenoir, North Carolina, and released their first batch of Carriage House apple brandy a year later. It's made with fresh cider from a nearby orchard and uses an old family recipe from Hollifield's bootlegger ancestors. In Mount Airy, Georgia, two brothers named Carlos and Fred Lovell, both of whom were in their eighties, founded the Ivy Mountain Distillery. The Lovells had learned to make moonshine as teenagers and operated illegally through the early 1960s, and after a fifty-year hiatus, they were making sour mash corn whiskey and apple brandy too.

In Powdersville, South Carolina, the guys at Six and Twenty Distillery took a slightly different path. After exploring the full range of possible grains, they turned their back on corn and went instead with wheat. They call it virgin wheat whiskey, and it's made with locally grown soft red winter wheat. "That wheat has a lot softer, more gentle palate to it," Robert "Farmer" Redmond told me. "Comparing our products to corn liquor is like comparing corn bread to angel food cake." If Redmond's name rings a bell for you, there's good reason. Farmer Redmond is related to the outlaw Lewis Redmond, who made the Upstate of South Carolina notorious for moonshining back in the 1870s. "I'm the only Redmond that's made whiskey in 106 years," Farmer says. "He was my grandfather's grandfather's youngest brother."

This resurgence in white whiskey will likely be short-lived. Even the smallest modern distillery operations are capital intensive, and bourbon and rye whiskey require years of barrel-aging before they are ready for market. White whiskey was an expedient way for fledgling distilleries to get some product out and bring in a little revenue while waiting for the good stuff to age. Now that these young microdistilleries have a few years under their belt, they are starting to bring to market aged spirits, and locally-made rye and bourbon are now becoming widely available across the South.

And that leaves only peach brandy. As this book was going to press, South Carolina, which produces twice as many peaches as the so-called Peach State of Georgia, was on the verge of having commercial peach brandy available once again. Scott and Ann Blackwell of Charleston's High Wire Distilling consulted with David Shields of the University of South Carolina, an expert in heirloom vegetables and fruits, to identify the best variety of peach to distill, and they worked with local farmers to secure a sufficient crop.

I'm still waiting for my first sip of a hailstorm julep made with real peach brandy. And I'm going to fancy it up, John Dabney style, with plenty of sliced fruit and colorful flowers. I can't imagine it will inspire me to the heights of purple prose that Irvin S. Cobb achieved with his bourbon mint juleps, but I do think it's going to be very refreshing indeed.

Acknowledgments

Many thanks are due to my editor, Kaitlin Ketchum, and designer, Tatiana Pavlova, and the rest of the team at Ten Speed Press for taking a horribly unwieldy manuscript and sculpting it into such a fine-looking book. Thanks also to copyeditor Jane Tunks Demel.

Thanks also to the brothers and sisters of the Charleston Brown Water Society for all of their support, encouragement, and fellowship. Much gratitude is due to Scott Blackwell and Ann Marshall at High Wire Distilling for patiently enduring two years of my badgering them to distill peach brandy—and for finally relenting and giving it a try. Some really tasty recipes were contributed by R. H. Weaver, the head barman at Husk, who has been trying for years to get the word cocktologist used in print. Mission accomplished.

David Wondrich, Wayne Curtis, and Mike Veach have blazed new territory in spirits history and provided me with much-needed clues and inspiration. Thanks also to Mark Jones, Charleston author and mobile historian, for contributing the great photo of the Palmetto Brewery.

David Hale Smith found this book a home and provided many helpful suggestions along the way—and tasty whiskey and barbecue, too.

And, finally, to my wife, Jennifer: thank you for patiently enduring yet another a project conceived primarily as a flimsy excuse for conducting "research." It probably won't be the last.

Bibliography

CHAPTER 1

Beverley, Robert. *The History of Virginia in Four Parts*. Rev. ed. (1722. Rpt. Richmond, VA: J. Randolph, 1855).

Bruce, Philip Alexander. *Social Life of Virginia in the Seventeenth Century* (Richmond, VA: Whittet & Shepperson, 1907).

Davidson, James West, and Mark Hamilton Lytle. *After the Fact: The Art of Historical Detection*. 3d ed. (New York: McGraw-Hill, 1991).

Glover, Thomas. *An Account of Virginia, Its Situation, Temperature, Productions, Inhabitants, and the Manner of Planting and Ordering Tobacco* (London: B. H. Blackwell, 1904).

Hening, William Waller. *The Statutes at Large: Being a Collection of All the Laws of Virginia* (New York: R & W & G Bartron, 1823).

Hess, Karen. *Martha Washington's Booke of Cookery* (New York: Columbia University Press, 1981).

Jeter, Annie Lash. *Domestic Life in Virginia in the Seventeenth Century* (Williamsburg, VA: Virginia 350th Anniversary Celebration Corporation, 1957).

McCord, David J. *Statutes at Large of South Carolina*. Vol. 7 (Columbia, SC: A. S. Johnson, 1840).

Meacham, Sarah Hand. *Every Home a Distillery: Alcohol, Gender, and Technology in Colonial Chesapeake* (Baltimore: Johns Hopkins University Press, 2009).

Morgan, Philip. *Slave Counterpoint: Black Culture in the 18th Century Chesapeake and Lowcountry* (Chapel Hill, University of North Carolina Press, 1998).

Pinney, Thomas. *A History of Wine in America: From the Beginnings to Prohibition* (Berkeley, CA: University of California Press, 1989).

Salinger, Sharon. *Taverns and Drinking in Early America* (Baltimore: Johns Hopkins University Press, 2002).

Smith, Frederick H. "Alcohol, Slavery, and African Cultural Continuity in the British Caribbean." *Drinking: Anthropological Approaches*, edited by Igor de Garine and Valerie de Garine, (New York: Berghahn Books, 2001).

Smith, John. *The Generall Historie of Virginia, New England & The Summer Isles* (New York: Macmillan, 1907).

Strachey, William. *The History of Travaile into Virginia Brittania*. Edited by R. H. Major (London: Hakluyt Society, 1849).

Temple, Sarah B. Gober, and Kenneth Coleman. *Georgia Journeys: Being an Account of the Lives of Georgia's Original Settlers* (1961. Rpt. Athens, GA: University of Georgia Press, 2010).

CHAPTER 2

Brown, Gregory J., Thomas F., Higgins, David F., Muraca, S. Kathleen, Pepper, and Roni H., Polk. *Archaeological Investigations of the Shields Tavern Site, Williamsburg, Virginia* (Williamsburg, VA: Colonial Williamsburg Foundation, 1990).

Burbidge, McDonald L., "Shepheard's Tavern" *Scottish Rite Journal* (June 1999). Available online at www.clansinclairsc.org/shepheardtavern.htm. Accessed January 22, 2013.

Byrd, William. *History of the Dividing Line and Other Tracts* (Rpt. Richmond, VA: Thomas Wynne, 1866).

Candler, Allen D. *Journal of the Trustees for Establishing the Colony of Georgia in America.* Vol. 1 (Atlanta, GA: Franklin Printing and Publishing Company, 1904).

Coleman, Kenneth. *A History of Georgia.* 2nd ed. (Athens, GA: University of Georgia Press, 1991).

Cooper, Thomas. *Statutes at Large of South Carolina.* Vol. 2 (Columbia, SC: A. S. Johnson, 1837).

Curtis, Wayne. *And a Bottle of Rum: A History of the New World in Ten Cocktails* (New York: Broadway, 2007).

Edgar, Walter B. *The Letterbook of Robert Pringle* (Columbia, SC: University of South Carolina Press, 1972).

Fraser, Charles. *Reminiscences of Charleston* (Charleston, SC: John Russell, 1854).

Gibbs, Pat. *Shields Tavern Historical Report, Block 9 Building 26B Lot 25* (Williamsburg, VA: Colonial Williamsburg Foundation, 1986).

Hewatt, Alexander. *An Historical Account of the Rise and Progress of the Colonies of South Carolina and Georgia.* Vol. 1 (London: Alexander Donaldson, 1779).

Horry, Harriott Pinckney. *A Colonial Plantation Cookbook.* Edited by Richard J. Hooker (Columbia, SC: University of South Carolina Press, 1984).

Lawson, John. *A New Voyage to Carolina* (London: 1709).

Marin, Craig Thomas. *Coercion, Cooperation, and Conflict Along the Charleston Waterfront, 1739–1785.* Ph D dissertation, University of Pittsburgh, 2007.

McWilliams, James E. *A Revolution in Eating* (New York: Columbia University Press, 2005).

Poston, Jonathan H. *The Buildings of Charleston: A Guide to the City's Architecture* (Columbia, SC: University of South Carolina Press, 1997).

Rice, Kym. *Early American Taverns: For the Entertainment of Strangers and Friends* (Chicago: Regnery Gateway, 1983).

Stephens, William. *The Colonial Records of the State of Georgia, Vol. 4: Stephen's Journal 1737–1740.* (Atlanta, GA: Franklin, 1906).

Urmston, John. Letter to the SPG. *The Colonial and State Records of North Carolina.* Vol. 1. Available online at docsouth.unc.edu/csr/index.html/document/csr01-0411. Accessed September 9, 2015.

Ward, Edward. *The Wandering Spy, or, the Merry Travellers* Part 2 (London, 1722).

Wondrich, David. *Imbibe! From Absinthe Cocktail to Whiskey Smash; A Salute in Stories and Drinks to "Professor" Jerry Thomas, Pioneer of the American Bar* (New York: Perigree, 2007).

Wondrich, David. *Punch: The Delights (and Dangers) of the Flowing Bowl* (New York: Perigee, 2010).

CHAPTER 3

Anburey, Thomas. *Travels Through the Interior Parts of America. Vol. 2* (1789. Rpt. Boston: Houghton Mifflin, 1923).

Bland, Theodorick. *The Bland Papers. Vol. 1.* Ed. Charles Campbell (Petersburg, VA: Edmund & Julian Ruffin, 1840).

Bradley, Richard. *The Country Housewife and Lady's Director. Part 2* (London: D. Browne, 1732).

Edelson, S. Max. *Plantation Enterprise in Colonial South Carolina* (Cambridge, MA: Harvard University Press, 2006).

Fithian, Philip Vickers. *Journals and Letters, 1767–1774* (Carlisle, MA: Applewood Books, 2007).

Greene, Jack P. *The Diary of Landon Carter of Sabine Hall, 1752–1778.* Vol. 1 (Charlottesville, VA: University Press of Virginia, 1965).

Hooker, Richard J., ed. *The Carolina Backcountry on the Eve of the Revolution: The Journal and Other Writings of Charles Woodmason, Anglican Itinerant* (Chapel Hill, NC: University of North Carolina Press, 1969).

Meacham, Sarah Hand. *Every Home a Distillery: Alcohol, Gender, and Technology in Colonial Chesapeake* (Baltimore: Johns Hopkins University Press, 2009).

Merrell, James Hart. *The Indian's New World: Catawbas and Their Neighbours from European Contact Through the Era of Removal* (Chapel Hill, NC: University of North Carolina Press, 1989).

Morgan, Philip. *Slave Counterpoint: Black Culture in the 18th Century Chesapeake and Lowcountry* (Chapel Hill, NC: University of North Carolina Press, 1998).

Pettigrew, Timmons. *The Charleston Beer Book* (Charleston, SC: History Press, 2011).

Quincy, Josiah. *Memoir of the Life of Joseph Quincy, Junior.* (Boston: Cummings, Hilliard, 1825).

Taylor, Joe Gray. *Eating, Drinking, and Visiting in the South: An Informal History* (Baton Rouge, LA: Louisiana State University Press, 1982).

Thorp, Daniel B. "Taverns and Communities: The Case of Rowan County, North Carolina." *In the Southern Colonial Backcountry: Interdisciplinary Perspectives on Frontier Communities.* Edited by David Colin Crass, et al. (Knoxville, TN: University of Tennessee Press, 1997): 76–86.

Walsh, Richard. "Edmund Egan—Charleston's Rebel Brewer." *South Carolina Historical Magazine* 16 (1955): 100–104.

CHAPTER 4

Grayson, William John. "Autobiography of William John Grayon." *South Carolina Historical and Genealogical Magazine* 49 (January 1948): 23–40.

Hailman, John. *Thomas Jefferson on Wine* (Oxford, MS: University of Mississippi Press, 2009).

Hancock, David. *Oceans of Wine: Madeira and the Emergence of American Trade and Taste* (New Haven, CT: Yale University Press, 2009).

——— "'A Revolution in the Trade': Wine Distribution And the Development of the Atlantic Market Economy, 1703–1807." In edited by John J. McCusker and Kenneth Morgan, *The Early Modern Atlantic Economy* (New York: Cambridge University Press, 2011): 105–153.

——— "Self-Organized Complexity and the Emergence of the Atlantic Market Economy, 1651–1815." *The Atlantic Economy During the Seventeenth and Eighteenth Centuries.* Edited by Peter A. Coclanis, 30–71 (Columbia, SC: University of South Carolina Press, 2005).

Hewatt, Alexander. *An Historical Account of the Rise and Progress of the Colonies of South Carolina and Georgia.* Vol. 1 (London: Alexander Donaldson, 1779).

Laurens, Henry. *The Papers of Henry Laurens.* Edited by Philip M. Hamer, George C. Rogers Jr., and Peggy J. Wehage (Columbia, SC: University of South Carolina Press, 1970).

Tuten, James. "'Have Some Madeira, M'dear': The Unique History of Madeira Wine and Its Consumption in the Atlantic World." *Juniata Voices* 8 (2008): 55–61.

CHAPTER 5

Anburey, Thomas. *Travels Through the Interior Parts of America. Vol. 2* (1789. Rpt. Boston: Houghton Mifflin, 1923).

Grizzard Jr. , Frank E. *The Papers of George Washington. Revolutionary War Series. Vol. 10,* 11 June 1777–18 August 1777 (Charlottesville, VA: University Press of Virginia, 2000).

Lengel, Edward G., ed. *The Papers of George Washington, Revolutionary War Series, vol. 13,* 26 December 1777–28 February 1778 (Charlottesville, VA: University of Virginia Press, 2003).

Taylor, Robert J., ed. *The Adams Papers: Papers of John Adams, Vol. 3. May 1775–January 1776* (Cambridge, MA: Harvard University Press, 1979).

CHAPTER 6

Buck, Solon J., and Elizabeth Hawthorne Buck. *The Planting of Civilization in Western Pennsylvania* (1939. Rpt. Pittsburgh, PA: University of Pittsburgh Press, 1995).

Carson, Gerald. *The Social History of Bourbon* (1963. Rpt. Lexington, KY: University of Kentucky Press, 2002).

Coxe, Tench. *A Statement of the Arts and Manufactures of the United States of America for the Year 1810.* (Philadelphia: A. Cornman, 1814).

An Essay on the Importance and the Best Mode of Converting Grain into Spirit (Lexington, KY: W. W. Worsley, 1823).

Fisher, David Hackett. *Albion's Seed: Four British Folkways in America* (New York: Oxford University Press, 1989).

Franklin, Benjamin. *The Papers of Benjamin Franklin.* Available online at www.franklinpapers.org. Accessed November 5, 2012.

Hall, Harrison. *The Distiller.* 2nd ed. (Philadelphia: J. Bioren, 1818).

Hogeland, William. *The Whiskey Rebellion* (New York: Simon & Schuster, 2006).

Hooper, Johnson Jones. *Some Adventures of Captain Simon Suggs* (Philadelphia: Carey and Hart, 1845).

Journals of the Continental Congress, 1774–178. Vol. 7, (Washington, DC: Government Printing Office, 1907.

McHarry, Samuel. *The Practical Distiller* (Harrisburg, PA: John Wyeth, 1809).

Pacult, F. Paul. *American Still Life: The Jim Beam Story and the Making of the World's #1 Bourbon* (Hoboken, NJ: John Wiley & Sons, 2003).

Pogue, Dennis J. "Shad, Wheat, and Rye (Whiskey): George Washington, Entrepreneur." cdm16829.contentdm.oclc.org/cdm/ref/collection/p16829coll4/id/17. Accessed November 11, 2011.

Rush, Benjamin. "An Account of the Progress of Population, Agriculture, Manners, and Government in Pennsylvania." *Edinburgh Magazine* 6 (1787): 99–104.

Stuart, James. *Three Years in North America.* Vol. 2 (New York: Harper, 1833).

Wilkeson, Judge. "Early Recollection of the West." *American Pioneer* 2 (May 1843): 203–17.

CHAPTER 7

Baird, Robert. *View of the Valley of the Mississippi* (Philadelphia: H. S. Tanner, 1834).

Durell, Edward Henry (aka H. Didimus) *New Orleans as I Found It* (New York: Harper & Bros., 1845)

Ingraham, Joseph Holt. *The Southwest. By a Yankee* (New York: Harper & Brothers, 1835).

Marryat, Captain Frederick. *Second Series of a Diary in America* (Philadelphia: T. K. & P. G. Collins, 1840).

Wilson Jr., Samuel "Maspero's Exchange: Its Predecessors and Successors." *Louisiana History: The Journal of the Louisiana Historical Association* 30, (Spring 1989): 191–220.

CHAPTER 8

Anburey, Thomas. *Travels Through the Interior Parts of America.* Vol. 2 (1789. Rpt. Boston: Houghton Mifflin, 1923).

Robert Cellem, *Visit of His Royal Highness The Prince of Wales to the British North American Provinces and United States* (Toronto, ONT: Henry Rowsell, 1861).

Davis, John. *Travels of Four Years and a Half in the United States of America* (London: R. Edwards, 1803).

Harwell, Richard Barksdale. *The Mint Julep* (Charlottesville, VA: University of Virginia Press, 1975).

Marryat, Captain Frederick. *Second Series of a Diary in America* (Philadelphia: T. K. & P. G. Collins, 1840).

Murray, Charles August. *Travels to North America During the Years 1834, 1845, and 1836* (London: Richard Bentley, 1839).

Ogg, David. "New College, Oxford, and South Carolina: A Personal Link." *South Carolina Historical Magazine* 59 (April 1958): 61–63.

Power, Tyrone. *Impressions of America During the Years 1833, 1834, and 1835.* Vol. 1 (Philadelphia: Carey, Lea & Blanchard, 1836).

Russell, William Howard. *My Diary North and South* (London: Bradbury and Evans, 1863).

Schwarz, Philip J. "Dabney, John." *Dictionary of Virginia Biography*. Vol. 3. Edited by Sara B. Bearss, et al. (Richmond, VA: Library of Virginia, 2006): 648–649.

Semmes, John E. *John H. B. Latrobe and His Times, 1803–1891* (Baltimore: Norman, Remington, 1917).

Sismondo, Christine. *America Walks into a Bar* (New York, Oxford University Press, 2011).

Weightman, Gavin. *The Frozen Water Trade* (New York: Hachette, 2004).

Norman R. Yetman, ed., *When I Was a Slave: Memoirs from the Slave Narrative Collection* (Mineola, NY: Dover, 2002).

CHAPTER 9

Brady, Roy. "America's Madeira Tradition." *History in a Glass: Sixty Years of Wine Writing from Gourmet* (New York: Modern Library, 2007).

Cote, Richard N. *Mary's World: Love, War, and Family Ties in Nineteenth-Century Charleston* (Mt. Pleasant: Corinthian Books, 2001).

Hailman, John. *Thomas Jefferson on Wine* (Oxford, MS: University of Mississippi Press, 2009).

Hancock, David. *Oceans of Wine: Madeira and the Emergence of American Trade and Taste* (New Haven, CT: Yale University Press, 2009).

McAlister, Ward. *Society as I Have Found It* (New York: Cassell, 1890).

McCulloch, John Ramsey. *A Dictionary, Geographical, Statistical, and Historical, of the Various Countries, Places, and Principal Natural Objects in the World*. Vol. 2 (London: Longman, Brown, Green, and Longmans, 1842).

Pinney, Thomas. *A History of Wine in America: From the Beginnings to Prohibition*, (Berkeley, CA: University of California Press, 1989).

CHAPTER 10

Annual Report of the Commissioner of Patents for the Year 1848 (Washington, DC: Wendell and Van Benthuysen, 1849).

Carson, Gerald. *The Social History of Bourbon* (1963. Rpt. University of Kentucky Press, 2002).

Coker, Joe. *Liquor in the Land of the Lost Cause: Southern White Evangelicals and the Prohibition Movement* (Lexington, KY: University of Kentucky Press, 2007).

Covey, Herbert C., and Dwight Eisnach. *What the Slaves Ate: Recollections of African American Foods and Foodways from the Slave Narratives* (Santa Barbara, CA: ABC-CLIO, 2009).

Dickinson, W. Calvin. "Temperance". *The Tennessee Encyclopedia of History and Culture*. Version 2.0. Available online at tennesseeencyclopedia.net/entry.php?rec=1302. Accessed March 12, 2014.

Douglass, Frederick. *Narrative of the Life of Frederick Douglass, an American Slave* (London: H. G. Collins, 1851).

Freedley, Edwin T. *Philadelphia and Its Manufactures* (Philadelphia: Edward Young, 1859).

Greenberg, Kenneth S. *Nat Turner: A Slave Rebellion in History and Memory* (New York: Oxford University Press, 2004).

Hoskins, Thomas. *What We Eat: An Account of the Most Common Adulterations of Food and Drink* (Boston: T. O. H. P. Burnham, 1861).

Jackson, John Andrew. *The Experience of a Slave in South Carolina* (London: Passmore & Alabaster, 1862).

Joyner, Charles. *Down by the Riverside: A South Carolina Slave Community* (University of Illinois Press, 1986).

McCord, David J., ed. *Statutes at Large of South Carolina.* Vol. 7 (Columbia, SC: A. S. Johnson, 1840).

Pacult, F. Paul. *American Still Life: The Jim Beam Story and the Making of the World's #1 Bourbon* (Hoboken, NJ: John Wiley & Sons, 2003).

Rorabaugh, W. J. *The Alcoholic Republic: An American Tradition* (New York: Oxford University Press, 1981).

Royall, Anne [Traveller]. *Sketches of the History, Life, and Manners of the United States* (New Haven, 1826).

Taussig, F. W. *The Tariff History of the United States.* 5th ed. (New York: G. P. Putnam's Sons, 1910).

Trollope, Frances. *Domestic Manners of the Americans.* 2nd ed. (London: Whittaker, Treacher, 1832).

Veach, Michael R.. *Kentucky Bourbon Whiskey: An American Heritage* (Lexington, KY: University of Kentucky Press, 2013).

CHAPTER 11

Ainsworth, Fred C., and Kirkley, Joseph. *War of the Rebellion: A Compilation of the Official Records of the Union and Confederate Armies.* Series 4, Vol. 2 (Washington, DC: Government Printing Office, 1900).

Coulter, E. Merton. *The Confederate States of America, 1861–1865* (Baton Rouge, LA: Louisiana University Press, 1950).

Daniel, Larry J. *Soldiering in the Army of Tennessee: A Portrait of Life in a Confederate Army* (Chapel Hill, NC: University of North Carolina Press, 1991).

Pringle, Elizabeth W. Allston. *Chronicles of "Chicora Wood"* (1922. Rpt. Atlanta, GA: Cherokee, 1976).

Robinson, William M. "Prohibition in the Confederacy," *American Historical Review* 37 (October 1931): 50–58.

Schroeder-Lein, Glenna R. *The Encyclopedia of Civil War Medicine* (Armonck, NY: M. E. Sharpe, 2008)

Schwarz, Philip J. "Dabney, John." *The Dictionary of Virginia Biography.* Vol. 3. Edited by Sara B. Bearss, et al. (Richmond, VA: Library of Virginia, 2006): 648–649.

Stewart, Bruce E. *Moonshiners and Prohibitionists: The Battle Over Alcohol in the Southern Appalachia* (Lexington, KY: University of Kentucky Press, 2011).

Vandiver, Frank E., ed. *Confederate Blockade Running through Bermuda, 1861–1865: Letters and Cargo Manifests* (Austin, TX: The University of Texas Press, 1947).

Wiley, Bell Irvin. *The Life of Johnny Reb: The Common Soldier of the Confederacy* (Baton Rouge, LA: Louisiana State University Press, 1943).

CHAPTER 12

Atkinson, George W. *After the Moonshiners, By One of the Raiders* (Wheeling, WV: Frew & Campbell, 1881).

Currey, Craig J. "The Army and Moonshiners in the Mountainous South During Reconstruction." Masters' thesis, US Army Command and General Staff College, Leavenworth, KS, 1994.

Davis, Robert Scott. "The North Georgia Moonshine War of 1876–77." *North Georgia History* 6 (Autumn 1989): 41–46.

"Law and Moonshine," *Harper's Weekly* (August 1878):

Miller, William R. *Revenuers & Moonshiners: Enforcing Federal Liquor Laws in the Mountain South, 1865–1900* (Chapel Hill, NC: University of North Carolina Press, 1991).

Stewart, Bruce E., ed. *King of the Moonshiners: Lewis R. Redmond in Fact and Fiction* (Knoxville, TN: University of Tennessee Press, 2008).

Stewart, Bruce E. *Moonshiners and Prohibitionists: The Battle Over Alcohol in the Southern Appalachia* (Lexington, KY: University of Kentucky Press, 2011).

Woolson, Constance Fenimore. "Up in the Blue Ridge." *Appleton's Journal* 5 (November 1878): 104–25

CHAPTER 13

Bready, James H. "Maryland Rye: A Whiskey the Nation Long Fancied—but Now Has Let Vanish." *Maryland Historical Magazine* 85 (Winter 1990): 345–378.

Browne, William Henry. *A Treatise on the Law of Trade-Marks and Analogous Subjects* (Boston: Little, Brown, and Co., 1873).

Carson, Gerald. *The Social History of Bourbon* (1963. Rpt. University of Kentucky Press, 2002).

Connelley, William Elsey, and E. M. Coulter. *History of Kentucky.* Vol. 5 (Chicago: American Historical Society, 1922).

Howard, George W., *The Monumental City: Its Past History and Present Resources* (Baltimore: J. D. Ehlers & Co., 1873).

Johnson, E. Polk. *A History of Kentucky and Kentuckians: The Leaders and Representative Men in Commerce, Industry and Modern Activities.* Vol. 3 (Chicago: Lewis, 1912).

Pacult, F. Paul. *American Still Life: The Jim Beam Story and the Making of the World's #1 Bourbon* (Hoboken, NJ: John Wiley & Sons, 2003).

Veach, Michael R. "20th Century Distilling Papers at the Filson," *The Filson Newsmagazine* 7(4). Available online at www.filsonhistorical.org/archive/news_v7n4_distilling.html. Accessed September 7, 2015.

Veach, Michael R. *Kentucky Bourbon Whiskey: An American Heritage* (Lexington, KY: University of Kentucky Press, 2013).

CHAPTER 14

Arthur, Stanley Clisby. *Famous New Orleans Drinks & How to Mix 'Em* (1937. Rpt. Gretna, LA: Pelican, 2011).

Hale, Walter. "The Passing of Old New Orleans." *Uncle Remus's Magazine* (March 1908): 9–11.

Hearn, Lafcadio. *La Cuisine Creole: A Collection of Culinary Recipes from Leading Chefs and Noted Creole Housewives, Who Have Made New Orleans Famous for Its Cuisine* (1885. Rpt. New Orleans: F. F. Hansell & Bro., 1903).

Hennick, Louis C., and E. Harper Charlton. *The Streetcars of New Orleans* (New Orleans: Jackson Square Press, 1975).

Morrison, Andrew. *The Industries of New Orleans* (J. M. Elstner, 1885).

Supreme Court of Louisiana, *Reports of Cases Argued and Determined in the Supreme Court of Louisiana*. Vol. 49, Part 2 (1897): 1119–1915.

CHAPTER 15

Charleston Receipts (Charleston, SC: Junior League of Charleston, 1950).

Emerson, W. Eric. *Sons of Privilege: The Charleston Light Dragoons in the Civil War* (Columbia, SC: University of South Carolina Press, 2005).

Ladies of the Guild of St. James Parish Church, *Favorite Food of Famous Folk* (Louisville, KY: John P. Morton, 1900).

Rhett, Blanche S. *Two Hundred Years of Charleston Cooking* (1930. Rpt. Columbia, SC: University of South Carolina Press, 1976).

Whaley, Emily. *Mrs. Whaley Entertains: Advice, Opinions, and 100 Recipes from a Charleston Kitchen* (Chapel Hill, NC: Algonquin, 1998).

CHAPTER 16

"Brewery Brought Taste to Augusta." *Augusta Chronicle* (February 13, 1999).

Dennée, Timothy J. *Robert Portner and His Brewing Company (Alexandria, VA: Parson Engineering Science, 2010). Available online at www.alexandriava.gov/uploadedFiles/ historic/info/archaeology/ARSiteReportHistoryPortnerBrewingCoAX196.pdf. Accessed September 8, 2015.*

Dubose, John Witherspoon. *Jefferson County and Birmingham, Alabama* (Birmingham, AL: Teeple & Smith, 1887).

Harris, Carl V. "Reforms in Government Control of Negroes in Birmingham, AL, 1890–1920." *Journal of Southern History* 38 (1972): 567–600.

Holland, Gerald. "The King of Beer." *American Mercury* (October 1929).

Kenny, D. J. *Cincinnati Illustrated: A Pictorial Guide to Cincinnati and the Suburbs* (Cincinnati: Robert Clarke & Co., 1879).

Merrill, Ellen C. *Germans of Louisiana* (Gretna, LA: Pelican, 2005).

Nau, John Frederick. *The German People of New Orleans* (Leiden: E. J. Brill, 1954).

Polak, Michael. *Warman's Bottles Field Guide* (Iola, WI: Krause Publications, 2010).

Smith, Ron, and Mary Boyle. *Atlanta Beer: A Heady History of Brewing in the Hub of the South* (Charleston, SC: The History Press, 2013).

CHAPTERS 17 and 18

Ayers, Edward L. *Promise of the New South* (New York: Oxford University Press, 2007).

Baum, Dan. "Jake Leg." *The New Yorker* (September 15, 2003): 50–5.

Blakely, Leonard Stott. *The Sale of Liquor in the South* (New York: Columbia University, 1912).

Cecil, Sam K. *The Evolution of the Bourbon Whiskey Industry in Kentucky* (Paducah, KY: Turner, 1999).

Coker, Joe. *Liquor in the Land of the Lost Cause: Southern White Evangelicals and the Prohibition Movement* (Lexington, KY: University of Kentucky Press, 2007).

Crowe, Charles. "Racial Violence and Social Reform—Origins of the Atlanta Riot of 1906." *The Journal of Negro History* 53, (July 1968): 234–56.

Dabney, Earl. *Mountain Spirits: A Chronicle of Corn Whiskey from King James' Ulster Plantations to America's Appalachians and the Moonshine Life* (New York: Scribner, 1974).

Edgar, Walter. *South Carolina: A History* (Columbia, SC: University of South Carolina Press, 1998).

Harris, Carl V. "Reforms in Government Control of Negroes in Birmingham, Alabama, 1890–1920," *Journal of Southern History* (1932): 567–600.

Huggins, Phillip Kenneth. *The South Carolina Dispensary* (1971. Rpt. Columbia, SC: Sandlapper, 1997).

Irwin, Will. "The American Saloon." *Collier's* (May 16, 1908): 9–12.

Minnix, Kathleen. *Laughter in the Amen Corner: The Life of Evangelist Sam Jones* (Athens, GA: University of Georgia Press, 2010).

Mixon, Gregory, and Clifford Kuhn. "Atlanta Race Riot of 1906." *New Georgia Encyclopedia.* Available online at www.georgiaencyclopedia.org/articles/history-archaeology/atlanta-race-riot-1906. Accessed April 2, 2015.

Moore, John Hammond. "The Negro and Prohibition in Atlanta, 1885–1887." *South Atlantic Quarterly* 69 (1970): 38–57.

Okrent, Daniel. *Last Call: The Rise and Fall of Prohibition* (New York: Simon & Schuster, 2010).

Parker, David B. "Sam Jones (1847–1906)." *New Georgia Encyclopedia.* Available online at www.georgiaencyclopedia.org/articles/arts-culture/sam-jones-1847-1906. Accessed April 3, 2015.

Pendergrast, Mark. *For God, Country and Coca-Cola: The Definitive History of the Great American Soft Drink and the Company That Makes It.* (New York: Basic Books, 1993).

Pettigrew, Timmons. *The Charleston Beer Book* (Charleston, SC: History Press, 2011).

Stuart, George R. *Famous Stories of Sam P. Jones* (New York: Fleming H. Revell, 1908).

Sullivan, Jack. "Who the Heck Was Irvin S. Cobb?" *Bottles and Extras* (Summer 2006): 38–41.

Veach, Michael R.. *Kentucky Bourbon Whiskey: An American Heritage* (Lexington, KY: University of Kentucky Press, 2013).

CHAPTERS 19 and 20

Campbell, Sally Van Winkle. *But Always Fine Bourbon: Pappy Van Winkle and the Story of Old Fitzgerald* (Louisville, KY: Limestone Lane Press, 1999).

Carson, Gerald. *The Social History of Bourbon* (1963. Rpt. University of Kentucky Press, 2002).

Cecil, Sam K. *The Evolution of the Bourbon Whiskey Industry in Kentucky* (Paducah, KY: Turner, 1999).

Cobb, Irvin S. *Irvin S. Cobb's Own Recipe Book* (Frankfort, KY: Frankfort Distilleries, 1936).

Dabney, Earl. *Mountain Spirits: A Chronicle of Corn Whiskey from King James' Ulster Plantations to America's Appalachians and the Moonshine Life* (New York: Scribner, 1974).

Foley, Bill. "Jax Beer: The Old Milwaukee of Another Era in Jacksonville." *Florida Times-Union* (June 1, 1996).

Kroll, Harry Harrison. *Bluegrass, Belles, and Bourbon: A Pictorial History of Whisky in Kentucky* (South Brunswich and New York: A. S. Barnes, 1967).

Mendelson, Richard. *From Demon to Darling: A Legal History of Wine in America* (Berkeley: University of California Press, 2009).

Pacult, F. Paul. *American Still Life: The Jim Beam Story and the Making of the World's #1 Bourbon* (Hoboken, NJ: John Wiley & Sons, 2003).

Sullivan, Jack. "Who the Heck Was Irvin S. Cobb?" *Bottles and Extras* (Summer 2006): 38–41.

"Whiskey: Newest U.S. business, Oldest U.S. problem." *Fortune* (November 1933).

Whitten, David O. *Handbook of American Business History* (Westport, CT: Greenwood, 1990).

Image Sources and Credits

Cover: Courtesy of the Library of Congress Photographs and Prints Division

Pages ii, iv, 25, 27, 39, 51, 86, 100, 134, 140, 148, 161, 169, 242, 244, 277: Courtesy of the Library of Congress Photographs and Prints Division

Page 13: George Smith, *A Compleat Body of Distilling* (1738)

Page 45: *The South Carolina and American General Gazette* (May 20, 1771)

Page 57: Illustration by G. G. White in *Heroes and Patriots of the South* (1860) by Cecil B. Hartley

Page 62: Benson John Lossing, *Our Country*, volume 1 (1875)

Page 73: R.M. Devens, *Our First Century* (Springfield, MA: C. A. Nichols, 1877)

Page 77: Harrison Hall, *The Distiller* (1818)

Page 96: Jerry Thomas, *How to Mix Drinks* (1862)

Page 97: Leo Engel, *American & Other Drinks* (1878)

Page 119: *Natchez Ariel* (November 21, 1825 and January 23, 1826)

Page 135: *Beadles Magazine* (1864)

Page 154, 157: George W. Atkinson, *After the Moonshiners* (1881)

Page 171: Courtesy of Buffalo Trace Distillery

Pages 185, 186, 187: *Reports of Cases Argued and Determined in the Supreme Court of Louisiana* (1897)

Page 205: *The Daily Review* (Wilmington, NC), March 28, 1889

Page 207: *Charlotte Observer*, January 9, 1897

Page 210: Phillip Kenneth Huggins, *The South Carolina Dispensary* (1997)

Page 211: Courtesy of Mark R. Jones and the Charleston County Public Library

Page 214: Courtesy of the University of North Texas Library

Page 225, 233, 235, 263, 265, 266: Author's collection

About the Author

Robert F. Moss is a food and drinks writer and culinary historian living in Charleston, South Carolina. He is the contributing barbecue editor for *Southern Living* and the Southern food correspondent for *Serious Eats*. He is a frequent contributor to the *Charleston City Paper*, and his work has also appeared in publications such as *Garden & Gun*, *Los Angeles Times*, *Charlotte Observer*, *Texas Monthly*, *Columbia Free Times*, and *Early American Life*.

Robert is the author of *The Barbecue Lover's Carolinas*, a guide to the restaurants, recipes, and traditions of barbecue in North and South Carolina; *Barbecue: The History of an American Institution*, the first full-length history of barbecue in the United States; and *Going Lardcore: Adventures in New Southern Dining*, a collection of essays about dining in the modern South.

A native of Greenville, South Carolina, Robert attended Furman University and received a PhD in English from the University of South Carolina.

Index

Four Roses whiskey, 257, 266, 267, 276

Frankfort Distilleries, 257, 262, 264

Franklin, Benjamin, 67

Franklin House Hotel, 138

Freitas, Ricardo, 50

French and Indian War, 39, 44

Fullsteam Brewery, 201

Fulton, Robert, 78

Fulton Brewery, 205

Funerals, 17–18

G

Gabor, Eva, 282

Gadsby's Tavern, 27

Gaines, William A., 170

Galveston-Houston Breweries, 255, 277

Garnet, Henry Highland, 122

Garrison, William Lloyd, 124

Gem Restaurant, 83

Georgia Spring Brewery, 205

Gin Fizz, The Ramos, 180

Glenmore, 257, 276

Glover, Thomas, 10

Gonzaullas, M. T. "Lone Wolf," 243

Goodrich, Samuel, 93

Goswick, Fred, 280

Grady, Henry, 219, 226

Grand brule, 178

Grand Ole Opry, 215

Grant, Ulysses, 145, 150

Grayson, William J., 56–57, 109

Great Awakening, 47, 124

Greene, Kenny, 288

Griffin, Bill, 271

Grimes, William, 91

Gross, Harry, 247

Guarino, Sam, 252

H

Haar, Carl, 242

Haar, Fred, Jr., 242

Haar, Frederick "Fred," 241, 242

Haar, William, 241, 247

Hailstorm julep, 95–97, 100, 102

Hall, Harrison, 76, 77, 116, 117

Hall, Roy, 272

Hamilton, Alexander, 71

Hampe, Frank, 239

Hampton, E. R., 144

Hampton, Wade, 145, 158, 159

Hancock, David, 54

Hancock, John, 63

Handy, Thomas H., 183–87, 188

Handy's Aromatic Cocktail Bitters, 184, 185, 186, 187

Hardin, John Henry, 272–73

Hardin, Paul, 273

Harris, Abraham, 121

Harris, John Newman, 247–48

Harrison, Benjamin, 226

Harwell, Richard Barksdale, 91

Hassell, Andrew, 123

Hasselmeyer, Henry Otto, 248

Hearn, Lafcadio, 177–78

Heaven Hill Distillery, 258, 276, 283, 285

Heileman, 278

Heiner Brau, 278

Hennessy, James, 58

Herbemont, Nicholas, 109

Herbers, G. H., 210

Herman, Edward W., 206–7

Hertzberg Foundation, 277

Heublein, 282

Hewatt, Alexander, 36–37, 56

Hewlett, John, 82, 87

Hewlett's Exchange, 82, 85, 86, 87

High Wire Distilling, 289

Himbeeressig (Raspberry Vinegar Syrup), 181–82, 183

Hipkins, Samuel, 40

Hiram Walker, 258–59

Hoffman, Charles Fenno, 98

Hoffman Distillery, 286

Holcombe, William H., Jr., 243, 244

Hollifield, Chris, 288

Hooks, Rebecca, 123

Hooper, Johnson J., 76

Hope Distillery, 112

N

Nation, Carrie, 213
National Brewing, 256, 277
National Distillers, 256–57, 261–62, 276
National Road, 78
Native Americans, 6, 20–21, 35–37
Navigation Acts, 69
Negus, 33
Neville, John, 72
New Exchange Coffee House, 82
New Orleans, 78–89, 95, 177–89, 201–3, 232, 234, 247
Newton, Francis, 53
New Yorker Hotel, 252
Nordan, Keith, 288
Norment, Frank, 223
Norton Simon, 285

O

Oak Hall, 137
O'Connor, Curly, 253
Oglethorpe, James, 34, 35
O'Grady, William, 145
Okrent, Daniel, 231
Old Canal Steam Brewery, 203
Old Crow whiskey, 115, 161, 170, 173, 257, 276
Old Fitzgerald, 160, 265, 268, 285
Old Forester, 269
Old Grand-Dad, 160, 257, 276
Old Judge Distillery, 268
Old Lewis Hunter, 276
Old Prentice, 276
Old Rip Van Winkle, 286
Old Sweet Springs, 140
Old Taylor, 170, 257, 276
Old Taylor Castle, 171
Old Tub Distillery, 115, 168, 169
Ordinaries, 16, 18–19, 47
Orgeat, Black Walnut, 60
The Original (Perhaps) Roffignac Cocktail, 182
O'Shaughnessy, P. J., 244

Ostner, William, 210
Otranto Club Punch, 197–98

P

Pabst, 276, 278
Painter, William, 203
Palmetto Brewery, 201, 211, 287
Pappy Van Winkle bourbon, 1, 275, 285, 286
Parker, M., 117
Parlor, 87
Patent Bourbon, 120
Patent stills, 76, 77
Paul Jones whiskey, 162, 267
Peach brandy
    aged, 42
    Brandy Punch, 38
    color of, 42
    history of, 40–41, 165
    Otranto Club Punch, 198
    Saint Cecilia Punch, 197
    today, 41–42, 289
Peach mobby, 10, 12
Peach Street Distillers, 42
Peacock, Isham, 124
Pearl Brewing Company, 277
Peek, James, 154, 155
Pemberton, John, 217
Pepper, Elijah, 115, 170
Pepper, James, 170
Pepper, Oscar, 170
Pernod Ricard, 276
Peychaud, Antoine Amédée, 79, 89, 183, 186
Peychaud's American Aromatic Bitter Cordial, 183–85, 188
Philip Morris, 278
Phillips, Carl, 280
Phillips, J. M., 154
Phoenix Brewing Company, 206
Phylloxera, 164, 188
Piedmont Distillers, 288
Pierce, Phineas, 95
Pike, S. J., 161
Pink House Tavern, 25

Van Winkle, Julian, Jr., 269, 285–86
Van Winkle, Julian, III, 1, 276, 285–86
Veach, Mike, 118, 269
Vest, C. C., 144
Vodka, 282
Volstead Act, 241, 250–51

W

Waldron, Gy, 281
Walker, F. G., 169
Walnut Orgeat, Black, 60
Ward, George, 227
Ward, John Joshua, 123
Ward, Ned, 22
Washington, Booker T., 226, 229
Washington, George, 42, 46, 49, 55,
    63–64, 71, 73, 74, 75, 192
Washington, Martha, 11, 31, 55, 74
Waterfill and Frazier Distillery, 237
Wathen, John A., 276
Watts, Edmund, 18
Weaver, R. H., 60
Webster, Bill, 272
Weiskopf, D. K., 256
Weiss, Seymour, 252
Welch, John, 157
Weller, W. L., 267–68, 285
Whaley, Emily, 195–96
Whiskey
    aging, 114, 116–18
    bottled in bond, 160, 172–75
    brands, 161–63
    during the Civil War, 127–33, 143
    counterfeit, 120, 174–75
    definition of, 21
    distribution of, 163
    early history of, 64–69, 71–78, 80,
        111–18, 123
    golden age of, 160–75
    marketing of, 163–64
    neat, 160
    in the post-WWII era, 276, 282–86
    during Prohibition, 237, 238–40
    during Reconstruction, 143–59

after repeal of Prohibition, 256–59,
    261–69
as substitute for brandy or rum,
    116–18
Whiskey Cobbler, 111
Whiskey Toddy, 65
See also Bourbon; Moonshine; Rye
    whiskey; White whiskey
Whiskey Rebellion, 71–73, 144
Whiskey Trust, 256
Whistle Pig, 284
White, John E., 227
White whiskey
    characteristics of, 142
    definition of, 142
    Moonshine Margarita, 143
    popularity of, 142, 288–89
Wild Turkey, 276, 286, 288
Wiley, Harvey W., 174, 175
Willard, Orsamus, 97
Willebrandt, Mabel Walker, 242–43
Williamsburg, 23, 24, 25–26, 27, 30
Williamson, William, 99
Wine
    Admiral Dewey's Artillery
        Punch, 193
    connoisseurship of, 105–6
    domestic production of, 7–10, 34,
        108–10
    imported, 19, 26, 54–56
    See also Catawba wine;
        Champagne; Madeira
Winters, Lance, 42
Witmer, Henry, 76
Woman's Christian Temperance
    Union, 213
Wondrich, David, 29, 32, 193
Woodmason, Charles, 47, 48
Woodward, James, 228
World War I, 195, 234

All rights reserved.

Published in the United States by Ten Speed Press, an imprint of the Crown Publishing Group, a division of Penguin Random House LLC, New York.

www.crownpublishing.com

www.tenspeed.com

Ten Speed Press and the Ten Speed Press colophon are registered trademarks of Penguin Random House LLC.

Library of Congress Cataloging-in-Publication Data

Moss, Robert F., author.
  Southern spirits : four hundred years of drinking in the American South, with recipes / Robert F. Moss.
      pages cm
  Includes bibliographical references and index.
  1. Cocktails—Southern States—History. 2. Alcoholic beverages—Southern States—History. 3. Drinking customs—Southern States—History.
  4. Southern States—Social life and customs. I. Title.
  TX951.M677 2016
  641.87'4—dc23
                                    2015025969

Hardcover ISBN: 978-1-60774-867-0
eBook ISBN: 978-1-60774-868-7

Printed in China

Design by Tatiana Pavlova

10 9 8 7 6 5 4 3 2 1

First Edition